golf courses of the world

365 days

Robert Sidorsky

golf courses of the world

365 days

Abrams, New York

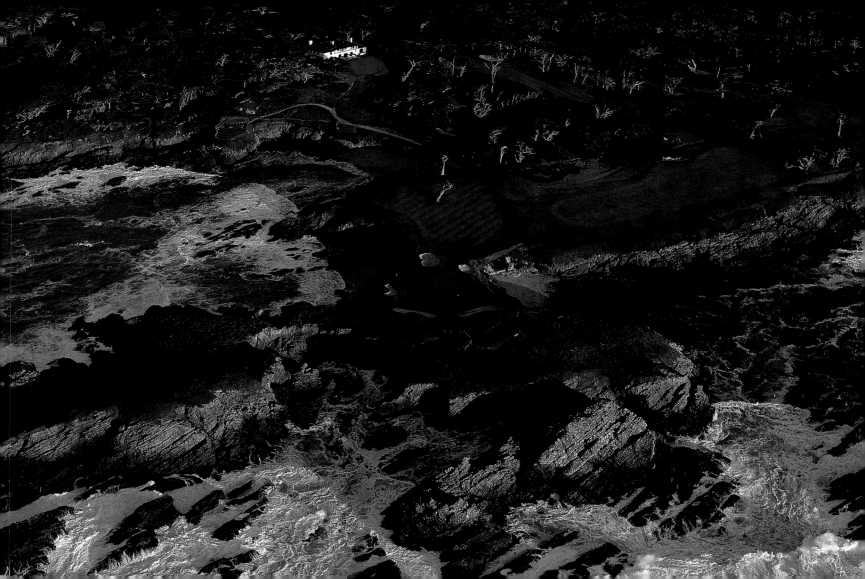

Introduction

Golf, more than any other sport, lends itself to journeys of discovery, and this book is in many respects the ultimate golfing journey. Here is every true golfer's most fervent fantasy—365 days of golf played on the most sensational courses, in blissfully balmy climes, circumnavigating the world of golf to visit a new site each day.

Some courses will be familiar favorites, while others will offer the lure of exotic surroundings in faraway places. It is a trip that I hope the reader will find both entertaining and educational, coming away with a newfound appreciation for the artistry and sheer beauty of golf courses around the world.

This stunning array of photographs taken by the world's leading golf course photographers goes a long way to explaining the appeal of golf on such a global scale. They vividly show that the attraction of golf is not just about the shared joys and frustrations of hitting the ball, but of experiencing the constant challenge of different courses and savoring their distinctive settings and delightful scenery.

These images also offer compelling proof that golf has flourished around the world in no small measure because of the adaptability of the game to every type of terrain and ecosystem. The golf courses featured span 60 countries around the world and 49 states, ranging from the antipodes of Paltamo near the Arctic Circle to Arelauquen in Patagonia. The result is a dazzling variety of courses adapted to their natural surroundings from the Alpine splendor of Banff in the Canadian Rockies to the swaying palms and sand-encircled fairways of the Ocean Course at Brazil's Ilha de Commandatuba, from Cabo del Sol in Mexico's cactus-cluttered Baja Desert to the jungle greenery of Handara in the Balinese highlands, from Sand Hills Golf Club in the grassland dunes of central Nebraska to Les Bordes in the bogland of the Loire Valley.

In our journey, we also gain much insight into the historical development and spread of golf. We can trace the game from its early roots in Scotland, beginning with the Honourable Society of Edinburgh Golfers and the Royal and Ancient Golf Club of St. Andrews, to Westward Ho! and Royal Liverpool in England. As went the British Empire, so went Scottish and English army officers and administrators spreading the game to the four corners of the earth. The introduction of golf in the United States in the 1890s came in part through the Scottish influence but also to a surprising extent via France, where American captains of industry and wealthy expatriates discovered the game on their visits to the French resorts of Biarritz, Pau, and Etretat.

Our 365 days of golf also give us a chance to explore the often overlooked creativity and skill of the world's foremost golf course architects. We can sample the work of the best architects past and present and view the characteristics that define their greatest achievements. Here are examples of the work of the early

Scottish and English masters: Willie Park, Jr., Harry Colt, Charles Alison, and Tom Simpson. The golden era of design in America is represented by the many courses designed by the likes of Charles Blair Macdonald, Seth Raynor, Donald Ross, Alister MacKenzie, A.W. Tillinghast, William Flynn, and George Thomas. In Canada, the genius of Stanley Thompson is on display.

In the post–World War II era, Robert Trent Jones developed a distinctly American style of design that became the international standard. He was followed by Pete Dye, who recognized the possibilities for golf architecture of rearranging the natural landscape on a massive scale, taking full advantage of the modern earth-moving equipment at his disposal to create a new style of design with sharply defined, sculpted features. Dye's work influenced the next generation of designers, including Jack Nicklaus, who has been a major force in building boldly conceived and ecologically sensitive modern courses all around the world.

Three of the most prominent active American golf architects are Tom Fazio, Robert Trent Jones, Jr., and Rees Jones. Rees Jones has made a name for himself both restoring classic courses, including a number of U.S. Open venues, and with his original designs. Trent Jones, Jr. has carried on the family tradition of designing courses over demanding and frequently spectacular terrain in far-flung locales. Fazio has designed courses with different looks and styles but with a consistent emphasis on the aesthetic shaping and framing of each hole. A number of American architects have also been engaged in exciting projects around the world, including Ronald Fream, Robert von Hagge, Jim Engh, and Kyle Phillips.

In recent years, a number of up-and-coming architects have been placing renewed emphasis on the strategic design principles and handcrafted look of the classic designs of the 1920s, with highly acclaimed results. In the vanguard of this back-to-the-future movement are Tom Doak, Ben Crenshaw and Bill Coore, Gil Hanse, and David McLay Kidd.

In selecting the 365 courses that comprise this global grand tour, the approach has been admittedly and intentionally subjective. The goal is to present the pageantry and poetry of golf around the globe rather than ranking courses by a set of criteria. Each of the courses has been selected because it has something of unique interest to offer through a combination of design, history, geographic setting, and plain old charm. No one could deny that Augusta National, which ambles around Rae's Creek and has its fairways pampered to a state of mint julep-green perfection, is a great course. The Himalayan Golf Club in Nepal, on the other hand, runs through a rocky river gorge, cattle wander the course, and its fairways are brown and scruffy most of the year, but who can deny the thrill of playing golf beneath the Annapurna Range of the Himalayas? Ballybunion in southwest Ireland, which may be the greatest of the world's seaside links, begins with a fairway that runs around a graveyard. The Delhi Golf Club in India might not provide the same test, but how many courses can claim that they play through the sandstone tombs of Moghul Emperors?

Golfers revel in finding and playing new courses around the world. The question I am continually asked by my golfing friends is whether it would be possible to actually make the 365-day journey and play each course along the way. With a private jet and perfect weather, it might not be completely out of the question, but the true aim of this book is to inspire more golfing adventures over many years. Any golfer who can play and enjoy the lingering memories of a fair number of these 365 courses over a lifetime should consider himself (or herself) fortunate indeed.

In an undertaking of this scope, I owe a debt of gratitude to many persons. I would like to thank Margaret L. Kaplan, Editor-at-Large at Harry N. Abrams, Inc., for her unwavering support of this project and her past and continuing commitment to publishing the finest illustrated golf books. Robert McKee and Russell Hassell deserve enormous credit for bringing together the vast collection of photographs and creating a coherent, colorful, and creative design. David Barrett was a diligent and dedicated editor who made my task much easier. I would also like to thank Amber Reed for her continued selfless editorial support and Steve Lapper for helping me to source the photographs.

The sumptuous photographs of courses around the world are the essence of this book and I am truly grateful to each of the talented and globe-trotting photographers who supplied images, including Phil Arnold, Aidan Bradley, Jordan Coonrad, Joann Dost, Dick Durrance, Markus Erdmann, William fforde, Jorge Gamboa, Matthew Harris, Jim Haver, John and Jeannine Henebry, Eric Hepworth, Paul Hundley, Russell Kirk, Mike Klemme, Bob Labbance, Larry Lambrecht, Jean-François Lefevre, Patrick Lim, Ken May, Taku Miyamoto, Robert Reck, David Scaletti, Phil Sheldon, and David Whyte.

I would also like to thank each of the golf architects who were exceptionally generous with providing information and photographs, including photographs of courses that were not even their own designs! The list includes Tom Doak, Ken Dye, Jim Engh, Ron Forse, Keith Foster, Lester George, Rees Jones, Stephen Kay, Tim Liddy, and Thomas McBroom. In particular, Ron Fream of Golfplan provided wonderful images of exotic courses. I am also very grateful to *Golfweek* senior writer and golf architecture maven Bradley Klein for giving me access to his personal photo archive.

Last but not least, I would like to thank my wife, Hilary, and my children, Alexander and Julia, without whom this book might have been completed a bit sooner, but with a lot less love and affection.

Robert Sidorsky
New York City, September 2004

▷ JANUARY 1   ▷ PRINCEVILLE RESORT (PRINCE COURSE)   ▷ HAWAII, U.S.A.

The Prince Course at the Princeville Resort is Hawaii's ultimate combination of the dramatic, exotic, and punishing. The nearby ocean cliffs and bosky green mountains of the island of Kauai are favorite settings for Hollywood forays into the jungle, including *South Pacific*, *Raiders of the Lost Ark*, and *King Kong*, with Mount Makana serving as the Bali Hai of *South Pacific*. Designed by Robert Trent Jones, Jr., the Prince's fairways are terraced through a lush jungle of mango trees, laced with ravines, and bisected by Anini Stream, which cascades from the red-ore rock walls on the 13th hole. Princeville is named after the Hawaiian prince, Albert Edward Kauikeaouli Leiopapa A. Kamehameha, the only child of Queen Emma and King Kamehameha IV, who died at age four. In 1860, when the Prince was two years old, his parents took him on their holiday at the ranch plantation of their foreign minister, a Scot named Robert Crichton Wyllie. Wyllie was so charmed by the little Prince that he named his 11,000-acre plantation Princeville.

▷ JANUARY 2 ▷ KAPALUA RESORT (PLANTATION COURSE) ▷ HAWAII, U.S.A.

The Plantation Course is part of the 1,650-acre Kapalua Resort on Maui. Opened in 1989, the Plantation Course put Maui on the world golf map and now hosts the Mercedes Championships, the season-opening event on the PGA Tour. Kapalua means "arms embracing the sea," and the course sits on a spectacular promontory high above the Pacific, where humpback whales can be seen breaching in the winter and spring. In designing the layout, Ben Crenshaw and Bill Coore had to take into account the fierce trade winds and steep pitch of the land. The result is a brawny, sweeping course with immense fairways and forced carries over jungly ravines. The 18th is a 633-yard par five that plunges downhill, where Tiger Woods and Ernie Els both made eagle in the final round of the 2000 Mercedes to go into a sudden-death playoff won by Woods. The Kapalua Resort also has two older courses, the Bay and the Village, which run through stands of Cook pines, ironwood, plumeria, and coconut palms. Kapalua was part of the vast surrounding pineapple plantation, which continues to be operated by the descendants of Dwight Baldwin, a missionary doctor who arrived in Maui in 1819.

▷ JANUARY 3   ▷ CHALLENGE AT MANELE   ▷ HAWAII, U.S.A.

Lanai was the Hawaiian Island known for its pineapples, but since 1991 it has been the home of two world-class resort courses, the Challenge at Manele and the Experience at Koele. Often referred to as Pineapple Island, Lanai is owned by Castle & Cooke's Dole Pineapple Company. A subsidiary of Castle & Cooke developed both the elegant Manele Bay Hotel, on the western shore of the island, and the Lodge at Koele in the central highlands of Norfolk and Scotch pine near Lanai City. The Challenge at Manele, designed by Jack Nicklaus, cascades across the bluffs on top of sheer rock cliffs that rise 150 feet above the Pacific. The 12th hole is one of the most dramatic par-threes in the world, with a carry across the chasm that rises above the Pacific to the cliff-top green. The hole was the site of Bill Gates's wedding to his wife Melanie in 1994.

▷ JANUARY 4   ▷ MAUNA KEA GOLF COURSE   ▷ HAWAII, U.S.A.

The luxurious Mauna Kea Beach Hotel was developed by Laurance Rockefeller in 1964 on the Big Island overlooking Kaunaoa Bay and set against the backdrop of Mauna Kea, or "White Mountain" in Hawaiian, a 13,784-foot-high volcanic peak that is dusted with snow. Rockefeller brought in Robert Trent Jones, the world's most renowned golf architect, to design the course. Rockefeller's main concern was whether a course could be built over the black lava fields. Jones, with typical bravado, assured him that grass could grow on the lava. It turned out that the crushed lava, pulverized using specially designed ribbed rollers, produced beautiful turf. Mauna Kea, with its contrast of plush green bordered by black, set the standard for what has become the hallmark of golf in Hawaii. It is a bold course designed on a large scale. The most famous hole is the par-three third, which plays from a tee perched on a great pile of lava to a green 210 yards across the inlet of the Pacific that is home to giant manta rays. Mauna Kea was inaugurated with a match between the Big Three of Arnold Palmer, Jack Nicklaus, and Gary Player.

▷ JANUARY 5　▷ OAHU COUNTRY CLUB　▷ HAWAII, U.S.A.

Oahu Country Club was founded in 1905 and the original nine-hole course opened in April 1907, making it the second-oldest course in Hawaii. A private club, the members have carried out constant revisions and lengthening of the course over the years, including some improvements suggested by Robert Trent Jones when he visited in 1960. The course rises and dips through the Nuuanu Valley, bounded by the Pali Highway and the surrounding mountains. Right from the elevated first tee, there are dazzling views of Waikiki, the Honolulu skyline, and the Pacific. The narrow fairways run through lush hills and are lined with banyan, paper bark, and giant monkeypod trees. The club hosts the Manoa Cup or Hawaii State Amateur Match Play Championship each year.

▷ JANUARY 6   ▷ OLYMPIC CLUB   ▷ CALIFORNIA, U.S.A.

The Olympic Club's Lakeside Course is known as the most claustrophobic in championship golf. The narrow, sloped fairways are overarched by an elaborate lattice of cypress, pine, and eucalyptus that must be negotiated from tee to green, demanding pinpoint driving accuracy and the ability to play a high fade through the narrow corridors. The Olympic Club actually acquired the course from the struggling Lakeside Country Club in 1922. The course is on the western edge of San Francisco, on the inland side of the ridges separating Lake Merced from the Pacific, while the club's other course, the Ocean Course, lies on the other side of the ridges. Olympic is known for producing underdog champions. In the 1955 U.S. Open, the unknown Jack Fleck defeated Ben Hogan in a playoff. In 1966, Arnold Palmer blew a big lead coming down the stretch and lost to Billy Casper in a playoff. In 1987, Tom Watson made his final hurrah in the U.S. Open but came up one stroke short of winner Scott Simpson. Lee Janzen won his second U.S. Open at Olympic in 1998, beating out Payne Stewart.

▷ JANUARY 7   ▷ HARDING PARK GOLF COURSE   ▷ CALIFORNIA, U.S.A.

Harding Park, located along the shores of Lake Merced, near Skyline Boulevard and the San Francisco Zoo, is San Francisco's legendary municipal track. Designed by Willie Watson in 1925, Harding Park had suffered from many years of neglect and fallen into disrepair. Former USGA president and San Francisco native Frank D. "Sandy" Tatum spearheaded a campaign that resulted in a $16 million refurbishment and lengthening of the course. With its makeover completed in 2003, Harding Park has been restored to its former glory so that it now rivals its famous neighbor, the Olympic Club. The course's distinguishing feature is groves of venerable redwoods and splayed cypress, with seven holes along Lake Merced. Harding Park, which hosted a PGA Tour event in the 1960s, returns to the Tour as the site of the WGC-American Express Championship in 2005.

▷ JANUARY 8   ▷ MAYACAMA GOLF CLUB   ▷ CALIFORNIA, U.S.A.

Mayacama is a private club that is tucked into secret valleys among the soft green hills of the Sonoma wine country near Santa Rosa. Designed by Jack Nicklaus and opened in 2001, the course wanders through clusters of old oaks and crosses streams and wetlands on its journey through the lush enfolding hills with the Mayacama Mountains in the distance. Mayacama has several of the region's highest-rated winemakers among its members, and as a condition of membership the vintners must annually provide the club with the equivalent of one barrel of their finest reserve wine. Each Mayacama member is issued a private wine locker in the club's wine cellar located beneath the clubhouse and adjacent to the 18th green.

▷ JANUARY 9   ▷ DRAGON AT GOLD MOUNTAIN   ▷ CALIFORNIA, U.S.A.

The Dragon at Gold Mountain is the golf course of the Nakoma Resort, located in the town of Clio, 45 miles northwest of Lake Tahoe. The owners of Nakoma are Dariel and Peggy Garner, who developed the resort on 1,280 acres they acquired in the Feather River Valley in northern California after earlier careers selling software programs to banks and growing gourmet baby vegetables in Mexico for the California market. The Dragon was designed by California-based course architect Robin Nelson, and Peggy Garner also hired LPGA Hall-of-Famer Patty Sheehan to make sure the course would be playable for women. The Dragon is surrounded by eight peaks of the Sierras, with the first tee facing Eureka Peak. It takes a dragon-slayer to conquer the course, with carries over ravines through narrow chutes of pines, and fairways teetering above deep gorges with the Feather River far below. The clubhouse at Nakoma is Frank Lloyd Wright's original design for the Nakoma Country Club in Madison, Wisconsin. Nakoma means "I do as I promise" in the Chippewa language. Wright designed the clubhouse in 1924 as a series of red cedar spires in the shape of wigwams, the highest soaring 60 feet, but it was never built. That is, until the Garners hired the Taliesin architectural group, which carries on Wright's tradition, to design the resort.

▷ JANUARY 10   ▷ LAHONTAN GOLF CLUB   ▷ CALIFORNIA, U.S.A.

Lahontan Golf Club is part of the gated community of Lahontan near Northern California's Lake Tahoe. The course is a scenic tapestry of the Northern Californian landscape—ridges of towering bottle-green pines, wetlands, flowering meadows alongside mountain lakes, and black rock outcroppings. Tom Weiskopf, who has become a top-notch golf course designer after a long career as one of the top pros of the 1960s and 1970s, has used the natural bounty at his disposal to full effect. Weiskopf's traditional-style design incorporates sentinel Ponderosa pines and Martis Creek, which appears for the first time on the eighth hole. There are views of Gooseneck Reservoir and to the west looms the Pacific Crest range between Tinker's Knob and Castle Peak, with Mount Rose and the Carson Range to the east. Lahontan takes its name from the Lahontan cutthroat trout, a prehistoric species that can still be found in Lake Tahoe and Martis Lake.

Above: Lahontan logo

▷ JANUARY 11   ▷ STANFORD UNIVERSITY GOLF COURSE   ▷ CALIFORNIA, U.S.A.

The Stanford University Golf Course, which opened in 1930, is located in the Palo Alto foothills above the Stanford campus, and from the 18th hole there is a spectacular view of downtown San Francisco. The course was designed by George C. Thomas and his construction superintendent Billy Bell, who produced many of California's most storied layouts, including Riviera and Los Angeles Country Club. It was built at the behest of Stanford's students, who found a dedicated supporter in Almon E. Roth, the university Comptroller, who convinced the trustees to provide the land and finance construction. When Bell first surveyed the property, he immediately recognized the benefit of incorporating San Francisquito Creek into the design, which required obtaining the land on the other side of the creek. Acquiring the additional property necessitated passage of an amendment to the California State Constitution to permit a land swap. Construction began in 1929, with great care taken to preserve the old oaks on the property, and Felt Lake was enlarged to provide water for the course. Many illustrious golfers have played their college golf at Stanford. The most famous of all is, of course, Tiger Woods, but other notable Stanford golfers include Tom Watson and Woods's teammates Notah Begay and Casey Martin.

▷ JANUARY 12   ▷ PEBBLE BEACH GOLF LINKS   ▷ CALIFORNIA, U.S.A.

Pebble Beach is to American golf what St. Andrews is to the game in Scotland. This greatest of all American seaside courses leapfrogs across the "Cliffs of Doom" above the cobalt water of the Pacific where the sea lions make their home. Surprisingly, the course was designed in the 1920s by two relative unknowns, California amateur champions Jack Neville and Douglas Grant. They were given the job by Samuel Morse, the grandnephew and namesake of the inventor of the telegraph, whose inspired vision resulted in the environmentally sensitive and exceptionally attractive development of the Monterey Peninsula. Pebble Beach is a favorite of the USGA and has hosted four U.S. Opens, including the particularly memorable 2000 event when Tiger Woods destroyed the field, winning by an astounding 15-stroke margin. Pebble annually hosts the PGA Tour's AT&T Pebble Beach National Pro-Am, the event formerly known as the Bing Crosby, and one of the game's great and colorful institutions. The Lodge at Pebble Beach, which overlooks the famous 18th fairway, is one of the world's legendary golf hotels.

The private Cypress Point Club, on California's Monterey Peninsula, is the ravishingly beautiful creation of Alister MacKenzie, the Scottish-born surgeon turned golf course architect. The 231-yard 16th hole, with its daredevil carry to a promontory of green perched above the frothy cauldron of surf below, is the most famous par three in the world. The concept for the hole, however, came not from MacKenzie but from Marion Hollins, the outstanding woman golfer who had won the U.S. Amateur in 1921. Hollins, who had been entrusted with developing the Cypress Point property in 1923, was directly responsible for hiring MacKenzie, and the two became close collaborators. The fairways fringed with ice plant gambol above the sea cliffs and through the groves of wind-warped cypress from which the course takes its name. MacKenzie wrote of the unique Monterey cypress: "It has an elbowed gnarled appearance and is twisted into such fantastic shapes as to be almost frightening. It is even beautiful when dead and the elbowed limbs give the impression of huge white gaunt skeletons of giant men. If one first visits Cypress Point in foggy weather, these weird white skeletons looming out of the mist are so terrifying that they are apt to create a depressing effect which is only dispelled when the sun breaks through the mist and brings to view a wonderful variety of color unsurpassed on any golf course."

▷ JANUARY 14　▷ SPYGLASS HILL GOLF COURSE　▷ CALIFORNIA, U.S.A.

Spyglass Hill Golf Course is Robert Trent Jones's storybook course on the Monterey Peninsula, a fantasy world of silvery sand ridges and secluded fairways shadowed by the Monterey pines and cypress of the Del Monte forest. Robert Louis Stevenson visited Monterey in 1879 and Spyglass takes its inspiration from *Treasure Island*. Each of the holes is named for a character in the novel, including Billy Bones and Long John Silver. Spyglass also brings to mind another Stevenson novel, *Dr. Jekyll and Mr. Hyde*. The first four holes loop around the exposed shelves of sand along the coast. Then the landscape changes dramatically and indelibly when the course darts into the woods, with long, narrow holes climbing to greens cut from the forest, and herds of deer nibbling on the fairways. The result is a swashbucklingly tough course. As Jim Murray put it: "If it were human, Spyglass Hill would have a knife in its teeth, a patch on its eye, a ring in its ear, and tobacco on its beard."

Riviera Country Club in Pacific Palisades is the most famous of the series of Southern California golfing gems designed by George C. Thomas and built by his construction superintendent Billy Bell. The site of the annual Nissan (formerly Los Angeles) Open on the PGA Tour, Riviera became known as Hogan's Alley after he won the 1947 and 1948 L.A. Opens and then also captured the 1948 U.S. Open at Riviera. The location shots for *Follow the Sun*, the 1951 movie about Hogan's life, were also filmed at Riviera. Laid out in the mid-1920s, the essential feature of the course is the barranca or ravine that figures on eight of the holes, while the fairways and rough consist of spiky kikuyu grass, which spread after it was introduced to stop erosion within the walls of the barranca. On the sixth hole, there is a small sand trap in the middle of the green. The 18th hole, which threads its way through a valley with the green perched below the Mediterranean palazzo of a clubhouse, is one of the most famous in golf. In 2004, Mike Weir duplicated Hogan's feat by winning his second consecutive Nissan Open at Riviera.

▷ JANUARY 16   ▷ RUSTIC CANYON GOLF COURSE   ▷ CALIFORNIA, U.S.A.

Rustic Canyon Golf Course is a public course, spread out over 350 acres on the floor of a secluded canyon in Ventura County north of Los Angeles. The broad green fairways hug the canyon base, separated by a sandy wash bristling with native broom. Rustic Canyon is a resounding affirmation of the vision of its designer, young American architect Gil Hanse, who collaborated with golf writer-historian Geoff Shackelford on the project. Hanse is a leading proponent of the minimalist, lay-of-the-land school of design that emphasizes the firm, fast-running ground game and strategic bunkering found at the great links courses of Scotland. Very little earth was moved at Rustic Canyon, but the natural features of the land were used to maximum effect, with the expanses of low-lying fairway strikingly offset by the sepia shades of the surrounding hills and the backdrop of the Santa Susana Mountains.

▷ JANUARY 17   ▷ LAS VEGAS PAIUTE RESORT   ▷ NEVADA, U.S.A.

There are three courses at the Las Vegas Paiute Resort operated by the Paiute Tribe on their ancestral lands in the open desert 25 miles northwest of the Las Vegas Strip. The Wolf Course, Snow Mountain, and Sun Mountain were all designed by Pete Dye, with wide panoramic views out to bare, beige and blue Mount Charleston and Sheep Mountain. The Wolf Course has broad fairways, flanked by desert ridges covered with a brocade of red and orange mission poppies, while yuccas and Joshua trees grow in the waste areas. There is plenty of water in play as a result of natural wells on the site, including the pond that surrounds the rock-strewn island green on the 15th hole, but the real strengths of the course are the natural flow of the holes and the overpowering desolation of the surrounding desert. *Above and right: Wolf Course*

▷ JANUARY 18   ▷ CASCATA GOLF CLUB, NEVADA   ▷ U.S.A.

When it comes to golf, Cascata Golf Club is the last word in Las Vegas extravagance. Designed by Rees Jones and built by the MGM Grand, the course is intended as the ultimate golf experience, open by invitation only to the highest of high rollers. In particular, MGM wanted to trump rival Steve Wynn's Shadow Creek course. But when MGM bought Wynn's Mirage Resorts in 2000, it sold Cascata to Park Place Entertainment, whose Las Vegas holdings include Caesar's Palace. Opened in 2001, Cascata is laid out in the desert mountains, with the fairways slippered through the canyons offering generous landing areas. Cascata is Italian for "waterfall," and the course takes its name from the 417-foot cataract that cascades down the mountain face and flows through the center of the opulent clubhouse. Jones created waterworks throughout the course by pumping water from nearby Lake Mead into an ancient dry riverbed that ran through the property, while the fairways are rimmed by tens of thousands of individually drip-irrigated date palms and desert plants. The price tag for the course came to a Caesar's ransom of nearly $60 million.

▷ JANUARY 19 ▷ REFLECTION BAY GOLF CLUB ▷ NEVADA, U.S.A.

Reflection Bay Golf Club, which opened in 1998, is a Jack Nicklaus-designed resort course at Lake Las Vegas, 17 miles east of the Strip in the town of Henderson. The course is an entrancing combination of rocky desert terrain and flatter holes traced around the 320-acre man-made lake. There are elevated tees, double fairways split by native vegetation, and three waterfalls with semi-tropical rock pools. Five of the holes play along or across the lake, complete with a white sandy shoreline and palm trees. Lake Las Vegas also recently unveiled the Falls Course designed by Tom Weiskopf that dramatically scales the desert escarpments on the back nine. The resort features a Florentine-inspired Ritz Carlton Hotel with a re-creation of the Ponte Vecchio.

▷ JANUARY 20   ▷ ENTRADA AT SNOW CANYON GOLF COURSE   ▷ UTAH, U.S.A.

Entrada, which is Spanish for entrance, is located in St. George, in the color country of southwestern Utah. The course lies at the base of the rugged and ruddy Navajo and Kayenta sandstone cliffs near the mouth of Snow Canyon. Opened in September 1996, Entrada was designed by golf legend turned television commentator Johnny Miller with Fred Bliss. The course is built on 700 acres of desert floor. Several of the holes play along the rust-colored cliffs, others wind through a desert wash lined with mesquite and reedy water holes, while three holes run through the ancient beds of scarred black lava.

▷ JANUARY 21   ▷ GREEN SPRING GOLF COURSE   ▷ UTAH, U.S.A.

Green Spring Golf Course is a public layout in Washington City, near St. George, in the southwestern corner of Utah. Designed by Gene Bates and opened in 1991, the course is sculpted through tessellated red rocks, with holes playing over canyons the color of smoky rubies and ponds lined with tall marsh grasses. Pine Valley Mountain hovers above the course to the north, and the mountains of Zion National Park loom further in the distance to the east. Washington City was founded by 38 Mormon families, all originally from southern states, who made the great trek west to Salt Lake, and were asked by Brigham Young to grow cotton in southern Utah—the so-called Cotton Mission. Washington City was the first of the cotton settlements along the basin of the Virgin River, earning the region the name of Utah's Dixie.

▷ JANUARY 22   ▷ FOREST HIGHLANDS GOLF CLUB   ▷ ARIZONA, U.S.A.

Forest Highlands Golf Club, located south of Flagstaff, is not the type of desert course one expects to find in Arizona. The original Canyon Course, designed by Tom Weiskopf and Jay Morrish in 1988, is carved out of majestic ponderosa pines with the back nine running through the canyon. To make maximum use of the canyon and create a variety of holes, they devised a routing with six par-threes, five par-fives, and only seven par-fours. Ten years later, Weiskopf returned to design the Meadows Course on his own. It is located on higher ground. There are tranquil streams fringed with orange grasses running through the course and views of the San Francisco Peaks. *Right: Canyon Course*

Desert Forest Golf Club is the unsung masterpiece of Robert "Red" Lawrence. Designed in 1962, Desert Forest was the first true desert-style course, the progenitor of all subsequent target-style designs in which there is no buffer between the distant fairway and the vast desert floor with its bristling armamentarium of pipes, spikes, and barrels of cactus—staghorn, agave, prickly pear, yucca, ocotillo, and saguaro. Desert Forest was built as part of the development of the newly founded town of Carefree, north of Scottsdale. Lawrence had moved to Arizona in the 1950s and designed a number of courses in the southwest, earning him the nickname of the Desert Fox. Born in White Plains, New York, in 1893, Lawrence worked early in his career for such legendary figures as Walter Travis in New York and the Philadelphia firm of Toomey & Flynn. Desert Forest also played an important role in the career of Tom Weiskopf, who is an honorary member of the club. Weiskopf first played the course in 1965, when he was 22, and was so captivated by the design and landscape that his round at Desert Forest contributed to his decision eventually to settle in Scottsdale and become involved in designing courses.

▷ JANUARY 24   ▷ DESERT MOUNTAIN CLUB   ▷ ARIZONA, U.S.A.

Desert Mountain, a private golf community in Scottsdale, has a horn of plenty—108 holes of Jack Nicklaus Signature golf. Renegade, the first of the Desert Mountain Club's six courses, is set up with two flagsticks on each green for players of different levels. The Cochise Course was the original home of the Senior PGA's Countrywide Tradition. Geronimo is a severe desert layout, with the par-three 18th requiring a tee shot over a desert canyon. Apache provides more traditional golf, with broader fairways and large greens. Chiricahua, named "the best golf course in Arizona" by the *Scottsdale Tribune*, serves up long views of the Valley of the Sun from the high elevations. Outlaw, the sixth and final of Nicklaus's creations, is bordered by the Tonto National Forest, with striking views of Four Peaks, Pinnacle Peak, and Superstition Mountain.

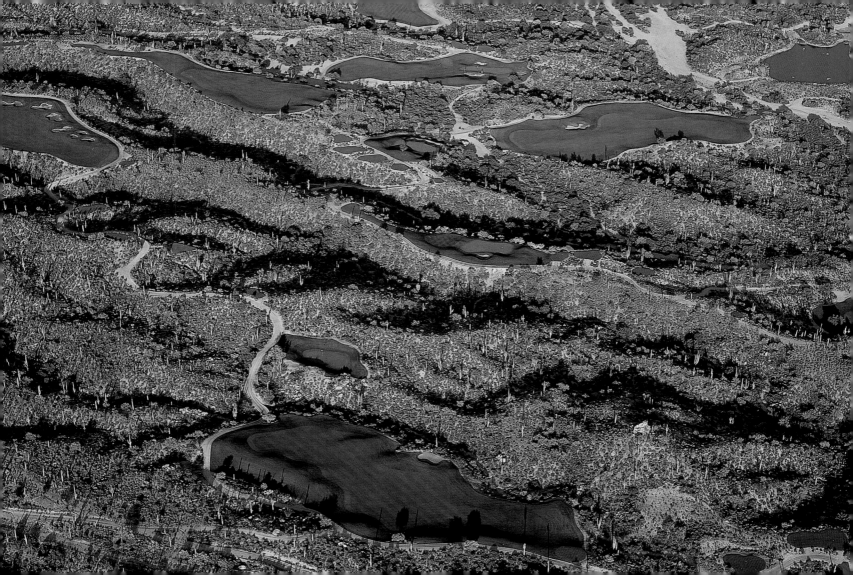

▷ JANUARY 25   ▷ APACHE STRONGHOLD GOLF COURSE   ▷ ARIZONA, U.S.A.

Apache Stronghold Golf Course is located in the austere desert wilderness of Arizona, guarded by the Chiricahuas, Aravipas, Superstition, and White Mountains. According to Apache legend, the Stronghold was a mystical haven in which the Apaches could pass unseen by their enemies. Located in the town of Globe, 90 miles east of Phoenix and 100 miles north of Tucson, the course is owned and operated by the San Carlos Apache Tribe as an adjunct to the Apache Gold Casino Resort. Designed by Tom Doak in 1999, the course exhibits his emphasis on fitting the holes to the natural features of the land, with careful shaping of the green contours. The broad fairways with bold cross bunkers are routed through secluded valleys, ridges, and across the many branches of the Gilson Wash that runs through the course, fretted with sage and mesquite trees. Apache Stronghold also offers desert variations on such classic Scottish links holes as the Redan and Principal's Nose.

Talking Stick Golf Club in Scottsdale features two courses, the North and the South, with the North ranked in *Golfweek's* Top 100 Modern Courses in America. Both courses were designed by the tandem of Ben Crenshaw and Bill Coore, and are prime examples of their emphasis on allowing the natural terrain to dictate the design, with broad fairways and carefully conceived cross-bunkers that dictate the angles of play. The North Course is a spare, treeless desert links, framed by wild native grasses, with long views across the landscape of palo verde trees, creosote, and mesquite to Camelback Mountain, the McDowell Range, and Pinnacle Peak. The South Course has a lusher, more parkland look. The courses were built on the lands of the Salt River Pima-Maricopa Indian community and take their name from the traditional Pima calendar stick, a wooden branch carved to mark significant historical events. *Right: North Course*

▷ JANUARY 27　▷ KIERLAND GOLF CLUB　▷ ARIZONA, U.S.A.

Kierland Golf Club is a 27-hole public course located in Scottsdale, with serene views of Camelback Mountain, Mummy Mountain, Pinnacle Peak, and the McDowell Range. Designed by Scott Miller, a former associate of Jack Nicklaus, and opened in 1996, the course is now part of Kierland Commons, which features an old-fashioned town square, including a town hall and the Westin-Kierland Resort. Miller moved a gargantuan 1.3 million cubic yards of earth to create the Acacia, Ironwood, and Mesquite nines. The result is holes contoured through broad ridges and banked hillsides, framed by blond desert grasses and mesquite trees. There are more than 300 saucer-shaped bunkers on the course, as well as lakes and dry desert washes. Kierland is also the home of a Golf Digest School run by Sandy and Mike LaBauve.

▷ JANUARY 28   ▷ ESTANCIA CLUB   ▷ ARIZONA, U.S.A.

The Estancia Club is the epitome of desert golf, laid out on the very doorstep of Scottsdale's Pinnacle Peak. Designed by Tom Fazio, Estancia garnered *Golf Digest's* award as the best new private course to open in the U.S. in 1996. The course starts off with greensites nestled in the rocky outcroppings, with their exclamation points of long-limbed sagauro cactus, before climbing the northern slope of Pinnacle Peak. There is no better testament to Fazio's adroitness at constructing courses that look entirely natural than Estancia, with the flowing green fairways spilling through the ferrous rock face of the mountainside.

▷ JANUARY 29　▷ PGA WEST　▷ CALIFORNIA, U.S.A.

PGA West is a country club community covering more than 2,200 acres near Palm Springs. There are six golf courses at PGA West—the TPC Stadium Course, the Jack Nicklaus Tournament Course, the Jack Nicklaus Private Course, the Arnold Palmer Private Course, the Tom Weiskopf Private Course, and the Greg Norman Course—set in the starkly barren desert of the Coachella Valley, against the backdrop of the crumpled San Jacinto Mountains. More than any other of his creations, the TPC Stadium Course, one of three courses at PGA West open to resort guests, earned Pete Dye his sobriquet as the Marquis de Sod when it opened in 1985. Intended to play as the world's toughest test, there had never been anything built quite on the scale of the Stadium Course. There are long forced carries over man-made lakes and bunker faces that rise 18 feet, dwarfing the hapless golfer below. The Stadium Course achieved notoriety when it hosted the Skins Game in 1986-1991, with Lee Trevino making an ace during the 1987 event when he one-hopped a six-iron into the hole on the rock-strewn, island-green 17th hole named "Alcatraz." The less severe Palmer Course was the site of one of the game's most historic rounds, when David Duval closed with an astounding 59 to win the 1999 Bob Hope Chrysler Classic, carding an eagle on the par-five 18th hole. *Above: Arnold Palmer Private Course Right: TPC Stadium Course*

▷ JANUARY 30   ▷ TORREY PINES   ▷ CALIFORNIA, U.S.A.

The Torrey Pines South Course in La Jolla, near San Diego, has long been recognized as the premier municipal course in Southern California and is familiar to golf fans as the site of the Buick Invitational. Rees Jones, "the Open Doctor," was hired in 2001 to strengthen the South Course, and he did just that, stretching it to a Herculean 7,600 yards from the tips and increasing the bunker tally from 44 to 72. Jones also added drama, shifting greens to bring the seaside cliffs and canyons more into play. The favorable reviews led to the USGA selecting Torrey Pines to host the 2008 U.S. Open, only the second municipal course ever to host the event. To go with the remodeled course, the luxurious Lodge at Torrey Pines opened in 2002. The Lodge, designed by Randell Makinson, emulates the Arts and Crafts Style that found great creative expression in Southern California in the early 1900s. The course adjoins the 2,000-acre Torrey Pines State Reserve, named for the rare torrey pine that is only found in the wild here and on Santa Rosa Island, forty miles off the coast from Ventura.

▷ JANUARY 3 1   ▷ CABO DEL SOL GOLF CLUB (OCEAN COURSE)   ▷ MEXICO

Cabo del Sol's Ocean Course may well be the best course ever designed by Jack Nicklaus and the setting in Mexico's Baja Desert, overlooking the splendor of the Pacific where Cortez once stood, is certainly one of the most bedazzling. Not long ago, the tip of the Baja Peninsula was an area visited only by serious fishermen in search of trophy marlin and billfish. Nowadays, Los Cabos, or "the Capes," the 20-mile stretch between the sleepy 17th-century mission village of San José del Cabo and the rowdy late-night bars of Cabo San Lucas, has become Mexico's top golf destination, with superb courses blossoming in the desert. Opened in 1994, Cabo del Sol is a memorable excursion through the profusion of the desert—organ-pipe and paddle cacti, palo verde, ironwood, wild plum, and fig trees—punctuated by peppermint fairways that spill onto the rocky coast surrounded by the searingly blue sea. The par-five 15th fans out to the Pacific and the lighthouse on *cabeza ballena,* or "whale's head," overlooking the waters where the right and gray whales spend the winter after their long migration from Alaska. Nicklaus has called the 16th through 18th three of the best ocean finishing holes in the world, with the par-three 17th playing over the sandy scimitar of beach to a raised green barricaded by the pink and gray sea rocks.

▷ FEBRUARY 1   ▷ CABO REAL GOLF CLUB   ▷ MEXICO

Cabo Real Golf Club is another Baja beauty in the Mexican golf constellation of Los Cabos. Designed by Robert Trent Jones, Jr. and opened in 1993, Cabo Real combines tropical seaside with mountain golf. Cabo Real's front nine climbs through the burnt orange ridges of the Sierra de la Laguna Mountains, with fairways careening along desert canyons. The more open back nine descends to the sea, with the par-three 12th plunging downhill, but not before taking in the long view out to the Pacific below. The par-three 15th plays across a powder puff of beach to a green that runs up to the backyard of the Las Ventanas al Paraiso Hotel. Of all the sybaritic resorts that line "The Corridor" between Cabo San Lucas and San José del Cabo, the most luxurious is Las Ventanas, its white adobes sprinkled around a sinuous lagoon of a swimming pool that runs through a desert garden of palms and barrel cactus out to the sea.

▷ FEBRUARY 2   ▷ FOUR SEASONS RESORT PUNTA MITA   ▷ MEXICO

The Four Seasons Resort Punta Mita is a shining example of Jack Nicklaus's flair for designing Edenic courses in tropical settings. The resort is spread out over nearly 1,500 acres on a peninsula between the Pacific and the Sierra Madre foothills some 45 minutes north of Puerto Vallerta. The course is routed around a narrow point, with five holes flirting with the Pacific, and three more wrapping around Banderas Bay. Some 1,800 palm trees frame the fairways, with waste bunkers of soft white sand. The showstopper at Punta Mita, or "Tip of the Arrow," is an optional 194-yard par-three hole, No. 3B, that plays across the ocean to a featherbed of green on a small rocky island. Golfers are ferried to the island by an amphibious golf cart.

▷ FEBRUARY 3   ▷ CLUB EL RINCÓN   ▷ COLOMBIA

There are several fine courses in Colombia but the most famous is El Rincón, located on the eastern outskirts of Bogotá. The course was designed by Robert Trent Jones in 1953, when he was gaining international prominence, on an open plain spotted with eucalyptus and pines near the Bogotá River. Jones planted numerous trees, seeded the fairways with kikuyu grass, and used the natural depressions to create lakes, so that water comes into play on 11 of the 18 holes. Jones also took into account the effect of the altitude in increasing the flight of the ball, since Bogotá is situated in the eastern range of the Andes, stretching the course to over 7,500 yards. The course has changed little over the years, except that the order of the two nines has been reversed, and Jones revised the par-three seventh to make it more closely resemble his famous par-three fourth over the water at Baltusrol. In 1980, El Rincón hosted the World Cup won by the Canadian pairing of Dan Halldorson and Jim Nelford.

▷ FEBRUARY 4   ▷ THE JOCKEY CLUB   ▷ ARGENTINA

The Jockey Club, with its Tudor clubhouse fit for a king, is located on Avenida Márquez in San Isidro, a suburb on the north side of Buenos Aires. One of the most famous and stylish of South American clubs, the Jockey Club has two 18-hole courses, the championship Red Course and the Blue Course, both designed by the illustrious Dr. Alister MacKenzie. The site of the courses, adjoining the club's racetrack and polo fields near the River Plate, is flat. MacKenzie therefore had to create features and give the courses definition, which he accomplished by constructing pushed-up greens, mounds, and clever use of bunkering. The courses opened in 1935, one year after MacKenzie's death. The Red Course hosted the World Cup in 1962, when the American team of Arnold Palmer and Sam Snead won, and in 1970, when the Aussie duo of Bruce Devlin and David Graham were victorious. *Right: Red Course*

▷ FEBRUARY 5   ▷ LLAO LLAO RESORT & HOTEL GOLF COURSE   ▷ ARGENTINA

Llao Llao Resort & Hotel is set in the Andean grandeur of Argentina's Nahuel Huapi National Park in Patagonia. Located 22 miles from the town of Bariloche and 17 miles from the main ski center of Cerro Catédral, the hotel sits on the hill between Lakes Nahuel Huapi and Moreno, with the snowcapped Andes as a backdrop and the golf course spread out below. The hotel, opened in 1940, is the work of the well-known Argentine architect, painter, and sculptor Alejandro Bustillo. Designed in the style of a Canadian mountain lodge, it features cypress logs, Norman red roof tiles, and a stone base. The golf course was situated and designed by Alberto Solar Dorrego. The course loops around the shores of ice-blue Lake Nahuel Huapi, with specimen trees of cypress, coigue, and arrayan. Above the course loom Mounts López and Capilla and the towering Tronador.

▷ FEBRUARY 6   ▷ ARELAUQUEN GOLF AND COUNTRY CLUB   ▷ ARGENTINA

Arelauquen Golf and Country Club is set in the mountain splendor of Patagonia, eight miles from Bariloche, surrounded by the Andes. The resort covers 1,400 acres, of which 1,000 are maintained as wilderness. The course, for which Argentine pro and Champions Tour player Vicente "Chino" Fernandez served as the design consultant, borders Gútiérrez Lake and is crossed by Longochinoco Stream. There are views throughout the course of the peaks of Cerro Otto and Cerro Catédral, the home of the area's main ski resort. There is also a five-star, 23-room mountain lodge at the course, built of native stone and timber.

▷ FEBRUARY 7   ▷ MARTINDALE COUNTRY CLUB   ▷ ARGENTINA

Martindale Country Club is located 35 miles outside of Buenos Aires in Pilar. The course was founded by John "Juan" Martin, an Argentinean of English descent, on the 1,000-acre estate and horse farm used for breeding polo ponies started by his father. Opened in 1989, the course was designed by local architects Diego Caprile and Marcos Capdepont, working with Houston-based Ken Dye. The mansion on the estate is now the clubhouse, while the course is routed through mature trees, with the brook on the property expanded to create a series of ponds within the centrifugal fairways. Martin was inspired to build the course by his father-in-law, the late Baron Marcel Bich, who created Les Bordes on his hunting estate in France's Loire Valley. Martin met his future wife when he was sent to resolve a dispute between Martin, Sr., who had acquired patent rights to the ballpoint pen process, and the Baron, who put his name on the Bic pen.

▷ FEBRUARY 8   ▷ GAVEA GOLF AND COUNTRY CLUB   ▷ BRAZIL

Gavea Golf and Country Club lies on the coast south of Rio de Janeiro, beyond Copacabana and Ipanema beaches. As Sir Peter Allen put it: "The location of Gavea—which Herbert Warren Wind tells us means Crow's Nest—is spectacular in the extreme as it is dominated by the huge monolithic Rock of Gavea which hangs 2,000 feet over the course like a great monster." The first nine holes and the final four are laid out through the hills, while the remaining five run through the palms and the flat sandy stretch near the shore. The second-oldest golf club in Brazil, Gavea was founded in 1923 by a group of Scots and Englishmen, with the course laid out by Arthur Morgan Davidson, a young assistant professional from Peterhead in Scotland, who continued as the pro for another 20 years.

▷ FEBRUARY 9   ▷ TERRAVISTA GOLF COURSE   ▷ BRAZIL

Terravista Golf Course is part of a new resort located in the Brazilian state of Bahia, a 90-minute flight north from São Paulo to Porto Seguro and then a 50-minute drive or, if you prefer, a ferry ride across the bay to Arraial D'Ajuda and a short drive to Trancoso. Terravista may not be easy to get to, but it is worth the journey, with spectacular holes spread out across the tabletop of the wrinkled sandstone cliffs that soar above the white sand beaches of the Atlantic. The 12th through 15th holes all run along the 120-foot high cliffs. This highwire act of a golf course, completed in 2004, was designed by Dan Blankenship, an American who worked with Pete and Perry Dye on the course at the Rio beach resort of Buzios, and decided to settle in Brazil. Trancoso is a tranquil fishing village and one of the earliest Portuguese settlements in Brazil, dating from 1586.

▷ FEBRUARY 10   ▷ COSTA DO SAUÍPE GOLF LINKS   ▷ BRAZIL

Costa do Sauípe Golf Links is part of the Costa do Sauípe resort located in Brazil's northern state of Bahia, some 50 miles from the capital of Salvador. The sprawling, 425-acre resort with five hotels is set in the environmentally protected area of Costa dos Coqueiros, consisting of miles of mangroves, *restingas* or natural levees, dunes, freshwater lagoons, coconuts, and stretches of Atlantic forest. The golf course, opened in November 2000, was designed by Brian Costello of JMP Golf Design Group. The beautifully maintained course features views of the sea and fairways elegantly hemmed by the powdery littoral sand dunes.

▷ FEBRUARY 11   ▷ COMMANDATUBA OCEAN COURSE   ▷ BRAZIL

The Commandatuba Ocean Course is a tropical idyll located on Ilha de Commandatuba off the coast of Brazil's Bahia province. Part of the Transamerica Ilha de Commandatuba Resort, the course, which opened in 2000, was designed by American Dan Blankenship, who is based in Brazil. The course is laid out on a flat spit of sand between the Atlantic beach and a mangrove swamp. The fairways run through scattered stands of centennial coconut trees, jupatis, and a patchwork of small lakes. The five finishing holes all skirt the beach, with fairways and greens stenciled on the surrounding sandy waste areas. The course is inhabited by capuchin monkeys, exotic birds, foxes, and anteaters.

▷ FEBRUARY 12   ▷ LAGUNITA COUNTRY CLUB   ▷ VENEZUELA

Lagunita is one of the finest and most venerable courses in Venezuela, located outside Caracas in a suburb of El Hatillo. Founded in 1956, the course is one of the few international designs of Dick Wilson, in contrast to his globetrotting rival in the design field during the 1950s and 1960s, Robert Trent Jones. The layout of the course is scissor-shaped, with many doglegs, beginning with the par-five first, which turns sharply to the left around an old quarry. There are five par-threes, with three of them measuring over 200 yards. Lagunita hosted the 1974 World Cup, which was won by the South African team of Bobby Cole and Dale Hayes.

▷ FEBRUARY 13   ▷ ROYAL WESTMORELAND   ▷ BARBADOS

Royal Westmoreland in Saint James Parish, on the west coast of Barbados, is a broad, tumbling course situated high above the Caribbean and fanned by the trade winds. Designed by Robert Trent Jones, Jr., the course has some of the most dramatic and challenging par threes in golf, with carries over coral rock, equatorial gorges, and water-filled quarries. While there is room off the tee, stray shots are likely to end up in one of the sugary bunkers or borders of purple feather grass and pandana, the spiky green and yellow cane lilies used to weave native baskets. Royal Westmoreland finishes with a flourish—a par five that requires a drive over a ravine brimming with mahogany, river tamarind, and dwarf bamboo. The course is surrounded by villas overflowing with bougainvillea and hibiscus, including "Lazy Days," the home of Masters champion Ian Woosnam that is just below the 18th tee.

▷ FEBRUARY 14   ▷ GREEN MONKEY GOLF COURSE AT SANDY LANE   ▷ BARBADOS

The Green Monkey Golf Course is a spectacular course overlooking the Caribbean at the ultra-luxurious Sandy Lane Hotel in Barbados, where Tiger Woods tied the knot with his Swedish valentine, Elin Nordegren, in the fall of 2004. Unofficially opened in 2003, the course took years to build, with the fairways blasted and chiseled in terraces through a coral stone quarry, its bare, 100-foot high walls striated with pinks and grays. The massive undertaking, including the creation of artificial lakes through the landscape of coral boulders, was orchestrated by Tom Fazio, who also completely reworked and expanded Sandy Lane's existing resort course. The Green Monkey owes its creation to Dermot Desmond and J.P. McManus, two Irish entrepreneurs and passionate golfers who purchased the Sandy Lane Hotel and rebuilt it from scratch. The course takes its name from the small green monkeys that came to Barbados as stowaways on slave ships 350 years ago. One of the bunkers is emblazoned with a grass island in the shape of a monkey.

▷ FEBRUARY 15   ▷ FOUR SEASONS RESORT GOLF COURSE   ▷ NEVIS

The Four Seasons Resort Course on Nevis begins at the base of Nevis Peak, the dormant volcano that dominates the small tear-drop shaped island in the West Indies that Columbus discovered in 1493. Columbus supposedly thought that the ring of clouds encircling the peak was snow, and christened the island Nuestra Señora de Los Nieves, or Our Lady of the Snows. Golf came to Nevis about 500 years later, in 1991, when the Four Seasons opened the course designed by Robert Trent Jones, Jr. The course is laid out on land that had once been Pinney's Plantation, Azariah Pinney having come to Nevis from England in 1685 to make his fortune in the sugar trade. The first few holes run through coconut and fan palms and the ruins of an old sugar mill. Then the course begins its climb along the 3,232-foot high Nevis Peak, with fairways carved through flamboyants, clammy cherry, sour-sop, and African sandbox trees. From the high holes, there are stirring views of the lush greenery of Nevis to the south and across Banana Bay to the bare mountains of St. Kitts to the north. The par-five 15th hole calls for a carry of 240 yards from the back tees over a river gorge that is home to green vervet monkeys, mongoose, and wild donkeys, before the course descends back to Pinney's Beach.

Palmas del Mar Resort and Country Club is a planned community in Humacao, Puerto Rico, developed by Charles Fraser, the man behind Sea Pines Plantation on Hilton Head Island and Florida's Amelia Island Plantation. The 2,100-acre resort with three and a half miles of beach has two courses, the Palms Course, a 1974 Gary Player design, and the Rees Jones-designed Flamboyan Course that debuted in 1999. The Flamboyan Course, which features Jones's swirling contours, wraps around a 23-acre lake, crosses the Candelero River, and dashes along the coast before climbing into the hills overlooking the ocean. The par-three 12th hole plays across a canal to a green backed by the ocean. *Right: Flamboyan Course*

Casa de Campo's Teeth of the Dog is Pete Dye's Dominican masterpiece, one of the world's truly great seaside courses and perennially ranked as the top course in the Caribbean. Dye first surveyed the site in 1969, when it was part of the vast holdings of Gulf & Western Corporation, whose CEO Charles Bludhorn launched the Casa de Campo resort. The course was painstakingly constructed by hand, with 300 local laborers chiseling the fairways from the sharp coral known as "dientes del perro" that gives the course its canine moniker. Topsoil was brought from the mountains by ox-drawn carts and the grass was all planted by hand. The entire course bears Dye's unmistakable stamp, from the cinnamon-colored waste bunkers to the coral tee boxes, to the small, contoured greens. Dye created a variety of inland holes but showed his true brilliance in letting Mother Nature take care of the seven holes that straddle and somersault across the azure waters of the Caribbean. Combined with the lavish tropical beauty of the setting, it is not hard to understand why Dye admits that Teeth of the Dog is the favorite of all his courses, and where he built a thatched-roof home alongside the fifth hole.

▷ FEBRUARY 18   ▷ CASA DE CAMPO (DYE FORE COURSE)   ▷ DOMINICAN REPUBLIC

The Casa de Campo Resort, located a two-hour drive southeast of Santo Domingo outside the town of La Romana, is the home of four Pete Dye-designed courses. In April 2003, Casa de Campo unveiled Dye's latest and long-awaited creation, dubbed Dye Fore. The course, built on an epic scale, spreads across cliffs and over chasms above the ominous, 300-foot deep gorge of the Chavon River, its banks lined with endless rows of palm trees. The course also overlooks Altos de Chavon, a cobble-stoned replica of a 16th-century Spanish village built by Casa de Campo developer Charles Bludhorn that houses restaurants, galleries, and artists' studios, as well as a stone amphitheater. The course follows the Chavon River out to the delta where it empties into the sea.

▷ FEBRUARY 19   ▷ PLAYA GRANDE GOLF COURSE   ▷ DOMINICAN REPUBLIC

The Dominican Republic has earned a well-deserved reputation as the Caribbean's leading golf destination. The courses that have received all the attention are in the southeast, with four Pete Dye-designed courses at Casa de Campo and courses by P.B. Dye and Jack Nicklaus at Punta Cana, with several more on the drawing board. Playa Grande Golf Course is a spectacular but unheralded layout east of Puerta Plata in a remote area of the Dominican Republic's north coast. The last course worked on by legendary archictect Robert Trent Jones, it was completed after many years in 1997. The course runs across tabletop cliffs 100 feet above the royal blue waters. With 11 holes circumnavigating the seaside cliffs, Playa Grande is truly the Pebble Beach of the Caribbean.

▷ FEBRUARY 20   ▷ THE WHITE WITCH   ▷ JAMAICA

The White Witch at the Rose Hall Plantation in Jamaica has become one of the top resort courses in the Caribbean since it opened in 2000. The course, designed by Robert von Hagge and Rick Baril, is spread out over 600 acres of lush, hilly countryside, splashed with big, ragamuffin bunkers, kettle ponds, and rambling stone walls. There are views over Montego Bay at every turn, with 16 of the 18 holes overlooking the sea. Developed and operated by the Ritz-Carlton, the course is named after Annie Palmer, the 19th-century mistress of the 4,000-acre Rose Hall sugar plantation. She was reputed to have murdered three of her husbands and many lovers before she met an untimely end herself at the hands of the plantation's overseer.

▷ FEBRUARY 21   ▷ FOUR SEASONS RESORT GREAT EXUMA AT EMERALD BAY   ▷ BAHAMAS

The Four Seasons Resort Great Exuma at Emerald Bay features a course designed by Greg Norman. The resort is 90 miles south of Nassau on Great Exuma, near the capital city of Georgetown, although most of the 365 islands that form the Exumas chain are uninhabited. Opened in 2003, the inland holes are routed around mangrove preserves and through palms on the higher ground overlooking the ocean. There is a sextet of seaside holes, Nos. 11 through 16, that wind along a peninsula studded with coral rock that is surrounded by the cornflower-blue Caribbean. The ample fairways are seeded with saltwater-resistant paspalum grass and the fine, milky-white sand in the bunkers was dredged from Emerald Bay. Norman has purchased a slip at the resort to moor his 228-foot motor yacht, christened *Aussie Rules*.

▷ FEBRUARY 22   ▷ SEMINOLE GOLF CLUB   ▷ FLORIDA, U.S.A.

Seminole Golf Club, ten miles north of Palm Beach, may have the most mystique of any club in the United States, in part because it was a favorite haunt of Ben Hogan, who was a member. Each year late in his career Hogan would play the course for 30 days straight to prepare himself for the Masters. Opened in 1929, Seminole was designed by Donald Ross, who made the most of the 40-foot high dune ridge running through the site. Seminole features the sloping, crowned greens for which Ross became famous at Pinehurst, but Seminole runs directly along the Atlantic, its fairways dotted with palms, and the wind is a constant factor. The nearly 200 swagged and sculpted bunkers encircling the greens and rippling across the fairways also weigh heavily on the player's mind. Ross was a modest man, but he was clearly pleased with his work at Seminole, declaring: "I don't say it is the best I have ever designed. Nevertheless, I like it very much." Claude Harmon, who was the professional at Seminole during the winter months and Winged Foot in the summer, shot the course record of 60 in 1947.

The Medalist Golf Club is a demanding private course laid out in the marshes adjoining Florida's Hobe Sound. Designed by Greg Norman and Pete Dye, the Medalist opened in 1994. The wide fairways run through ramrods of pines to small, angled greens, requiring a number of forced carries over marshes and waste bunkers frocked with ruby red grasses. Norman has had a close association with the Medalist, continuing to revise the design over the years. The course is known in particular for the sophisticated chipping areas around its greens, which have become something of a Norman trademark. The old-fashioned sod-walled bunkering is also unusual, particularly for a course in Florida, but reflects the deep affinity of Dye and Norman for traditional links golf.

▷ FEBRUARY 24   ▷ RED STICK GOLF CLUB   ▷ FLORIDA, U.S.A.

Red Stick is a private, high-end club located by Kings Highway in Vero Beach that opened in November 2000. The founders sought to create a "modern classic" and brought Rees Jones on board to design the course on a 320-acre site that includes part of the piney dune ridge running from Sebastian to Jupiter Hills, as well as seams of wetlands blanketed by white fountain, pink muhly, and marsh grasses. Jones routed the opening holes through the wetlands, followed by a pine barren sequence, and then sculpted rolling features through what had been an open, flatter area. The pine barren portion of the course, which runs from holes seven through 14, was enhanced with the planting of almost a thousand oak, slash pine, and loblolly trees, while fill from the three lakes that were built on the course was used to add dimension to the finishing holes. The club takes its name from the Redsticks, Creek Indian warriors who carried red sticks into battle and were allies of the Seminoles during Florida's Indian wars.

▷ FEBRUARY 25 ▷ BLACK DIAMOND RANCH (QUARRY COURSE) ▷ FLORIDA, U.S.A.

Black Diamond Ranch's Quarry Course is one of the most dazzling designs in the impressive portfolio of architect Tom Fazio, whose skill in enhancing the aesthetic appeal of any landscape is unsurpassed. Located in Lecanto, in Florida's Citrus County just 15 minutes from the Gulf of Mexico, Black Diamond Ranch is a 1,320-acre private golf club community. The Quarry Course, which opened in 1987, plays through a limestone quarry with fairways bracketed by live oaks, dogwoods, myrtles, and magnolias. The quarry holes begin with the 13th, a par-three that plays 180 yards over the smaller of the two quarries, with the back tee perched over 80 feet above the quarry floor. The next four holes bob and weave through the limestone escarpments, with the green of the 218-yard par-three 17th guarded by 30-foot cliffs. Dan Jenkins called this stretch of holes "the best five consecutive holes of golf anywhere in the world."

▷ FEBRUARY 26   ▷ WORLD WOODS GOLF CLUB   ▷ FLORIDA, U.S.A.

World Woods Golf Club, located 50 miles north of Tampa in Brooksville, defies all stereotypes of golf in Florida. The two courses, Pine Barrens and Rolling Oaks, are laid out on 2,100 acres of pristine, sandy pine forest. The president of World Woods, Yukisha Inoue, set out to build courses that would rival the best in the world, hiring preeminent golf course architect Tom Fazio for the job. Fazio's design for the Pine Barrens course, which opened in 1993, is both a stunning homage to Pine Valley Golf Club, the world's top-ranked course set in the pine barrens of New Jersey, and a unique achievement. Unlike the exclusive Pine Valley, where Fazio is a member, World Woods is open to the public. At Pine Barrens, the fairways are curving green atolls set among scooped-out sandy reefs sprinkled with brush and wiry grasses. Taken all together, the golfer must negotiate 44 acres of waste bunkers. *Above and right: Pine Barrens Course*

▷ FEBRUARY 27   ▷ HYATT REGENCY GRAND CYPRESS RESORT   ▷ FLORIDA, U.S.A.

The Hyatt Regency Grand Cypress Resort in Orlando already had 27 holes of golf designed by Jack Nicklaus when in 1988 the resort unveiled Nicklaus's New Course. The New Course is a Sunshine State tribute to the Old Course in St. Andrews, Scotland. Many features of the Old Course are usefully and entertainingly woven in, including a recreation of the Swilcan Burn, although this one is inhabited by alligators. There are also recreations of Hell Bunker, the pot bunkers known as the Beardies, and the Principal's Nose, not to mention several double greens. The 17th hole plays as the Road Hole, including a stone wall along the pebble-dash road, and the pronounced dip in front of the 18th green is a Floridian version of the famous Valley of Sin. The courses are laid out on 1,500 acres one mile north of the hotel.

▷ FEBRUARY 28   ▷ TPC AT SAWGRASS (STADIUM COURSE)   ▷ FLORIDA, U.S.A.

Located at Ponte Vedra Beach near Jacksonville, the Stadium Course at the Tournament Players Club at Sawgrass is a landmark course in the annals of golf course architecture. Designed by Pete Dye as the first TPC course and opened in 1981, Sawgrass came to define a new style of target golf, in which the player had to find the salvation of fairway amidst a diabolical array of waste bunkers and lagoons. The course was conceived by Deane Beman, the then-Commissioner of the PGA Tour, specifically to hold the Players Championship, with spectator mounds used to create the concept of stadium golf. While the pros found the course hellish, and complained long and loud (leading to the course being revised two years after it opened), the golfing public relished the dramatic spectacle that builds to a crescendo on the three finishing holes. Dye became a household name among golfers and the term "signature hole" entered the golf lexicon with the famous par-three, 17th island hole. While there had been earlier island greens, none matched the stark severity of Dye's creation—a green omphalos surrounded by a sea of blue.

▷ MARCH 1   ▷ FANCOURT RESORT AND HOTEL (MONTAGU COURSE)   ▷ SOUTH AFRICA

The Fancourt Resort and Hotel near George, South Africa, is in the heart of the "Garden Route," the strip of coastline east of Cape Town that stretches from Heidelberg in the west to the Tsitsikamma Forest and the Storms River in the east. All three of Fancourt's courses, the Montagu, the Outeniqua, and the Links, were designed by Gary Player, South Africa's paragon of golf. Framed by the Outeniqua Mountains, the Montagu Course offers lush green fairways, sapphire lagoons, and bands of the brilliant heathland vegetation, known as *fynbos* or "fine bush" in Afrikaans, that exemplifies the Edenic landscape for which the Garden Route is famed.

▷ MARCH 2   ▷ FANCOURT RESORT AND HOTEL (LINKS COURSE)   ▷ SOUTH AFRICA

The Fancourt Resort and Hotel hosted the 2003 President's Cup, played on the resort's Links Course, the most recent of the resort's Gary Player-designed courses. The potboiler of a President's Cup ended in a controversial tie agreed to by team captains Jack Nicklaus and Player with darkness approaching, after Tiger Woods and Ernie Els had played three holes of a pressure-packed sudden-death playoff. The Links Course is an exposed, rumpled layout with authentic links features, spread out against the unkempt savannah grasses with the Outeniqua Mountains hovering above.

▷ MARCH 3   ▷ WILD COAST COUNTRY CLUB   ▷ SOUTH AFRICA

Wild Coast Country Club is routed through a dramatic site in the Transkei hills, some 80 miles south of Durban on the south coast of KwaZulu-Natal. The hotel complex adjoining the course is built on the edge of the Umtamvuna River and Thompson's Lagoon. Designed by Robert Trent Jones, Jr. and opened in 1983, the course is a rugged, untamed journey through narrow valleys and over ravines brimming with native vegetation, with the first hole playing above Thompson's Lagoon. The elevated tees provide views of the Indian Ocean, while the greens have been cultivated with grass from Durban Country Club, making for exceptionally fine putting surfaces.

▷ MARCH 4   ▷ DURBAN COUNTRY CLUB   ▷ SOUTH AFRICA

Durban Country Club, just two miles from the downtown Durban skyline, is South Africa's premier course and one of the best in the world on any score. The course runs parallel to the Indian Ocean with its wide sandy beach, separated only by the coastal highway. The heaving fairways, built over the coastal sand hills, crest and dip through indigenous trees and thick bush. The most famous hole is the par-five third, with the tee atop a dune and the drive down to the chute of rolling fairway below. The short par-three 12th is named for the Prince of Wales, who took 17 shots when he played here in 1924. Durban was designed in 1922 by the South African professional Laurie Waters working with George Waterman. Waters had been an assistant to Old Tom Morris at St. Andrews before emigrating to South Africa in 1901 for his health.

Mauritius, discovered by Portuguese explorers in the late 1400s, is a tropical green paradise that lies 1,200 miles off the coast of southern Africa, out beyond Madagascar, in the middle of the Indian Ocean. There are four 18-hole courses on the island, with the venerable Gymkhana Club at Vacoas having been built by and for the British army back in 1902. There are also five nine-hole courses, with more golf on the way. The Belle Mare Plage Resort, 45 minutes from the capital of Port Louis on the east coast, is home to both the Legend Course designed by South African professional Hugh Baiocchi and opened in 1994, and the Links Course designed by Peter Alliss and Rodney Wright, which opened in 2003. The Legend, home to the Mauritius Open each December, features holes carved from volcanic rock and running along the lagoon of the coastal lowland plain, with native Javanese deer flitting across the fairways. Four holes on the front nine of the Links Course slither around the lagoon, while the back nine takes advantage of the rolling, wooded site. Mauritius was named by the Dutch, who claimed it in 1598, before it passed to the French in the early 1700s, while the British held the island from 1814 to 1968 and introduced golf. *Right: Legend Course*

▷ MARCH 6 ▷ HANS MERENSKY COUNTRY CLUB ▷ SOUTH AFRICA

Hans Merensky Country Club is located in Phalaborwa in South Africa's Limpopo or Northern Province. The course is laid out in the bushveld adjoining the famous Kruger National Park, which runs along the entire length of the Hans Merensky Estate's eastern boundary. The course is South Africa's ultimate golf-in-the-wild experience, set in the estate that includes an elegantly landscaped, thatched-roof hotel and its own private game reserve. The wildlife wandering the course includes giraffes, lions, warthogs, hippos, and several varieties of antelope. Originally established by the Phalaborwa Mining Company, the course was designed in 1966 by Bob Grimsdell and is beautifully maintained, with tranquil ponds and native trees. While efforts were made in the past to build fences to keep wildlife off the course, these proved unsuccessful and golfers must be wary of the big game, particularly elephants and buffalo. *Above: waterbuck on the course*

▷ MARCH 7   ▷ LOST CITY GOLF COURSE   ▷ SOUTH AFRICA

The Lost City Golf Course is one of two courses designed by Gary Player at Sun City, the lavish playground and casino built by Sol Kerzner in South Africa's North West Province. The desert-style, boulder-strewn course lies beneath the hills of the Pilanesberg bushveld, with the backdrop of the domed towers of the Palace of the Lost City, a fantasy of African fable turned into stunning reality. The ninth and 18th holes both circle the central lake, and several holes on the back nine adjoin the Pilanesberg Game Reserve. The green of the par-three 13th is in the shape of the African continent, with each of the three bunkers filled with a different color sand to symbolize the country's racial diversity. The hazard just left of the green is home to some 40 crocodiles.

There are many fine courses in Zimbabwe, the former Rhodesia, dating back to Bulawayo Golf Club founded in 1895, followed by Salisbury Golf Club, now Royal Salisbury, founded in 1899. The Elephant Hills Golf Course in Victoria Falls, opened in 1970, is two miles upstream on the Zambezi River from the fabled falls. Indeed, the plumes of spray can be seen from the balconies of the adjoining 276-room Elephant Hills Inter-Continental Hotel. The Gary Player-designed course cuts through the broad plain of bush with fairways frequented by grazing antelope and gaggles of baboons. The Scottish explorer David Livingstone became the first European to witness Victoria Falls on his excursion down the Zambezi in 1855, writing that "scenes so lovely must have been gazed upon by angels in their flight."

It should come as no surprise that there are several fine courses in Kenya, which was colonized by the English as British East Africa, with golf in Nairobi dating back to 1906. Karen Golf Club is located in the genteel Nairobi suburb of Karen, named for Baroness Karen Von Blixen, the Danish author who wrote *Out of Africa* under the pen name Isak Dinesen. In her book, which was made into an Oscar-winning movie, she describes her love affair with Denys Finch-Hatton and how she eventually came to leave the coffee plantation where she had lived for nearly 20 years, selling the land in 1931. The golf course was established in 1938, and was one of the first courses in Kenya to have grass greens, rather than sand to create "browns." The course is adorned with a profusion of flowering native trees and shrubs framed by the Ngong Hills. Von Blixen allowed the club to use the center portion of her coat of arms in the design of its flag and her stone farmhouse now houses the Karen Blixen Museum.

▷ MARCH 10 ▷ TABARKA GOLF CLUB ▷ TUNISIA

For many years the Carthage Golf Club in La Soukra, six miles from Tunis, was the only course in Tunisia, laid out near the Punic and Roman ruins of ancient Carthage. In recent years, however, Tunisia has become a major vacation destination for golfers from Northern Europe. Tabarka, like several other courses in Tunisia, was designed by California-based golf course architect Ronald Fream. The course is located two hours northwest of Tunis, near the Algerian border. Opened in 1992, it takes its name from the nearby fishing and coral harvesting village of Tabarka that traces its history to Carthaginian times. The course is laid out through the cork oaks and dunes running along the seaside cliffs, making this the Cypress Point of Tunisia. From the 14th hole there is a good view of the 16th-century Genoese fort that sits on the crest of a small island off of Tabarka's harbor, and inland are the mountains covered with oak forest.

▷ MARCH 11　▷ ROYAL DAR ES SALAAM (RED COURSE)　▷ MOROCCO

Golf in Morocco dates to Royal Tangier, opened in 1917, but flourished in the last few decades under the royal patronage of the late King Hassan II, an avid golfer who commissioned many courses. In 1971, Robert Trent Jones was hired to design the Red Course at Royal Dar Es Salaam near Rabat, which remains Morocco's top course. The course is carved through a forest of thousands of cork oaks and flowering trees and shrubs, including mimosa, bougainvillea, and orange trees, in the 1,000-acre forest of Zaers, near the royal hunting ground. Jones created the lakes that form the water hazards, and which are now home to colonies of flamingos and waterfowl. The course is the site of the annual Hassan II Trophy tournament, an invitation-only pro-am that attracts top pros from around the world.

▷ MARCH 12   ▷ CLUB DE GOLF VALDERRAMA   ▷ SPAIN

Valderrama is the crown jewel of golf in Spain, and the top-ranked course in continental Europe. It is tucked away in a quieter corner of the Andalusian coast—
to the west of the Costa del Sol and close to the Rock of Gibraltar—in the hills above Sotogrande with its swank marina. The patriarch and guiding force of
Valderrama is Jaime Ortiz-Patiño, heir to the Bolivian tin fortune, who has worked relentlessly to bring the course into the forefront of world golf. While
Valderrama's manicured fairways and pampered greens earn it comparisons to Augusta National, the abundant ancient cork oaks and flowering mimosa give it a
distinctively Andalusian character. Two of the most memorable holes are the par-five fourth, with the green guarded by a waterfall, and the par-five 17th, where
the sloped green fronted by the pond creates havoc for the pros. There is a good mix of short, tight par-fours and longer holes, and each of the four par threes is
memorable. Valderrama was designed by Robert Trent Jones and originally known as Los Aves, before Patiño and a few friends acquired the course in 1985, and
brought Jones back for further refinements. In 1997, Valderrama elevated Spanish golf to new heights when it became the first course in continental Europe to
host the Ryder Cup, with the European team captained by Seve Ballesteros holding off the favored Americans to claim a one-point victory.

▷ MARCH 13 ▷ TORREQUEBRADA ▷ SPAIN

Torrequebrada is located in the heart of the Costa del Sol, between Benalmádena and Fuengirola. Designed by Spaniard José (Pepe) Gancedo, once described as the Picasso of golf course architects, the course opened in 1976 and quickly became one of the most popular of the 30 or so courses clustered around the jet-set playground of Marbella and Puerto Banus. The course is laid out in the billowing hills above the Mediterranean, with the fairways lined by palms and pines and over 100 species of trees. Gancedo is known for working with dramatic terrain and Torrequebrada is no exception. Water comes into play on nine of the holes, most notably on the 16th, where lakes have to be navigated on both the drive and the approach. Torrequebrada is the home course of European PGA Tour star and Ryder Cup veteran Miguel Angel Jiménez. *Above: White village of Casares*

▷ MARCH 14   ▷ MONTECASTILLO HOTEL GOLF RESORT   ▷ SPAIN

Montecastillo Hotel Golf Resort is located just outside Jérez de la Frontéra, in the heart of Spain's sherry country between Cadiz and Seville, an area also known for its equestrian heritage. Montecastillo is the centerpiece of golf in western Andalucia, as golf spreads to the Atlantic coast, opening up a new frontier for golfers playing the boatload of glamorous courses along the Costa del Sol. Designed by Jack Nicklaus and opened in 1992, the course runs through ridges dotted with olive trees and the oversized, cookie-cutter shaped bunkers that line the fairways are filled with Marmolada sand. From 1997 to 2001, Montecastillo hosted the Volvo Masters, one of the top events on the European tour. The luxurious hotel with its castellated walls overlooks the course.

▷ MARCH 15   ▷ SAN LORENZO GOLF CLUB   ▷ PORTUGAL

During the past 30 years, Portugal's southernmost province, the Algarve, has become a hotbed of golf, with splendid courses spread among modern hotels and whitewashed villas along the Atlantic. Of all the Algarve's courses, the most stunning is San Lorenzo, or São Lourenço, one of four courses that make Quinto do Lago the Algarve's leading resort. Designed by the late Joe Lee and opened in 1988, the course straddles the western edge of the Ria Formosa Nature Reserve, a wetlands sanctuary for aquatic birds migrating from the Arctic to Africa. The elevated tee of the sixth hole offers a view of the fairway curving along the Ria's expansive salt marsh with a rickety wooden bridge leading out to the coastal dunes beyond. The seventh continues along the marsh, while the eighth and ninth skirt a large lagoon echoing with the cries of egrets, cranes, and purple gallinules, where once there had been a tomato field. The course returns to the lagoon on the 17th and 18th, with the final hole requiring a heroic shot across the lagoon to a headland of green. The course is named for the Church of São Lourenço, one of the most beautiful of the blue-and-white-tiled churches in the Algarve, located just outside the nearby town of Almancil.

▷ MARCH 16   ▷ VILAMOURA GOLF CLUB (OLD COURSE)   ▷ PORTUGAL

Vilamoura Old, one of several courses at the resort complex of Vilamoura with its glitzy marina, is one of the oldest and indisputably one of the best courses in the Portuguese Algarve. Designed by Frank Pennink in 1969, the course is a superb example of strategic design in the English parkland style, with doglegs and tight bunkering through the umbrella pines. The four par threes are exceptionally good and distinct from one another, with the fourth playing over water to a green flanked by trees and the 10th requiring a carry over a ravine. Pennink also designed the delightful Palmares Golf Club, which is a few miles further west near Lagos, where outdoor cafes line the old harbor that was once the stronghold of Henry the Navigator during the 15th century.

▷ MARCH 17   ▷ VALE DE PINTA   ▷ PORTUGAL

Vale de Pinta is a course that tends to be overshadowed by its better-known neighbors on the Algarve Coast, such as Penina, Vilamoura, and San Lorenzo, but it is one of the best that Portugal's golfing Riviera has to offer. Located near the lively beach resort of Carvoeiro, six miles east of Portimão, Vale de Pinta was designed by American Ronald Fream in 1992. The course is one of the most pastoral in the Algarve, with long views out to the Monchique Mountains to the north and across copper-colored rock outcroppings. The broad, bumpy fairways are generously sprinkled with white-flowering almond trees, first brought to the Algarve from North Africa by the conquering Moors, as well as fig, carob, and olive trees. The stout olive trees on the course are 400 to 600 years old, with one ancient, gnarled specimen estimated to be more than 1,500 years old.

▷ MARCH 18   ▷ PENHA LONGA GOLF CLUB   ▷ PORTUGAL

Penha Longa is a strikingly panoramic and punctiliously maintained course laid out in the foothills of the craggy Sintra Mountains near Lisbon. Part of the Caesar Park Penha Longa Resort, the clubhouse adjoins what was the first convent of the Order of St. Jerome, built in 1355, and later owned by the Count of Penha Longa. Over the centuries, the Portuguese royal family built a palace and homes on the grounds, beginning with the retirement house of King Manuel I, where he went into mourning after the death of his wife, Maria, in 1517. Robert Trent Jones, Jr., who designed the course in 1992, took full advantage of the steep terrain and magnificent backdrops, with the par-five sixth hole tumbling downhill to a green framed on the right by a 16th–century stone aqueduct and water tower and by the pond of Adens to the left. The par threes are particularly memorable, with the fifth plunging off an elevated tee and the seventh and 15th playing over ponds. The course finishes strongly, with a tough par-four 16th snaking through the valley to an elevated green and the par-five 18th running back to the palace. The course takes its name from the Penha Longa, or long rock, a spear of granite jutting from the hillside above the 18th hole.

▷ MARCH 19   ▷ FURNAS GOLF CLUB   ▷ AZORES

Furnas Golf Club is located on São Miguel, the largest of the islands comprising the Portuguese possession of the Azores in the north Atlantic, 900 miles from the Portuguese coast. Built between 1936 and 1939 as a nine-hole course, Furnas was designed by Scottish architect Philip Mackenzie Ross, whose portfolio includes the revamped Ailsa Course at Turnberry. A second nine was added in 1990 by the British firm of Cameron & Powell. The course overlooks the town of Furnas near Furnas Lake, an area renowned for its *calderas*, thermal springs that gush boiling water and mud. The local cuisine features *cozido* or a stew of meat and vegetables cooked by burying the pots in the volcanic earth. The course is designed in the traditional British style, its fairways separated by the Japanese cryptomeria introduced to the Azores about a hundred years ago, with sprays of hydrangeas, azaleas, and pink pampas grass.

▷ MARCH 20   ▷ TRÓIA GOLF CLUB   ▷ PORTUGAL

Tróia is one of Portugal's great courses and its secluded location, on the narrow sandbar of Tróia that is reached by a 20-minute ferry ride across the Sado Estuary from Setúbal, only adds to its mystique. The sandy promontory by the sea was the ideal landscape for Robert Trent Jones to create a Portuguese-style Pine Valley. The narrow, rippling fairways run through tall sentinel pines and are engulfed by the sandy scrub that substitutes for rough, with the course bracketed by the coast and the Arrábida Mountains. Opened in 1980, Tróia quickly proved its mettle at the 1983 Portuguese Open, when the winner Sam Torrance was the only player in the field to break par.

The grandiloquently named Real Sociedad Hipica Española Club de Campo or Royal Spanish Equestrian Society Club de Campo is located some 15 miles north of Madrid, next to the Jarama auto race track and the Spanish Royal Automobile Club's course. There are actually two golf clubs named Club de Campo near Madrid, the other being the well known Club de Campo Villa Madrid, which is located on the outskirts of Madrid, just across the valley and in clear sight of another championship course, Puerta de Hierro Golf Club. Hipica was founded separately from Villa Madrid in 1929, but when the equestrians based their stables at Villa Madrid, the two clubs merged in the 1940s. After Villa Madrid was purchased by the city of Madrid and became a municipal facility, the equestrians decided to demerge, and bought their own land for a new club. The result is two 18-hole courses, the North and the South, both designed by the American architect Robert von Hagge. The North Course, one of the highest rated in Spain, runs though puffy pines with fairways layered around four ponds. *Right: North Course*

▷ MARCH 22 ▷ CAMPO DE GOLF EL SALER ▷ SPAIN

Located outside Valencia with its orange groves and rice fields, El Saler is recognized as the masterpiece of the Spanish architect Javier Arana, who was responsible for designing the classical courses that continue to set the standard in Spain. More than half the holes run through a pine forest, beginning with the first four, but El Saler is best known for its links-style holes bordering the Gulf of Valencia. The waste areas of powdery sand are drizzled with myrtle and mimosa bushes and succulents known as "catclaws." The Parador de El Saler, one of Spain's state-owned hotels, adjoins the 18th green. El Saler hosted the Spanish Open in 1984, 1989, and 2001, and also was the site of the 2003 Seve Trophy Competition, pitting the top pros from Great Britain and Ireland against the Continental European team captained by Seve Ballesteros himself.

▷ MARCH 23   ▷ CLUB DE GOLF MASIA BACH   ▷ SPAIN

Masia Bach is located a half-hour drive west of Barcelona, adjoining the Masia Bach vineyard and overlooking the village of Sant Esteve Sesrovires with its dou-

ble-spired church. In the distance, rising abruptly from the valley floor, are the sheer stone peaks of Montserrat. Designed by Spain's José Maria Olazábal and

opened in 1990, Masia Bach is a bustling club. The course is carved out of the flanking mountainside in two nine-hole loops. The front nine is particularly strik-

ing, with fairways burrowing through rock walls and traversing water-filled gorges rimmed with pines. With plenty of elevation changes, there are long views

at every turn over the valley and the Catalan countryside.

▷ MARCH 24   ▷ PGA GOLF DE CATALUNYA   ▷ SPAIN

PGA Golf de Catalunya is one of the newer and better courses in Spain, adding to the superb cadre of courses around the Costa Brava that includes Masia Bach, Mas Nou, and Pals. Situated at Caldes de Malavella, the course is inland, with greens guarded by ponds, and fairways shorn from pines, cork oaks, and olives, framed by the Montseny Mountains. Designed by European Senior Tour veterans Neil Coles and Angel Gallardo, the course was developed by the PGA European Tour and opened in 1999. Golf de Catalunya hosted the Gene Sarazen World Open in 1999, won by Thomas Bjorn, and the 2000 Spanish Open. The course is 10 miles from the ancient walled city of Girona dominated by the cathedral tower overlooking the River Onyar.

▷ MARCH 25 ▷ REAL GOLF CLUB DE PEDREÑA ▷ SPAIN

Real Golf Club de Pedreña is where Seve Ballesteros, Spain's conquering hero, learned the game as a caddie and honed his short-game legerdemain, hitting rocks on the beach with a hand-me-down three-iron. While golf has boomed in the Costa del Sol to the south, the roots of the game in Spain are in the royal courses of the north, with Pedreña having been bestowed with its royal title by King Alfonso XIII, himself a dedicated golfer, shortly after it opened in 1928. Designed by the preeminent English architect Harry Colt, the course occupies a small, wooded peninsula that unfurls into the Bay of Santander, with the Cubas River estuary flanking both sides of the peninsula. The course is typically reached by ferry and provides fine views across the bay to the town of Santander, with the mountains beyond. In 1991, the members engaged Ballesteros to design an additional, and very challenging, nine holes that run around the hilly terrain with the estuary coming into play on seven of the nine holes. The clubhouse was originally a summer home for Alfonso XIII's wife, Queen Victoria Eugenia; Ballesteros's new home overlooks the course. *Above: fishing boats in Pedreña harbor*

▷ MARCH 26   ▷ GOLF DE CHIBERTA   ▷ FRANCE

Biarritz, the sophisticated resort on the Côte Basque first popularized by Napoleon III and the Empress Josephine, has the strongest golfing tradition of any part of France, and the most exciting combination of old and new courses. Golf in Biarritz began with the famous course laid out in 1888 by the Scottish pros Willie and Tom Dunn near the lighthouse or le Phare, which is still thriving, although in modified form, today. Chiberta is an exceptionally elegant seaside course just north of Biarritz, in Anglet, founded in 1927 by the immensely wealthy Belgian banker Albert Lowenstein. Designed by the patrician English architect Tom Simpson, who did much of his best work in France, the first hole runs down to a green framed by a Moorish-style palace. Simpson created a syncopated balance between the hushed holes that run through the woods and others that burst exuberantly into the open linksland along the beach of Chiberta, with its scores of surfers riding the long Atlantic rollers.

▷ MARCH 27   ▷ GOLF DE SEIGNOSSE   ▷ FRANCE

Golf de Seignosse is about 20 miles north of Biarritz, located in Les Landes—a marshy area of ferns and bracken, where the inhabitants used to get around on stilts. The dominant feature of this sparsely inhabited area is the seemingly endless colonnades of straight umbrella pines planted in the 19th century to curb erosion of the sandy soil. Designed by American architect Robert von Hagge and opened in 1989, the course's narrow fairways are cut through the secluded valleys and ridges of the Landaise Forest. There are dramatic elevation changes, with the high holes looking across the pine forest out to the Bay of Biscayne. There is also a small golf hotel adjoining the clubhouse, built in the style of a wood-frame New Orleans villa, painted a bright maroon.

▷ MARCH 28 ▷ CANNES MANDELIEU GOLF CLUB ▷ FRANCE

Golf was introduced to the French Riviera by Grand Duke Michael of Russia, who founded Cannes Golf Club in 1891, making it the fourth-oldest club in France. Grand Duke Michael's own introduction to the game came while on a partridge shoot in Scotland, when his curiosity was aroused by distant sightings of golfers on the Old Course at St. Andrews. The Grand Duke and his wife, Countess Sophie de Turbie, granddaughter of the poet Pushkin, had been exiled from Russia by Czar Alexander III and had taken up residence in Cannes. Having cultivated an enthusiastic band of fellow golfers, the Grand Duke inaugurated a nine-hole course through the parasol pines. The course was subsequently expanded to 18 holes, with Harry Colt having a hand in the redesign, but the esplanades of parasol pines remain the overriding feature. The River Siagne runs through the course, with a little ferry transporting golfers between the second and third and 12th and 13th holes. The rustic, half-timbered clubhouse was originally a hunting lodge.

▷ MARCH 29   ▷ MONTE CARLO GOLF CLUB   ▷ FRANCE

The Monte Carlo Golf Club at Mont Agel in La Turbie, France, is a showstopper, its fairways teetering on the mountainside plateau overlooking the Principality of Monaco. Indeed, at times the course can be shrouded in clouds, but on a typical clear day there are giddy views of Monte Carlo out to San Tropez and across the cerulean Mediterranean all the way to the outline of Corsica on the horizon. The first 11 holes unfold with unspoiled views of the mountains, while the final seven overlook the sea. The course has undergone substantial revisions in recent years, but was laid out by William Parker in 1911 at the request of the Société des Bains de Mer. Not surprisingly, the course is steep but the fairways are generous and clustered with elegant cypress. Prince Rainier has played the course regularly and the Monte Carlo Open, a European Tour event, was held here from 1984 to 1992.

▷ MARCH 30 ▷ PEVERO GOLF CLUB ▷ SARDINIA, ITALY

Pevero Golf Club is on the Costa Smeralda, the northeast coast of Sardinia developed by the Aga Khan as the playground for the international jet set. Designed by Robert Trent Jones in 1971 at the height of his career, Pevero is one of his grandest and most scenic creations. The course is laid out in two loops, rising and tumbling through a valley with the front nine curving around Pevero Bay and the back nine overlooking the beach of Cala di Volpe (Bay of Foxes). The fairways are hewn from the coastal rock and run through dwarf pine, broom, and gorse, with the ponds created by Trent Jones coming into play on the sixth and seventh and the 16th and 17th holes. From the fourth tee, with the green far below, the snow-capped mountains of Corsica can be seen across Pevero Bay.

Golf Club de Chamonix in the Rhone Alpes region of France offers breathtaking vistas of the Mont Blanc range and the massif of the Aguilles Rouges. Robert Trent Jones designed the course along the fairly flat valley at the base of the Alps, which is used for cross-country skiing in the winter months, while rock-bound streams wind through the fairways. Golf at Chamonix dates back to 1935, when the original nine-hole course was completed for the benefit of the English guests at the hotel. Work began on the expanded and redesigned 18-hole layout by Jones in 1977, and the course opened in 1982. Other Alpine courses in the region include Aix les Bains, Les Gets, Megève, and Annecy.

▷ APRIL 1   ▷ GOLF DE FRÉGATE   ▷ FRANCE

The Frégate course, which is part of the Dolce Frégate resort, is located in the foothills of Provence on the western edge of the Riviera, near the villages of Saint Cyr sur Mer and Castellet on the road to Bandol. Designed by American Ronald Fream and opened in 1992, the course is laid out along the ridges of a fan of land that runs through the Bandol vineyards and olive groves on the hills overlooking the Mediterranean. The par-three third is enclosed by the walls of an old quarry with marmalade-colored sandstone, rising to 50 feet high. The 10th hole at the far end of the course offers the best view over the sea and along the coastline with the westerly wind playing a major factor. The final hole climbs along a waterfall with five ponds. Much of the rock excavated during construction was used in building various hotel, clubhouse, and villa foundations, walls, and garden terraces. Over 100,000 cubic yards of topsoil was purchased from inland farmers to cover the exposed rock and allow grass to grow on the fairways. The stone clubhouse is adjacent to an attractive Mediterranean-style four-star hotel with a terra-cotta roof.

▷ APRIL 2   ▷ DALLAS NATIONAL GOLF CLUB   ▷ TEXAS, U.S.A.

Dallas National, a private course that opened in 2002, is built on 388 acres of rolling land crowned by woods of cedar, elm, and oak, and fields of wildflowers, defying all preconceptions of the topography of North Texas. Founder John MacDonald brought in designer Tom Fazio to build a demanding course that plays a whopping 7,326 yards from the Texas tees. The layout traverses creeks, canyons, and two plateaus on the Dallas-Duncanville-Grand Prairie borders, only six miles from downtown Dallas, with elevation changes of more than 170 feet. There are eight wood-trellised bridges to link the holes across the dramatic terrain. The members of Dallas National include Texas Ranger turned Yankee slugger Alex Rodriguez, baseball's wealthiest player and a dedicated golfer, hockey's Brett Hull, and golf legend and Dallas native Lee Trevino.

▷ APRIL 3   ▷ BARTON CREEK RESORT AND COUNTRY CLUB   ▷ TEXAS, U.S.A.

Barton Creek Resort and Country Club, located in the Texas Hill Country just 15 minutes west of downtown Austin, features a cornucopia of outstanding courses by Tom Fazio, Ben Crenshaw and Bill Coore, and Arnold Palmer. Fazio designed the Foothills Course in 1986 and followed it with the Canyons Course in 2000. Native son Crenshaw and his partner Coore are responsible for the Crenshaw Cliffside layout. Palmer's Lakeside Course is located 25 miles away on the shores of Lake Travis. Laid out over 210 acres, the Canyons Course runs through a box canyon with Short Springs Branch Creek coming into play. The course is terraced through hillsides ribbed with limestone, with prickly pear cactus, Spanish oaks, red oaks, junipers, sycamore, and orange-skinned madrone trees along the fairways. From 1990 to 1994, Barton Creek hosted the Legends of Golf tournament on the Champions Tour.   *Right: Canyons Course*

▷ APRIL 4   ▷ THE QUARRY GOLF CLUB   ▷ TEXAS, U.S.A.

The Quarry Golf Club, located near the San Antonio airport, is a sterling example of a golf course as a successful environmental reclamation project. Opened in 1993, the course is the first solo design of Keith Foster, a longtime associate of Arthur Hills. Routed through an abandoned limestone quarry, the front nine is laid out over 80 acres of land that was covered by kiln dust that had to be sealed in clay vaults. Lakes were excavated and the fill used to create the fairways. The back nine is a show-stopping tour through the 100-acre quarry, boxed in by 80- to 100-foot-high vertical walls. The quarry floor is sprinkled with native grasses, creased by chasms crossed by narrow bridges, and dominated by a lake tied directly to the San Antonio aquifer that comes into play on the 12th and 13th holes.

▷ APRIL 5 ▷ SHADOW HAWK GOLF CLUB ▷ TEXAS, U.S.A.

Shadow Hawk Golf Club is a private club in Richmond, a suburb of Houston. Opened in November 1999, Shadow Hawk's honorary members include the senior President George Bush. Designed by Rees Jones, the course is enclosed by oaks, mesquite, and mature pecan trees. Adjoining Shadow Hawk is the Houstonian, a public course designed by Jones, creating a powerful one-two punch. The dominant feature of the Houstonian is a natural oxbow lake that comes into play on the 13th through 17th holes, with the 17th a par-three that plays across the lake. The head pro at Shadow Hawk is Paul Marchand, one of the game's most respected teachers.

Money Hill Golf & Country Club, which wraps around a 200-acre lake fed by an artesian spring, is the centerpiece of the private community of Abitha Springs in southeastern Louisiana. Money Hill acquired its name in the 1800s because it was reputed to be where the Barataria pirates, the most infamous of whom was Jean Lafitte, had buried their stolen treasure. Treasure hunters continued to explore and excavate the site until well into the 1930s. Designed by Ron Garl and opened in 1998, the interior holes at Money Hill play across hills and valleys. The final five holes hug the shoreline, including the par-three 16th, with its green set in the lake. The home of many protected species of birds and plants indigenous to the longleaf pine ecosystem of this part of the Louisiana coast, Money Hill is a conservation priority site.

▷ APRIL 7   ▷ DANCING RABBIT GOLF CLUB   ▷ MISSISSIPPI, U.S.A.

Dancing Rabbit Golf Club is built on the ancestral lands of the Mississippi Band of the Choctaw Indians, most of whom were forcibly relocated to Indian Territory in Oklahoma in the 1830s. This resort in central Mississippi, near Tupelo, consists of two courses, The Azaleas and The Oaks, both designed by Tom Fazio and Jerry Pate, the 1976 U.S. Open champion. The courses are carved through gently rolling forests of high-canopied pines and hardwoods, with more than two miles of spring-fed creeks and streams weaving across the fairways. The clubhouse is located at the headwaters of Wolf Creek. Dancing Rabbit is named for the traditional Choctaw assembly grounds along the banks of the Big and Little Dancing Rabbit Creeks a few miles from the clubhouse.

Above: clubhouse   Right: Azaleas Course

▷ APRIL 8   ▷ COTTON CREEK CLUB AT CRAFT FARMS   ▷ ALABAMA, U.S.A.

The Craft Farms Golf Resort on Alabama's Gulf Coast originated as a gladiolus farm founded by R.C. Craft in 1963. Craft expanded his gladiolus operation over the years but since the flowers only bloom for five to six weeks a year, starting in 1975 he decided to switch to other crops to ensure a year-round income stream. That same year, his son also started a successful sod farm after graduating from Auburn University. By the 1980s, the Crafts had the land and the turf-grass experience to build a golf course, and they persuaded none other than Arnold Palmer to design their course. Palmer's Cotton Creek Club opened in 1988, followed by a second 18, Cypress Bend, completed in 1997. In 1993, Craft Farms also acquired the Woodlands Course, designed by Larry Nelson, from a Japanese company that was unable to complete the project, giving the resort 54 holes of golf. Cotton Creek runs through the original course, crossing the dogleg 17th hole and flowing into the marsh that separates the two nines.

East Lake Golf Club is closely associated with the brilliant career of Bobby Jones, for it was here that he learned to play the game under the instruction of the Carnoustie-born professional Stewart Maiden. The East Lake property was acquired in 1904 by the six-year-old Atlanta Athletic Club for its new golf course. During the 1890s, the area had been an amusement park, Atlanta's version of Coney Island. The course opened on July 4, 1908, with six-year-old Bobby Jones present at the opening reception. Jones's father, "Colonel" Robert T. Jones, was a member from the outset and served as president of the club from 1937 to 1942. In 1915, when he was 13, Bobby defeated his father in the final to win the club championship. By the 1960s, East Lake had become an inner-city neighborhood and in 1970 a public housing project was built on the site of what had once been East Lake's No. 2 Course, designed by Donald Ross in 1928. Surrounded by urban blight, the original East Lake Course, which had been completely remodeled by Ross in 1913, was all but forgotten and the Atlanta Athetic Club moved to the northern suburbs. In a remarkable tale of urban renewal, a local charitable foundation headed by Tom Cousins purchased East Lake in 1993 and a year later course architect Rees Jones was brought in to restore Ross's lost masterpiece. The grandiose Tudor clubhouse overlooking the lake was also restored to its 1926 design. The reborn East Lake dazzled the golfing world when it was unveiled at the 1998 Tour Championship and has been the centerpiece of the revitalization of the neighboring community.

▷ APRIL 10   ▷ REYNOLDS PLANTATION   ▷ GEORGIA, U.S.A.

Reynolds Plantation is a resort and residential community set around Lake Oconee in central Georgia, 75 miles east of Atlanta. The resort developed by Mercer Reynolds boasts four top-drawer courses—the Great Waters Course designed by Jack Nicklaus, the National Course designed by Tom Fazio, the Plantation Course created by Bob Cupp, and the recently completed Rees Jones-designed Oconee Course—as well as a new Ritz-Carlton hotel. The Great Waters Course that opened in 1992 is carved from the Georgia pines around the nooks and crannies of the lakeshore. Nine holes play along or across Oconee, including the par-five 18th with water down the entire left side of the fairway and sickled green. Lake Oconee is Georgia's second-largest lake with 374 miles of shoreline and it makes a literary appearance in the opening paragraph of James Joyce's *Finnegan's Wake*. *Above and right: Great Waters Course*

▷ APRIL 11   ▷ AUGUSTA NATIONAL GOLF CLUB   ▷ GEORGIA, U.S.A.

Augusta National Golf Club, the home of the Masters Tournament that signals the coming of spring every April, was founded by Bobby Jones as his dream course. Jones started with the ideal property, a former nursery named Fruitlands founded by the Belgian horticulturalist Baron Prosper Berckmans. The old manor house is now one of the world's most famous clubhouses and the pitching fairways and greased lightning-fast greens are surrounded by floral fireworks in the form of azaleas, rhododendrons, camellias, and redbud. Jones engaged Dr. Alister MacKenzie as the architect and together they created a course that brilliantly reflected their shared belief in strategic design based on the model of the Old Course at St. Andrews. The 11th through 13th holes, which play around Rae's Creek, embody the risk-reward strategy of Jones and MacKenzie. This stretch of holes is known as Amen Corner, a name that the *New Yorker* golf writer Herbert Warren Wind came up with based on the jazz song "Shouting at Amen Corner." The Masters began in 1934 as the Augusta National Invitational and quickly blossomed into one of golf's four major championships. Through the Masters, Augusta National has come to symbolize the perfectly maintained and abiding beauty of the American parkland course.

▷ APRIL 12   ▷ SEA ISLAND GOLF CLUB   ▷ GEORGIA, U.S.A.

The Sea Island Resort was started by Howard Coffin, an automotive engineering whiz who founded the Hudson Motor Company. While visiting the Savannah racetrack in 1910, Coffin and his wife made a trip to Sapelo, a small island south of Savannah, and became enchanted with the beauty of the Georgia coast. Coffin purchased the 20,000-acre island in 1911 and continued to acquire additional land over the next decade, including the small island that was to become known as Sea Island. Coffin enlisted his cousin Alfred W. "Bill" Jones as his business partner, originally envisioning construction of a grandiose hotel on the scale of the Waldorf Astoria. Jones came up with a more realistic plan for an "overnight inn" and in 1928 the Cloister was born. The hotel has endured and flourished as a landmark of American golf and a popular honeymoon destination for newlyweds, including George and Barbara Bush, who spent their honeymoon there in 1945 and returned for their 50th wedding anniversary. The original course consisted of the Plantation Nine designed by Walter Travis and the Seaside Nine designed by the famed team of Harry Colt and Charles Alison; later, the Retreat Nine designed by Dick Wilson was added. In 1998, Rees Jones modified and seamlessly combined the Plantation and Retreat nines, creating the Plantation Course. At the same time, Tom Fazio created a completely redesigned and stunning 18-hole Seaside Course that unfolds through the lowland scenery of marsh and moss-draped live oaks with powder-puff bunkers of talcum white sand. *Above and right: Seaside Course*

▷ APRIL 13   ▷ OCEAN FOREST GOLF CLUB   ▷ GEORGIA, U.S.A.

Ocean Forest lies on the northern tip of Sea Island, laid out through a landscape of pristine palmettos, pines, and oaks that rustle across the relic sandbars formed by the estuary of the Hampton River. The private course was developed by the Sea Island Resort's CEO Bill Jones III, the grandson of the co-founder of Sea Island Golf Club. Rees Jones, who had already successfully renovated the Plantation Course at Sea Island Golf Club in 1992, was selected to design Ocean Forest. Completed in 1994, Rees Jones adopted an understated approach and allowed the rich natural topography of lowland marsh, sandy swells, and undisturbed coastal forest to dominate the course. The 18th hole sweeps along the sea to the left, with a skinny finger of marsh pinching the fairway from the right. In 2001, Ocean Forest hosted the Walker Cup Match won by the team from Great Britain and Ireland.

▷ APRIL 14   ▷ HARBOUR TOWN GOLF LINKS   ▷ SOUTH CAROLINA, U.S.A.

Harbour Town Golf Links on Hilton Head Island is the inspired design of Pete Dye that in many ways came to define the modern school of golf course architecture. When Dye designed the course in 1967, he was largely unknown outside his native Midwest, and his player consultant, Jack Nicklaus, was just getting
started in the design business. Dye created small greens, Scottish-style pot bunkers, waste areas, and used railroad ties and telegraph poles as bulkheads for the
hazards, all of which was very avant garde at the time, and represented a reaction to the designs of Robert Trent Jones, the leading American golf course architect. Harbour Town was a phenomenal success and became the centerpiece of the Sea Pines Resort developed by Charles Fraser. In 1969, the PGA Tour started
playing the Heritage Classic at Harbour Town, with the inaugural tournament won by Arnold Palmer. With the marsh and Calibogue Sound fronting the tee and
running along the entire left side of the fairway, and the famous red and white candy-striped lighthouse of the Hilton Head marina behind the green, the 18th at
Harbour Town is one of the great finishing holes in golf.

▷ APRIL 15   ▷ HAIG POINT GOLF CLUB   ▷ SOUTH CAROLINA, U.S.A.

Haig Point Golf Club is a private course designed by Rees Jones on Daufuskie Island, which can only be reached by ferry across Calibogue Sound from Hilton Head. The demanding layout has a routing that alternates with rhythmic cadences between open holes that wend through immense live oaks festooned with Spanish moss, holes hemmed by forests and ponds, and forced carries across the tidal marsh along the sound, which comes into play on the par-three eighth and 17th holes. The clubhouse is the former Strachan mansion, which was built in 1910 on St. Simons Island, Georgia. The mansion was saved from destruction by the International Paper Company, the developer of Haig Point, and moved by barge 100 miles up the Intracoastal Waterway to Daufuskie. *Above: Daufuskie Island Resort*

Yeamans Hall Club, near Charleston, is one of the most fascinating courses in the United States, both in terms of its design and its social history. It occupies what had once been the 1,000-acre plantation granted by the Lords Proprietors of Carolina in 1674 to Lady Margaret Yeamans, widow of Sir John Yeamans. The club was founded as a winter resort by well-to-do northerners, with 10 gentlemen holding an organizational meeting at the Downtown Association in New York on April 20, 1925. By the spring of 1926, the Yale golf team made the journey from New Haven to Charleston to play the inaugural rounds. Yeamans Hall was one of the last designs of Seth Raynor, who designed many of the courses of the high-society clubs of the 1920s. The juxtaposition of traditional cross-bunkers and huge, squared-off greens in the midst of the low country landscape of marsh and live oaks is particularly striking. Over the years, many of the distinctive features of Raynor's design were lost, but in 1998 the club hired course architect Tom Doak, an admirer of Raynor's work, to return the course to its original design, right down to the sunken bathtub contour in the middle of the par-three third hole. The overall plan for the club was developed by Frederick Law Olmsted, Jr., who described the grounds as "diversified and picturesquely undulating." The clubhouse and several quadrangles of cottages to house the visiting members were designed by James Gamble Rogers, the architect of Yale's Harkness Quadrangle and of the Yale Club in New York.

▷ APRIL 17 ▷ THE OCEAN COURSE AT KIAWAH ISLAND ▷ SOUTH CAROLINA, U.S.A.

The Ocean Course at Kiawah Island, near Charleston, is one of the few truly great links or duneland courses in the United States and one of the few great links courses to be constructed, rather than routed through the natural hollows and bowls. The Ocean Course also has the distinction of having been awarded the 1991 Ryder Cup before it was even built. Pete and Alice Dye began work on the course in 1989 and despite the fanfare and pressure that went with it, they produced a bold and dramatic layout that remains true to the Scottish linksland ideal. The course is laid out in a figure eight, with the front nine looping clockwise and the back nine running counterclockwise as it hugs the shoreline. The first few holes are both excruciatingly difficult and exciting, followed by a series of holes that saunter along the salt marsh. The back nine is uninhibited seaside golf, with a string of fairways that tumble along the ocean before arriving at the famous par-three 17th, with its petrifying carry over the eight-acre lake that was created at the suggestion of Alice Dye. The Ocean Course produced one of the most epic encounters in the history of the Ryder Cup, with the U.S. winning the "War by the Shore" when Bernhard Langer missed an agonizing six-foot putt on the 18th hole of the final match that would have given him a win over Hale Irwin and the point the Europeans needed to keep possession of the Cup.

▷ APRIL 18   ▷ CASSIQUE GOLF CLUB   ▷ SOUTH CAROLINA, U.S.A.

Cassique is a private course that is part of the Kiawah Island Club, although it is actually located just across the Kiawah River on Seabrook Island. The course, opened in 2000, is a creative and gorgeous fusion of Carolina Low Country and Scottish-style hill country golf. Designed by five-time British Open champion Tom Watson, the front nine occupies what was once flat farmland. More than a million cubic yards of earth were moved to transform the land into rolling hills, with "Mount Watson," the highest point, rising to 45 feet. The world's largest tree spade was brought in to relocate 67 live oaks. Watson also introduced features from classic links courses, including a recreation of the Spectacles, the famous twin bunkers at Carnoustie, on Cassique's No. 6. The back nine is a series of enchanting lowland holes along the marsh with long views out to the Ocean Course and the Atlantic. Cassique is named for the Chief of the Kiawah Indians who in 1670 led the English colonists to settle in what would become Charleston.

▷ APRIL 19   ▷ CALEDONIA GOLF & FISH CLUB   ▷ SOUTH CAROLINA, U.S.A.

Caledonia Golf & Fish Club in Myrtle Beach, which opened in 1994, is a public course that is deeply rooted in the antebellum South. Caledonia was originally a large rice plantation, having been founded by Dr. Robert Nesbit, a Scottish immigrant, who adopted the Roman name for his native country. Nesbit acquired the plantation in the 1700s by marrying Elizabeth Pawley, whose family settled nearby Pawleys Island, and the Nesbit family continued to operate Caledonia until 1940. The drive up to the colonnaded clubhouse, through ancient live oaks draped in Spanish moss, is as impressive as any in golf. By the time Caledonia was acquired in 1971 for use as a hunting and fishing club, only 152 acres of the once vast plantation remained. Two decades later, when a golf course was built, designer Mike Strantz made the most of the tight site, creating a variety of holes that feature sculpted waste areas, live oaks, and water hazards. The 18th hole is a resounding finish with water down the right side and views of the old rice fields stretching out beyond the Waccabuc River.

▷ APRIL 20   ▷ PINEHURST RESORT (NO. 2 COURSE)   ▷ NORTH CAROLINA, U.S.A.

The Pinehurst Resort is the most famous American golf resort and the one that most often draws comparisons with St. Andrews, for although it is far from the sea in the sandy wastes of central North Carolina, it is a planned village that has become dedicated to golf. The irony is that when Pinehurst was founded in 1895 by James Tufts, the wealthy Bostonian manufacturer of soda fountains, there was no golf there at all. In its first few years, Pinehurst was a retreat for New Englanders of modest means who were convalescing from respiratory illnesses, where the favorite pastime was roque, a form of croquet. The recreational picture began to change in 1899 when a nine-hole course was built. In 1900, Tufts hired Donald Ross, the transplanted Scottish professional, to come to Pinehurst to embark on designing what was to become a series of courses. Ross's Pinehurst No. 2 is an endless source of inspiration and fascination—a course that appears relatively benign but whose challenging angles of play and crowned greens with fall-away slopes make it inordinately difficult. The 310-room hotel is a national landmark and the resort also owns the Holly Inn. In 1999, Pinehurst hosted its first U.S. Open, which proved to be a worthy and exacting test for the pros, with the late Payne Stewart winning the championship. The Open returns to Pinehurst in 2005. *Above: Statue of Donald Ross*

▷ APRIL 21 ▷ PINE NEEDLES LODGE AND GOLF CLUB ▷ NORTH CAROLINA, U.S.A.

Pine Needles Lodge and Golf Club in Pinehurst tends to be overshadowed by the more famous and much larger Pinehurst Resort, but Pine Needles has a charm and bonhomie all its own that should not be overlooked. Pine Needles was designed by Donald Ross, the sage of Pinehurst, in 1927. Though not as demanding or intricate as Pinehurst No. 2, Pine Needles is pure Ross and a sheer pleasure to play, while still providing plenty of challenge. The holes are deceptively difficult and water does come into play, particularly on the short third hole, one of Ross's most memorable par threes. The course hosted the U.S. Women's Open in 1996 and 2001, won by Annika Sorenstam and Karrie Webb, respectively, and the event is returning to Pine Needles in 2007. It is fitting that the Women's Open should be held there, since the resort is owned and run by Peggy Kirk Bell, a charter member of the LPGA and one of America's top teachers, who acquired the course with her late husband Warren "Bullet" Bell in 1953. The resort has a cozy, down-home style and Peggy Bell seems like she is always on hand to greet guests.

▷ APRIL 22   ▷ WADE HAMPTON GOLF CLUB   ▷ NORTH CAROLINA, U.S.A.

Wade Hampton Golf Club is set in the heart of the Blue Ridge Mountains of western North Carolina, near the village of Cashiers. The course is named after the famous Confederate general, who also served as governor of South Carolina and as U.S. Senator. The property was the summer retreat of the Hampton family for more than 150 years. In 1922, the Hampton estate was purchased by E. Lyndon McKee, who converted it into the High Hampton Inn, which has remained a popular rustic mountain getaway for generations of Southerners seeking to escape the heat of summer. McKee's grandchildren, A. William McKee and Ann McKee Austin, developed Wade Hampton as a private and refined golf club that opened in 1987. The course is one of designer Tom Fazio's loveliest and most natural creations, lying directly below the imposing stack of Chimney Top Mountain. The course flows effortlessly through tall pines and rushing mountain streams with rocky beds banked with rhododendron that guard the greens of the par threes.

The Grove Park Inn Resort & Spa was built as a grand mountain retreat in western North Carolina overlooking Asheville and the Blue Ridge Mountains. Built on Sunset Mountain at an elevation of 2,500 feet, the hotel was founded in 1913 by Edwin Grove, owner of Grove's Pharmacy and Paris Medical Company of St. Louis, and inventor of such elixirs as Grove's Chill Tonic and Grove's Bromo Quinine. Grove had begun spending summers in Asheville in the 1890s on the advice of his physician. As Grove's son-in-law and co-developer explained: "The idea was to build a big home where every modern convenience could be found, but with all the old-fashioned qualities of genuineness, with no sham. All attempts at the bizarre, the tawdry and flashily foolish to be omitted." The same could be said of the golf course. While golf has been played at the site since 1899, the course is the work of the legendary Donald Ross, who was brought in to redesign the layout in 1924 after having established his reputation at Pinehurst.

The Honors Course in the town of Ooltewah, just north of Chattanooga, was developed by Jack Lupton to honor the spirit of amateur golf. Lupton selected as his designers Pete and Alice Dye, who were themselves top-notch amateur golfers, Pete having won the 1958 Indiana State Amateur while Alice won the Indiana Women's Amateur seven times. Opened in 1983, the course is exceptionally tranquil, with softly sculpted, natural fairways winding around two lakes and through groves of southern red oak, shagbark hickory, pines, and dogwoods in an isolated valley beneath the ridge of White Oak Mountain. A distinguishing feature of the Honors Course is the striking array of specimen grasses planted by David Stone, the greenkeeper at the course since its inception. When Stone first accepted the position, he undertook a comprehensive study of the native grasses in the Chattanooga Valley, and began introducing them around the fairways and bunkers. The result is a rich medley of purple, brown, beige, and tan fescues and sedges.

▷ APRIL 25   ▷ THE HOMESTEAD RESORT   ▷ VIRGINIA, U.S.A.

The Cascades Course at The Homestead Resort in Hot Springs is the Allegheny Mountain masterpiece of William Flynn, the great Philadelphia golf course architect of the golden era of design. Opened in 1923, the course's strength is how seamlessly the narrow, sloping fairways are contoured through the valley floor, surrounded by the dense overgrowth of white and red oaks, red, sugar, and silver maples, white pines, and Norway spruce. A mountain stream comes into play on many of the holes, particularly the final three. The course finishes with a 192-yard par-three over the stream, with the green overlooking the clubhouse that was once the summer home of New York Stock Exchange trader Jakey Rubino. In 1967, Catherine LaCoste, the daughter of French tennis star René "the Crocodile" LaCoste, won the U.S. Women's Open at the Cascades as a 20-year-old amateur, the only amateur ever to win the championship. The resort has two other courses: The Old Course is a 1913 Donald Ross design and the Lower Cascades Course is a Robert Trent Jones design from 1963. *Above: Lower Cascades Course   Right: Cascades Course*

▷ APRIL 26   ▷ KINLOCH GOLF CLUB   ▷ VIRGINIA, U.S.A.

Kinloch Golf Club, or "By the Lake," is a private club that opened in April 2001 twelve miles northwest of Richmond. The centerpiece of the course is the 70-acre lake, which is also home to a fishing club. The lake was built by Richmond real estate developer C.B. Robertson, who showed the property to Marvin "Vinny" Giles, the 1972 U.S. Amateur Champion who is now an agent representing a number of Tour players. Giles persuaded Robertson that they should create an exceptional course, and they proceeded to work with Richmond-based course architect Lester George. Kinloch is routed through forests of pines, fruit trees, and dogwoods, and the construction crew was given leaf packages to enable them to identify and preserve specimen flowering trees during clearing. Most of the holes on the back nine skirt the lake, which is overlooked by the Tudor-style clubhouse with its steeply pitched, oversized roof.

▷ APRIL 27   ▷ ROYAL NEW KENT   ▷ VIRGINIA, U.S.A.

Royal New Kent, located in New Kent County, is an interesting fusion of links golf with the modern sculpted style of Mike Strantz, who headed several projects for Tom Fazio before embarking on a solo design career. The course is in the town of Providence Forge, named for a forge that was destroyed in the Revolutionary War and one of the earliest settlements in New Kent County, but takes its inspiration from Royal County Down and Ballybunion in Ireland. Strantz created the stone walls that run through the course. While it bears only a distant resemblance to its Irish cousins, Royal New Kent is an altogether striking design in its own right, with the fairways nestled in big, sinewy coils and humps of land. Strantz used shaggy red and brown fescue grasses to demarcate the roiling mounds and added 134 plunging bunkers, many with fringed edges that recall the "eyebrow" bunkers of Royal County Down. The back tees at 7,291 yards are named Invicta, the Latin word for "unconquerable."

▷ APRIL 28   ▷ ROBERT TRENT JONES GOLF CLUB   ▷ VIRGINIA, U.S.A.

The Robert Trent Jones Golf Club is a tribute to its designer, who dominated golf course architecture both in the United States and internationally, leaving his indelible mark on some 450 courses in 45 states and 29 countries. RTJ, which coils around Lake Manassass, the 850-acre reservoir in northern Virginia's Prince William County, is a gathering place for movers and shakers from inside the Beltway. Jones first discovered the sylvan property in the late 1970s, but it was not until his Ft. Lauderdale neighbor, Wendy's founder Dave Thomas, put him in touch with developer Clay Hamner in the mid-80s that the project became a reality. Completed in 1990, when Jones was at the end of his career, half of the holes cavort along the banks of the lake, including six on the back nine, and there are two inland ponds to boot. All of this has made for high drama at the Presidents Cup, which the club has hosted three times beginning with the inaugural match in 1994, with the U.S. team victorious each time. RTJ will host the Presidents Cup again in 2005. The clubhouse is presidential in stature, a red-brick Georgian mansion with a colonnaded rotunda.

▷ APRIL 29   ▷ THE GREENBRIER   ▷ WEST VIRGINIA, U.S.A.

The Greenbrier is one of America's grandest and oldest golf resorts, set on 6,500 acres in the Allegheny Mountains in White Sulphur Springs. Over the years the resort has been a favorite golfing haven for presidents and high-powered Washington politicians. Twenty-two presidents have slept in the white Georgian hotel with its towering portico. There are three courses at the Greenbrier. The Old White Course, named for the original hotel that stood from 1858 to 1922, was designed by Charles Blair Macdonald in 1913, and remains one of America's finest mountain courses. Robert Trent Jones chose the first hole of the Old White for the dream 18-hole course he put together for an article that appeared in *Town & Country* in 1938. The Greenbrier Course, designed by Seth Raynor in 1924, was revised by Jack Nicklaus when the course was selected as the site for the 1979 Ryder Cup Matches. From the ninth tee, there is a view of the Midland Gap in the Allegeheny Mountains, where the early settlers passed through on their way to the West. In 1999, the Lakeside Course, designed by Dick Wilson in the 1960s, was completely revamped by Bob Cupp. The Course was renamed the Meadows, harkening back to the original nine-hole course built in the stream valley known as "the meadows." *Right: Meadows Course*

▷ APRIL 30   ▷ PETE DYE GOLF CLUB   ▷ WEST VIRGINIA, U.S.A.

The Pete Dye Golf Club in the town of Bridgeport, near Clarksburg, is one of the most unusual and creative courses in the United States. The course is a testament to the perseverance of Dye, the most inventive golf course architect of the modern era, and to the dream of the club's founder, James LaRosa, of building a golf course over land that had been used for coal mining that would commemorate the tradition of the region. LaRosa, who became interested in golf through his son, invited Dye to West Virginia in 1979, and 16 years later the project was finally completed. The final product is a tour de force, with carries over creased, stream-laced countryside and along the plateaus created by strip mining of the wooded hillsides. There is a 40-yard walk or cart ride through a replica mineshaft between the sixth and seventh holes and the par-five eighth incorporates a 120-foot high wall exposing the Pittsburgh seam of coal and a ventilation entry. Pete Dye Golf Club is a private national golf club, with members from 27 states and five countries.

The Camargo Club is a private club situated in the rolling countryside outside of Cincinnati. It is not a particularly well-known course, but it is one that is especially revered by students of classic golf course architecture, and it has long been a favorite of architect Pete Dye. Camargo was designed by Seth Raynor in 1921. Raynor had worked with Charles Blair Macdonald in the design of the National Golf Links of America in Southampton, New York, and thereafter he emerged from Macdonald's shadow to design many of the classic layouts of the 1920s. What makes his designs so intriguing is that he excelled in taking certain strategic design principles found on famous holes in Scotland and adapting them to the terrain of each of his courses. This is the blueprint that Macdonald followed at the National and Raynor used it with particular flair and creativity in the parkland setting of Camargo. Camargo's par threes feature an Eden based on the 11th hole at St. Andrews, a Short modeled on the fifth at Royal West Norfolk, a Redan based on the 15th hole at North Berwick, and a Biarritz. Tom Doak, who is responsible for the restoration of Raynor's original features at Yeamans Hall in South Carolina, has also done a restoration at Camargo. One of Camargo's members is Neil Armstrong, the first man on the moon.

▷ MAY 2   ▷ VALHALLA GOLF CLUB   ▷ KENTUCKY, U.S.A.

Valhalla Golf Club, named for the resting place for warriors in Norse mythology, is a course of lusty proportions that has put Louisville on the world golf map. Designed by Jack Nicklaus and opened in 1986, the course was developed by leading Louisville businessman Dwight Gahm and his three sons. Nicklaus was given a ruggedly rustic 263-acre site as his canvas, consisting of two farms and an old Boy Scout camp crossed by a stream called Floyd's Fork. The first nine is laid out through relatively open land, while the back nine is hewn from more rolling terrain covered with sycamore, oak, locust, and walnut trees. The PGA of America was so smitten with the design that it purchased a stake in the course and selected it to host the 1996 PGA Championship won by Mark Brooks. In 2000, Valhalla was again the site of the PGA, with Tiger Woods clawing his way to a spine-tingling victory over Bob May in sudden death.

▷ MAY 3   ▷ VICTORIA NATIONAL GOLF CLUB   ▷ INDIANA, U.S.A.

Victoria National Golf Club is routed through a former strip-mining site near Evansville in southern Indiana. Terry Friedman, the developer of the course, wanted to create a private club with a demanding course of the highest caliber. He looked long and hard to find an unusual and dramatic site that would serve as the canvas for one of Tom Fazio's more distinctive creations. Fazio made the most of the jagged contours on the 400-acre site, creating deep, sinuous lakes in the pits left by the strip mines by reaching underwater springs during the construction process. The spoil heaps left over from the mining process resemble shaggy dunes, and Fazio poured the fairways through and, in some instances, across them. With only 27 acres of fairway, and trouble all around, Victoria National is both visually exhilarating and constantly challenging.

▷ MAY 4   ▷ SPRINGHOUSE LINKS AT GAYLORD OPRYLAND RESORT   ▷ TENNESSEE, U.S.A.

The Springhouse Links at Gaylord Opryland is located in the country music capital of Nashville. Designed by former U.S. Open and PGA champion Larry Nelson, the course is an exposed, linksy layout that features tracts of wetlands and is bordered by limestone bluffs. The course takes its name from the century-old springhouse located behind the fourth hole. Springhouse is owned by the Gaylord Opryland Hotel, which is adjacent to the historic 4,400-seat Grand Old Opry, America's showcase for country music. From 1994 through 2003, the course was the home of an event on the Champions Tour.

▷ MAY 5   ▷ BLESSINGS GOLF CLUB   ▷ ARKANSAS, U.S.A.

Blessings Golf Club, a private course in the town of Johnson, just outside Fayetteville in the northwest corner of Arkansas, made its debut in June 2004. Designed by Robert Trent Jones, Jr., the course was developed by Jim Tyson of Arkansas-based Tyson Foods. The dominant design feature is Clear Creek, with holes rimmed by wild grasses swooping over the steep elevation changes along and across the creek. Indeed, the course was going to be called the Course at Clear Creek right up until opening day, when Tyson decided to count his blessings. Blessings is the home of the University of Arkansas golf team, whose most famous product is John Daly. The Fred and Mary Smith Razorback Golf Center has six indoor/outdoor practice bays, an indoor video swing analysis station, and locker facilities for the men's and women's teams, while the state-of-the-art practice range was created by leading golf teacher and CBS commentator Peter Kostis. The Golf Center and clubhouse were designed by University of Arkansas architecture professor and emerging international architect Marlon Blackwell.

▷ MAY 6   ▷ SOUTHERN HILLS COUNTRY CLUB   ▷ OKLAHOMA, U.S.A.

Southern Hills Country Club in Tulsa is one of the great championship courses in American golf. A traditional course that runs over gently undulating land, Southern Hills demands accurate driving to avoid the high, cloying Bermuda rough on the many doglegs. The greens are small and the bunkers are filled with a sand called "No. 6 Wash" that comes from the nearby Arkansas River. Southern Hills was designed by Perry Maxwell of Ardmore, Oklahoma, in 1935, making it a leap of faith by the members during the depths of the Depression. Southern Hills has hosted three PGA Championships and three U.S. Opens, the most recent major being the 2001 Open. South African Retief Goosen three-putted from 12 feet on the green of the treacherous, uphill 18th hole to blow his lead in the final round, but held on to defeat Mark Brooks in an 18-hole playoff the next day.

▷ MAY 7　▷ KARSTEN CREEK GOLF CLUB　▷ OKLAHOMA, U.S.A.

Karsten Creek Golf Club in Stillwater is the home course of the Oklahoma State Cowboys, and one of the best public courses in the United States. When Mike Holder became coach of the Oklahoma State golf team in 1974, he dreamed of building a championship course for his squad. He located an ideal site and contacted renowned architect Tom Fazio in 1983 about designing the course. Fazio drew up a plan for the course but the project remained on the drawing board for another eight years, until the late Karsten Solheim, founder of equipment-maker Karsten Manufacturing, agreed to provide the funding. In 1994, Holder's 20-year quest was realized and Karsten Creek opened. Karsten Creek is a luscious, rolling course of secluded holes through blackjack oaks and hickory trees with long meadow grasses lapping the fairways and a creek ambling around the 11th hole. The final three holes open up to the 110-acre Lake Louise created by Fazio and named for Solheim's wife. The lake runs all along the left side of the long, par-four 17th, while the 18th curves around the opposite shore back to the clubhouse.

▷ MAY 8   ▷ PAA-KO RIDGE GOLF CLUB   ▷ NEW MEXICO, U.S.A.

Paa-Ko Ridge is a public course of exquisite beauty set in the eastern foothills of the Sandia Mountains above Albuquerque, just off New Mexico's scenic, winding Highway 14, named the Turquoise Trail after the turquoise mines that once flourished in the area. There are ruins of ancient Anasazi Indian dwellings nearby, and Paa-Ko takes its name from the Anasazi "root of the cottonwood tree." The course features stunning elevation changes and carries to broad, bluegrass fairways garlanded with piñon pines, cedars, prickly pear, and barrel cacti, with views of the Estancia Valley below. Golf course architect Ken Dye and his partner Baxter Spann have made their reputations creating courses that flow effortlessly through the mesas and mesquite of New Mexico's high mountain desert.

Black Mesa Golf Club is a stunning course that streams through the New Mexican high desert on the Santa Clara Pueblo 30 minutes north of Santa Fe. Opened in 2003, Black Mesa was designed by Baxter Spann of the firm of Finger Dye Spann, whose partner Ken Dye is responsible for two other New Mexico gems, Piñon Hills and Paa-Ko Ridge. Spann did not try to alter the terrain, but instead fitted swirling fairways and dollops of green between crowns of sandstone and rocky gullies cut by ancient arroyos. Spann created big pinwheeling bunkers and oversized greens in the natural depressions that are surrounded by wiry wild grasses and juniper bushes.

The Golf Club at Redlands Mesa is set in the rugged red sandstone wonderland of southwestern Colorado near Grand Junction. The course was molded with great care to fold within the surrounding grandeur by its designer, Jim Engh. Redlands Mesa bows and bends through jumbles of boulders, its coils of green spread out 5,000 feet above sea level, with 350 feet of elevation change throughout the course. From the many elevated tees, there are magnificent views of the purple faces of the Bookcliffs to the north and the Grand Mesa, the world's highest flat-top mountain, to the east. Just to the west of the course is the Colorado National Monument, with its sheer sandstone canyons in shades of vermilion and brown and its forests of piñon trees and Utah junipers inhabited by bighorn sheep.

▷ MAY 11   ▷ RIVER VALLEY RANCH   ▷ COLORADO, U.S.A.

River Valley Ranch in Carbondale, some 30 miles from Aspen, is one of the best and most breathtaking public courses in Colorado. Designed by Jay Morrish and opened in 1996, the course plays at an altitude of 6,200 feet, lying beneath the snow-crowned 7,953-foot Mount Sopris in the Roaring Fork Valley. The course rolls across open countryside that had previously been cattle ranches dating back to the days of the Homestead Act. Seven holes run along or across the Crystal River, with large swirling greens split by swords of sand and long views across the sagebrush and piñon pines that veil the valley.

▷ MAY 12   ▷ IRONBRIDGE GOLF CLUB   ▷ COLORADO, U.S.A.

Ironbridge Golf Club is located outside Glenwood Springs, 45 miles north of Aspen, near the Roaring Fork River. The course takes its name from the Hardwick Bridge, an old trellised iron bridge that crosses the river. Designed by Arthur Hills and opened in May of 2003, four of the holes—the 10th through 13th—swoop through the rust-colored mountains. The 12th drops 200 feet from tee to green with views of Mount Sopris and Five Mile Mountain. Several of the holes on the front nine are laid out on what had previously been a nine-hole course and the 14th through 18th holes stretch across the old Rose Ranch.

▷ MAY 13   ▷ CHERRY HILLS COUNTRY CLUB   ▷ COLORADO, U.S.A.

Cherry Hills Country Club is a traditional and elegant parkland course outside Denver. Opened in 1923, it was designed by William Flynn, the Philadelphia architect of the golden era whose portfolio includes Shinnecock Hills and the Cascades Course in West Virginia. More than any other course, Cherry Hills is associated with the stardom of Arnold Palmer. It was here in the final round of the 1960 U.S. Open that Palmer famously drove the green on the 346-yard first hole for an easy birdie, and kept on making birdies for a 30 on the front nine. Eventually, Palmer passed 14 golfers who were ahead of him going into the last round to win the championship. The 1960 Open was also a crossroads in golf history, marking the emergence of a young Jack Nicklaus, who finished second as an amateur, and the last hurrah of an aging Ben Hogan, who was in contention until he found the water that rings the island green of the par-five 17th hole. The U.S. Open was last held at Cherry Hills in 1978, when Andy North was the victor.

▷ MAY 14   ▷ WALKING STICK GOLF COURSE   ▷ COLORADO, U.S.A.

Walking Stick Golf Course in Pueblo, an hour and a half south of Colorado Springs, is laid out in the harsh high desert terrain of jagged red and tan rocks and sagebrush. A municipal course owned by the town of Pueblo, it has been rated one of the best affordable public courses in America since it opened in 1991. The course is routed along and around cavernous arroyos that crease the landscape and is named for the abundant cholla cacti, which when dried have the appearance of a walking stick or cane. Walking Stick was designed by Arthur Hills and Keith Foster, who created big, flowing greens on the desert floor that take their inspiration from the rolling greens designed by Perry Maxwell at Prairie Dunes in Kansas.

▷ MAY 15   ▷ PRAIRIE DUNES COUNTRY CLUB   ▷ KANSAS, U.S.A.

Prairie Dunes Country Club is the great inland links of the American heartland, and the masterpiece of its designer, Perry Maxwell. Prairie Dunes was established by the four sons of Emerson Carey, who had founded the Carey Salt Company after vast deposits of sodium chloride were discovered in Hutchinson, the remnants of what had once been a great saltwater sea covering central Kansas. Dedicated golfers, the Careys hired Maxwell in the mid-1930s to design a course on 480 acres northeast of Hutchinson. Maxwell immediately recognized the potential offered by the rolling sandhills. His son Press, who became a successful golf course architect, recalled: "It seemed to him, as it did to many others, that this part of Kansas looked just like parts of Scotland. He thought that the area would be a wonderful site for a Scottish-type course in the valleys of the sandhills." Maxwell designed 18 holes through the crests and dips of the dunes and the lovely old cottonwood trees, with fairways brushed by wild plum bushes, yucca plants, bluestem, sunflowers, milkweed, and crowfoot grass. Only nine of the holes were built in 1937, with the additional nine completed by Press Maxwell nearly two decades later in 1956. The wildly tossing greens are known as the "Maxwell rolls." In 2002, Juli Inkster shot a sizzling final-round 66 at Prairie Dunes to capture her second U.S. Women's Open.

▷ MAY 16   ▷ SAND HILLS GOLF CLUB   ▷ NEBRASKA, U.S.A.

Sand Hills Golf Club lies amidst the vast sand hills of central Nebraska near the village of Mullen—golf's ultimate fulfillment of the credo "build it and they will come." Sand Hills has been lauded as a masterpiece of the highest order, and is ranked by *Golfweek* as the No. 1 course opened in the United States since 1960. The course was developed as a private club by Omaha-based Dick Youngscap and his partners on a thousand acres of boundless inland dunes left by receding glaciers. Youngscap hired Ben Crenshaw and Bill Coore, the leading practitioners of old school, lay-of-the land golf course architecture, to design the course. They were presented with the dilemma of such an astonishing site that it offered literally hundreds of different options for laying out holes among the dunes. Through countless hours of inspecting the property, they gradually arrived at an ideal routing in which they "found" 18 superb and unique holes lying in the sandhills blanketed with blood-orange and brown native grasses. Virtually no earth was moved in laying out the course, completed in 1994, but Coore and Crenshaw in their typical fashion paid meticulous attention to the contours of the greens, allowing for shots to run onto the putting surfaces, and created enormous, raggedy-edged bunkers that look like they are part of the landscape.

▷ MAY 17   ▷ WILD HORSE GOLF CLUB   ▷ NEBRASKA, U.S.A.

Wild Horse Golf Club, opened in 1997, is located in Gothenburg, a whistle-stop village on the Union Pacific railroad. The course was built after a group of Gothenburg residents raised $1.6 million through a share offering to state residents. The inspiration for the project came from Sand Hills Golf Club, the majestic course routed through the massive sandhills of central Nebraska. Dave Axland and Dan Proctor, two of the contractors who were instrumental in shaping the Sand Hills course, were hired to lay out a prairie links with a similar minimalist sensibility at Wild Horse. The result is an enchanting course that follows the low expanse of the landscape, with blowouts of sand creating large, irregular bunkers fringed with blond prairie grass. While Sand Hills is a private course, Wild Horse is open to the public, with a welcoming clubhouse perched on the open prairie at the southeastern edge of Nebraska's Sand Hills region.

▷ MAY 18   ▷ SUTTON BAY CLUB   ▷ SOUTH DAKOTA, U.S.A.

Sutton Bay Club, which lies in the flyspeck town of Agar, 40 miles north of Pierre, is a transcendent golf course in an out-of-the-way place. The course takes its spiritual inspiration from Sand Hills Golf Club, the field-of-dreams prairie links in central Nebraska, which harkens back to Prairie Dunes in Kansas, the first of the great American inland links. While Sand Hills paved the way by proving that a private national club with an other-worldly layout could exist at a seemingly unreachable destination, Sutton Bay is unique in many respects. The course was designed by Graham Marsh, an Australian playing on the Champions Tour, who was shown the property by Mark Amundson, the director of his U.S. design office and a native of South Dakota. Both men were enthralled by the site, which was part of the Sutton family ranch of several thousand acres that dates back to 1896. Opened in 2003, the course is laid out over wind-blown dunes created by glaciers, while the back nine is also flanked on the left by a vast mesa. The fairways bubble and spill through the endless sierras of coffee-colored grasses. Unlike at Sand Hills or conventional links courses, the soil is not sand-based but consists of shale, with thousands of boulders pitting the landscape. This landlocked links also comes with a bay view. The course overlooks Lake Oahe, the immense lake that was formed when the Missouri River was dammed in the 1960s, measuring three miles wide and 230 miles long, and visible from every hole.

The Powder Horn Golf Club is a semi-private development located at the base of the Bighorn Mountains in Sheridan, 80 miles south of where Custer made his last stand at Little Big Horn. The course consists of three nines designed by Dick Bailey—Mountain, Stag, and Eagle. The Mountain nine features exposed, links-style golf, right down to a replica of the Swilcan Burn Bridge at St. Andrews on the first hole. The Stag nine runs through groves of cottonwoods and incorporates a number of stream crossings and beaver ponds, with the holes revolving around an old red barn. The par-three 15th plays diagonally across Little Goose Creek with the two-tiered green set in what had once been the corral of the old barn behind.

▷ MAY 20   ▷ TETON PINES RESORT AND COUNTRY CLUB   ▷ WYOMING, U.S.A.

Teton Pines Resort and Country Club is located in Wyoming's Jackson Hole Valley, at the base of the massifs of the Teton Mountain Range. Seven miles west of the town of Jackson, the resort's course was designed by Arnold Palmer and Ed Seay over a former cattle ranch. Opened in 1987, the course is ringed with 40 acres of ponds and streams, with water coming into play on 16 of the 18 holes. The verdant, flat course runs along the valley floor sandwiched between the creased spires of the Tetons and the Snake River, which flows the entire length of the 50-mile-long valley.

▷ MAY 21   ▷ SUNRIVER RESORT (CROSSWATER COURSE)   ▷ OREGON, U.S.A.

The Sunriver Resort is the centerpiece of central Oregon's golf haven. Located just south of the town of Bend, and shielded by the Cascade Mountains to the west, Sunriver can boast 300 days of sunshine a year. Of Sunriver's three courses, the premier 18 is the Crosswater Course, completed in 1995 by the design team of Bob Cupp and John Fought. The course spreads over a bucolic meadow, its fairways surrounded by colorful native grasses, wetlands, and solitary ponderosa pines with the Cascades and Mount Bachelor in the background. Crosswater is criss-crossed by the Deschutes and Little Deschutes Rivers, requiring as many as 16 forced carries, which give rise to the course's self-descriptive name. The long, rippling meadow is where two John Wayne Westerns, *True Grit* and *Rooster Cogburn*, were filmed.

▷ MAY 22   ▷ RUNNING Y RANCH RESORT   ▷ OREGON, U.S.A.

Running Y Ranch Resort is located on the shore of Upper Klamath Lake, 10 miles west of the town of Klamath Falls in southern Oregon, not far from the California border. The 10,000-acre Running Y Ranch was formerly owned by Walt Disney's brother, Roy. Nearly 30 miles long and up to eight miles wide, the lake is the largest body of freshwater west of the Rockies. Opened in September 1997, the Running Y course was designed by the Arnold Palmer Design Company. The front nine plays through open meadow, along ten acres of wetlands, and through ponderosa pines. The back nine begins along a pond and winds through Payne Canyon. The surrounding wetlands are home to more than 250 species of birds, including sandhill cranes, pelicans, and bald eagles, with the Lower Klamath National Refuge having been established by President Theodore Roosevelt in 1908 as the nation's first waterfowl sanctuary.

Bandon Dunes, the resort on Oregon's remote southwest coast just north of the town of Bandon, has become a world-renowned golf destination, with two resounding links courses set in the tempestuous dunes with their tiaras of yellow flowering gorse high above the Pacific. Bandon Dunes is the brainchild of Michael Keiser, who was determined to build a low-key resort with out-of-this-world golf, and after looking at sites throughout the U.S., found his golfing nirvana when he acquired 1,200 acres adjoining Bullards Beach State Park that had been mainly used by dirt bikers. Keiser, who had made his fortune in the greeting-card business, took a leap of faith in hiring a young, unknown Scottish golf course architect, David McLay Kidd, to design Bandon Dunes. Kidd, whose father is the course manager at Gleneagles, designed a swashbuckling course where each nine loops out to the coast and back, with deep, sod-walled bunkers and broad, rumpled fairways creating different angles of play.

▷ MAY 24   ▷ PACIFIC DUNES   ▷ OREGON, U.S.A.

The Bandon Dunes Resort burst onto the golf scene in 1998 when it unwrapped an honest-to-goodness, Scottish-style seaside links on the rough and tumble dunes high above the Pacific in southern Oregon. Michael Keiser, the developer of the resort, commissioned Tom Doak, an intrepid believer in the virtues of classic design principles, to design the resort's second course. Doak had a tough act to follow but Pacific Dunes, opened in 2001, is, if anything, even more stunningly picturesque and varied in its artistry. Doak was able to lay out holes on the cliffs above the windswept beaches with their sculpture gardens of gargantuan driftwood. Other holes run through blowout sand ridges and across swaths of huckleberry bushes and red fescues, while everywhere there are wildflowers and ferns and splashes of yellow gorse. As much as the setting, it is the strategic options, thrilling shots, and challenging green complexes that have lifted Pacific Dunes near the top of most golf course rankings. The no-frills resort is dedicated to golf, while the quaint old village of Bandon offers seafood restaurants overlooking the Coquille River, vintage stores, and the Cranberry Sweets candy store.

▷ MAY 25   ▷ ASTORIA COUNTRY CLUB   ▷ OREGON, U.S.A.

Astoria Country Club is located on the northern Oregon coast, in the lower Columbia River region, laid out on land that was claimed by an early settler who had reached the Clatsop Plains by wagon train over the Oregon Trail in 1845. The golf course dates from 1924, a wonderful vintage links that funnels through the deep valleys between the high dunes one mile from the Pacific. The town of Astoria was founded in 1811 in the triangle formed by the Columbia and Young's Rivers pointing westward to the Columbia Bar and the Pacific. The Astoria Column, built in 1926 atop Astoria's highest hill, is etched with a pictorial frieze of Captain Robert Gray's discovery of the Columbia River in 1792. The reward for climbing the winding steps to the top of the 125-foot-high column is an immense panoramic view of the girdling rivers, ocean beaches, surrounding forests, and the volcanic cone of Mount St. Helens.

▷ MAY 26　　▷ PORT LUDLOW GOLF CLUB　　▷ WASHINGTON, U.S.A.

The Resort at Port Ludlow is located 28 miles west of Seattle, across Puget Sound, and can be reached by a half-hour ferry ride. The Port Ludlow Golf Club has three nines, Tide, Timber, and Trail, designed by Robert Muir Graves. The holes are carved out of a dense evergreen forest of Douglas fir and cedar that was once a logging site. Prior to its opening in 1976, the first 18 holes were cleared by a team of 60 lumberjacks who spent months wielding chainsaws and machetes. Giant cedar stumps, clogged with ferns, mosses, and wild berries, protrude from the fairways and the peat bog that comes into play on several holes. The tee boxes are roped with the old boom chains that were used to bundle logs in the harbor. The resort overlooks Ludlow Bay and Hood Canal, with Olympic National Forest just to the west, and the snow-capped Olympic Mountains in the distance.

▷ MAY 27   ▷ TPC AT SNOQUALMIE RIDGE   ▷ WASHINGTON, U.S.A.

The TPC at Snoqualmie Ridge is located in the town of Snoqualmie, a half-hour drive east of Seattle. Designed by Jack Nicklaus and opened in 1999, the course is cradled by Mount Si and the foothills of the Cascades. Built on an exceptionally rugged site with over 300 feet of elevation change between the third and 16th tees, Snoqualmie Ridge features carries over ravines and generous fairways splashed with 107 bunkers of pure white Idaho sand. The Snoqualmie Falls are visible from the 12th tee, and from the back tees the course stretches to 7,264 yards. Snoqualmie Ridge will host a Champions Tour event starting in 2005.

▷ MAY 28   ▷ DESERT CANYON GOLF CLUB   ▷ WASHINGTON, U.S.A.

Desert Canyon Golf Club is indeed a course fashioned through a canyon in the high desert, but the desert is in the unlikely locale of eastern Washington State. Located in Orondo, the course provides dazzling views of the Columbia River and the triangular folds of the toffee-colored North Cascades Mountains that border the course. Designed by Desert Canyon's director of golf, Jack Frei, the target-style layout is divided between the Lakes and the Desert nines. There is also an 18-hole, par-72 putting course replete with lakes, traps, and rock formations designed by Frei and PGA tour player Rick Fehr.

▷ MAY 29   ▷ CHATEAU WHISTLER GOLF CLUB   ▷ CANADA

Chateau Whistler Golf Club is set in the midst of the slopes of the Coastal Mountains of southwestern British Columbia, with magnificent views across the Whistler Valley. Designed by Robert Trent Jones, Jr. and opened in 1993, the course is built on the benchlands of Blackcomb Mountain, carved through stands of Douglas firs and the granite-studded mountainside. The course crosses creeks and ponds as it rises and descends a total of more than 400 feet. Whistler has become a major golf destination, with Chateau Whistler now joined by the Nicklaus North Golf Club, the Arnold Palmer-designed Whistler Golf Club, and the nearby Big Sky Golf and Country Club.

▷ MAY 30   ▷ BIG SKY GOLF AND COUNTRY CLUB   ▷ CANADA

Big Sky Golf and Country Club is located in British Columbia's Pemberton Valley, some 20 miles north of the Chateau Whistler Resort. Opened in July 1994, the course is on flat land, at an elevation of 600 feet, roughly 1,600 feet lower than the ski village at Whistler, which allows for golf from mid-April through mid-October. Designer Bob Cupp transformed a marshy site that had previously been used to grow seed potatoes, building a dyke around the course to facilitate irrigation. Cupp routed the course around seven lakes that are linked by the serpentine Green River and other creeks. The granite, snow-capped face of 8,450-foot Mount Currie towers above the south end of the course.

Capilano Golf and Country Club, set in coniferous West Vancouver, is a scenic course of the first magnitude, with a matchless view of the Vancouver skyline from the first tee. Designed by Stanley Thompson, the course owes its establishment to A.J.T. Taylor, an investment broker born on Vancouver Island in 1887. Taylor purchased 6,000 acres across the inlet from Vancouver, and then began selling lots to well-to-do individuals in Britain. Taylor was able to use the financial resources of Guinness Brewery, a major investor in the property, to arrange for the building of the Lions Gate Bridge as the link to West Vancouver. The bridge, at the time the second-longest suspension bridge in the world after the Golden Gate, was opened by King George VI in 1939, the same year as the Capilano clubhouse. The course was designed seven years earlier by Thompson on Hollyburn Mountain, west of the Capilano River. Thompson did a masterly job of routing the course along the hillside, with the first six holes descending 300 feet in elevation. The clubhouse, built on the high ground to resemble a Norman-style chateau, was the site of the wedding reception of Pierre and Margaret Trudeau in 1971.

▷ JUNE 1   ▷ BANFF SPRINGS GOLF COURSE   ▷ CANADA

The Banff Springs Hotel and Golf Course was developed by the Canadian Pacific Railway as a resplendent playground in the Banff National Park in the Canadian Rockies, 80 miles west of Calgary, Alberta. The golf course, which opened in 1928, was designed by Stanley Thompson, the legendary Canadian architect of the golden era of golf course architecture. The course is laid out in the Bow Valley along the confluence of the Bow and Spray Rivers. The arching fairways trace the serpentine of the Bow, with the granite faces of Mount Rundle, Sulphur Mountain, and Tunnel Mountain flanking the course. Blasted from the bedrock and carved from an immense fortress of evergreens, Banff Springs is reputed to have been the first course to cost over $1 million to build. The most famous hole is the "Devil's Cauldron," a 170-yard par-three from an elevated tee across a glacial pond to a green at the base of Mount Rundle. The 800-room Banff Springs Hotel, which officially opened on June 1, 1888, rises like a vast baronial palace above the course. *Above: Banff Springs Hotel*

Jasper Park Lodge Golf Course is another tour de force in the Canadian Rockies of Alberta designed by the incomparable Stanley Thompson. Opened in July 1925, the course is set in Jasper National Park, just outside the town of Jasper, on the diaphanous green waters of Lac Beauvert. Above the fairways tower the purple-blue snow-capped peaks called the Whistlers (not to be confused with Whistler Mountain in British Columbia). Thompson supposedly patterned the bunkers after the snow formations on the mountains. The course is routed in a clockwise loop, with the 14th through 16th holes running along a flinthead of land that juts into Lac Beauvert, where the loons can be heard in the early morning. The ninth is a 230-yard par three, known as "Cleopatra," that plays downhill from a steeply elevated tee. Thompson originally shaped the fairway to resemble the figure of a voluptuous woman when viewed from the tee. The management of the Canadian Pacific Railway, which developed the course, had Thompson revise the fairway contours, but the name stuck.

▷ JUNE 3 ▷ STEWART CREEK GOLF COURSE ▷ CANADA

Stewart Creek Golf Course is near the old coal mining town of Canmore, Alberta, on the eastern slopes of the Rundle Range 15 minutes from Banff. The mines at Canmore date back to 1886, and several of the mine shafts are visible along the course, their entries refurbished to serve as rain shelters. Designed by Alberta architect Gary Browning, Stewart Creek is an exceptionally pristine layout, with staggered rows of pines, granite ledges, and the clear waters of Stewart Creek, framed by the peaks of the Three Sisters looming above. With over 50 miles of tunnels running under the course, the risk of fairways sinking or collapsing was a major concern. To reinforce the fairways, 120,000 square feet of geo-fabric mesh was used to line the most susceptible areas, the same type of material used for the bright orange fences at World Cup downhill ski races. The first hole kicks off with a specatacular 100-foot drop to the fairway.

▷ JUNE 4 ▷ HIDDEN LAKES GOLF RESORT ▷ IDAHO, U.S.A.

Hidden Lakes Golf Resort is located at Sandpoint, in the panhandle of northern Idaho that is surrounded by Lake Pend Oreille, Idaho's largest lake. The golf course at Hidden Lakes is the realization of the dream of Jim Berg, whose older sister Eugenia and her husband Thurston Thomas "T.T." McGhee ran the property as a cattle ranch starting in 1924. Berg and his family began construction of the golf course in 1983 and it was completed in 1986, with additional revisions in 2000. The course offers vistas of the Selkirk and Cabinet Mountains, with the lower Pack River creating water hazards that are traversed by railroad-car bridges on 16 of the 18 holes—hence the course's name. The groves of cedar, birch, and evergreen that line the fairways are home to elk, deer, bear, muskrat, and especially the moose that roam the course. The clubhouse, situated along the banks of the Pack River, is built of rough-hewn logs from the area with walk-in stone fireplaces. The center support of the interior is a six-foot-thick cedar trunk with a life-size moose head carved from one of its limbs. *Above: Carved moose head in clubhouse*

The Coeur D'Alene Resort Course is on Lake Coeur D'Alene, located in Idaho's upper panhandle some 30 miles from Spokane. Designed by Scott Miller and opened in 1991, the experience is that of a manicured lakeshore park with immaculate bentgrass fairways and bluegrass rough straddled by rocky outcroppings and slender rods of Austrian pines. Players are taken to the course from the resort on mahogany launches named Eagle and Double Eagle, with a lakeside practice range where floating balls are hit to floating targets in the water. Several holes play along the shore of the lake and over Fernan Creek. But what makes Coeur D'Alene world-famous is the par-three 14th hole, which features the world's only floating green. Built of foam-filled concrete, the 15,000-square-foot, 7,500-ton green comes complete with a pair of bunkers, small pines, and a bed of red geraniums. Each day the yardage is adjusted from 100 to 175 yards offshore by moving the green using cables and winches. After the tee shots, players are ferried out to the green, where the boat's skipper rakes the sand, tends the flagstick, and records the scores.

▷ JUNE 6   ▷ OLD WORKS GOLF COURSE   ▷ MONTANA, U.S.A.

Old Works Golf Course is laid out over what had once been the site of one of the world's largest copper smelters, which began production in 1884 to process the ore from the Butte mines. Designed by Jack Nicklaus in 1994 and opened as a public course, Old Works transformed what had been an EPA Superfund site into a green expanse offset by swirling bunkers filled with jet black slag, a by-product of the smelting process. Nicklaus cleverly incorporated remnants of the actual 19th-century Old Works into the design, including the stone furnaces of the Calciner that line the par-five third hole and the massive brick flue that gapes from the hillside above the fourth. The elevated tees offer views of the Anaconda-Pintler Mountains while Warm Springs Creek comes into play on the first, 10th, and 11th holes. The holes have names such as Flue #5, Convertor, Copper Kings, and Anode. Old Works plays a hefty 7,700 yards from the back or "Slag" tees.

▷ JUNE 7   ▷ LINKS OF NORTH DAKOTA   ▷ NORTH DAKOTA, U.S.A.

The Links of North Dakota is located on a prairie in northwest North Dakota, about half an hour from Williston, population 15,000, and 164 miles northwest of Bismarck. The course was named the Red Mike Resort when it opened in 1995. While the "resort" consists of little more than an RV park, there is a world-class golf course on the bluffs overlooking Lake Sakakawea. Red Mike, as it is popularly known, was designed by New York-based golf course architect Stephen Kay, working on a shoestring budget. Kay hardly moved any dirt, but laid out wide-open fairways through the undulating bluffs and created 82 bunkers. The main challenge comes from the wind and the high, cocoa-colored native prairie grass that frames every hole. Lake Sakakawea, which is a dammed portion of the Missouri River, is known for its excellent fishing, with Chinook salmon, walleye, northern pike, bass, and perch. Lewis and Clark camped near the upper bays of the lake on April 17, 1805, during their transcontinental expedition.

▷ JUNE 8   ▷ HAWKTREE GOLF CLUB   ▷ NORTH DAKOTA, U.S.A.

Hawktree Golf Club is a big, hummocky course that unfolds through the high plains prairie bluffs of Bismarck, North Dakota. Hawktree was designed by Jim Engh, a native of Dickinson, North Dakota, who is now based in Castle Rock, Colorado. Engh has developed a reputation for designing intensely attractive courses in beautifully forbidding landscapes in the American West, including the Golf Club at Redlands Mesa in Grand Junction, Colorado, and the Sanctuary in Sedalia, Colorado. Hawktree is designed around Burnt Creek, a tributary of the Missouri River that comes into play on eight holes, with the course edging the wetlands, and lakes featuring on another three holes. The fairways are framed with high, tan prairie grasses and the bunkers are ebony, filled with black coal slag instead of sand.

▷ JUNE 9 ▷ DEACON'S LODGE ▷ MINNESOTA, U.S.A.

Deacon's Lodge, which opened in September 1998, is the most recent golfing addition to Grand View Lodge in the Brainerd Lakes District of Minnesota. Designed by Arnold Palmer, the course is named after his father Deacon Palmer, the pro and superintendent at Latrobe Country Club in western Pennsylvania. Carved out of 499 acres of pristine Norway pine and birch, the course is hugged by three wilderness lakes, and the waste bunkers and chipping areas are engulfed by thick wetlands. The natural waste bunkers were created by peeling off the five-inch layer of topsoil to expose the 170-foot-deep sand base below. There are five sets of tees—Winnie, Lodge, Deacon, King, and Palmer. Brainerd is where the Paul Bunyan Trail begins its 100-mile route north to Bemidji.

Hazeltine National Golf Club outside Minneapolis had a rocky start as a championship course, but has now earned a reputation as a fair and dramatic test of the game's best players. Opened in 1961, Hazeltine was a brawny creation of Robert Trent Jones featuring many doglegs. Hazeltine was heavily criticized by the pros at the 1970 U.S. Open won by Tony Jacklin, and it was unclear whether the course would again be selected to stage the Open. Jones made substantial changes, including new 16th and 17th holes, and then Rees Jones, Trent's younger son, was brought in to further polish the design before the 1991 Open. The result was a pronounced success. Payne Stewart tied with Scott Simpson in regulation, and came back from two strokes behind with three holes to play to win the 18-hole playoff. Rich Beem was the enthralling and ebullient winner of the 2002 PGA Championship at Hazeltine, overcoming birdies on the last four holes by Tiger Woods to earn a one-stroke victory. He clinched the title on Hazeltine's marquee 16th hole, which has a fairway shoehorned between a creek down the left and Lake Hazeltine to the right, by rolling in a 35-foot birdie putt.

▷ JUNE 11   ▷ THE HARVESTER   ▷ IOWA, U.S.A.

The Harvester, outside Ames, is the home course of the Iowa State Cyclones. The course represents the fulfillment of the dream of Dickson Jensen, a young, self-made entrepreneur, who majored in engineering at Iowa State and taught at the university before becoming a successful real estate investor. Jensen hired Keith Foster to design the course, and the two agreed to build it on a 300-acre site that had been a cattle farm and a campground with a 60-acre dammed lake. Foster describes the course, which opened in 2001, as "man-sized," built on a large scale with sweeping fairways through towering oaks and native grasses and with elevation changes of 40 to 70 feet. Lake Harvester comes into play as the backdrop to the downhill, par-three eighth and runs parallel to the ninth. The lake is in play again on the par-three 17th and the boomerang par-five 18th, hugging the entire right side of the fairway.

▷ JUNE 12   ▷ WAKONDA GOLF CLUB   ▷ IOWA, U.S.A.

Wakonda is an Indian word denoting the supernatural, roughly translated as "great spirit." Wakonda Golf Club was established by several of the old-line families of Des Moines and completed in 1922, at the then-staggering cost of $650,000. The course is very hilly, with fairways enclosed by monumental burr oaks, elm, and locust trees. Wakonda was designed by the little-known but highly accomplished Midwest golf course architect William Langford, working with civil engineer Theodore Moreau. Their work together includes Lawsonia Links in Wisconsin and Skokie Country Club outside Chicago.

▷ JUNE 13 ▷ THE CLUB AT PORTO CIMA ▷ MISSOURI, U.S.A.

The Club at Porto Cima on the Lake of the Ozarks was developed by the Four Seasons as the centerpiece of a private golf community. While the site on the Shawnee Bend peninsula of the Lake of the Ozarks is just across the water from The Lodge of the Four Seasons, the property was inaccessible and could not be developed until the Lake of the Ozarks Community Bridge was completed on May 1, 1998. Designed by Jack Nicklaus as a signature course and opened in 2000, Porto Cima loops around the lake and through a forest of native oak trees, with seven holes straddling the water. The inspiration for the Mediterranean motifs of the Porta Cima development, which includes a yacht club, comes from the resort village of Portofino on the Italian Riviera.

▷ JUNE 14   ▷ ST. LOUIS COUNTRY CLUB   ▷ MISSOURI, U.S.A.

St. Louis Country Club, which opened in 1914, is one of the classic designs of the great architectural tandem of Charles Blair Macdonald and Seth Raynor, who first worked together when Macdonald hired Raynor as the engineer for the National Golf Links of America. As at many of their other courses, they designed par threes modeled on the most strategically perplexing and enjoyable one-shotters found in the Old World, including a Short, an Eden, a Redan, and a Biarritz hole, as well as a novel fifth par-three named the Crater. In typical fashion, the bunkers are elongated with steep grass walls, with the fairways of the fifth and par-five 13th separated by tentacles of sand known as the Snakes. Located in the suburb of Ladue, St. Louis Country Club hosted the 1947 U.S. Open, when Sam Snead came agonizingly close to capturing the championship that would forever elude him, losing by one stroke to Lew Worsham in an 18-hole playoff.

▷ JUNE 15   ▷ MEDINAH COUNTRY CLUB (NO.3 COURSE)   ▷ ILLINOIS, U.S.A.

Medinah Country Club's No.3 Course is the famed championship course of Chicago. With its massive red-bricked and minareted mock-Moorish clubhouse, Medinah was founded in 1928 by the Shriners, who are members of the Arabic Order of Nobles of the Mystic Shrine. The club is named for Islam's second holiest city. The Shriners were started by a New York City Freemason in 1871 after he returned from a trip to Europe, where lavish parties in Arabic costumes were then in vogue. Medinah is a big-shouldered and taxing course, measuring more than 7,400 yards, with nine doglegs. The central feature of the course is Lake Kadijah, named after Mohammed's wife. Medinah's signature holes, the par-three 13th and 17th, both play across the lake, with the glassy greens sloped so that a tee shot hit with too much backspin risks rolling back into the water. In one of the more memorable U.S. Opens, Hale Irwin caught journeyman Mike Donald on the final hole of regulation in 1990 and then won the championship in the 18-hole playoff the next day. Medinah will host the PGA Championship in 2006. *Above: member's fez*

▷ JUNE 16   ▷ CHICAGO GOLF CLUB   ▷ ILLINOIS, U.S.A.

The Chicago Golf Club was founded in 1892 by Charles Blair Macdonald, who was one of the great early pioneers of golf in America. A native of Chicago, Macdonald learned the game as a student at St. Andrews University in the 1870s. He later became a leading amateur golfer, established golf course architecture as a discipline in the United States, and wrote an interesting memoir entitled *Scotland's Gift—Golf*. In 1894, the original nine-hole course was replaced with an 18-hole layout designed by Macdonald in the suburb of Wheaton, making it the first 18-hole course in America. Chicago hosted three early U.S. Opens, beginning in 1897. Harry Vardon, the dominant English professional, won the Open at Chicago in 1900, while Philadelphia's Johnny McDermott became the first native-born American to win the Open in 1911. Nowadays, Chicago is a rarefied, private club, where Macdonald's design endures as a masterpiece.

▷ JUNE 17   ▷ OLYMPIA FIELDS COUNTRY CLUB   ▷ ILLINOIS, U.S.A.

Olympia Fields Country Club, located about 28 miles south of downtown Chicago, hosted the 2003 U.S. Open won by Jim Furyk, 75 years after dapper Johnny Farrell beat Bobby Jones in a playoff in the 1928 Open. Founded in 1915, Olympia Fields was originally a 72-hole facility, with the No. 4 Course, now the North Course, the site of the U.S. Open. The other three courses were combined into the South Course when the club was forced to sell land during the Depression. The stone clubhouse, with its famous 80-foot high Tudor clock tower, is one of golf's great landmarks. The North Course was designed by Willie Park, Jr., scion of the golfing dynasty of Parks from Musselburgh, Scotland. A classic parkland course laid out across ridges and farmland, the dominant design feature is the serpentine Butterfield Creek. Park was a talented and resourceful designer at a time when golf course architecture in America was in its infancy. *Right: North Course*

▷ JUNE 18   ▷ HARBORSIDE INTERNATIONAL GOLF CENTER   ▷ ILLINOIS, U.S.A.

There are many vaunted courses in Chicago's suburbs, but Harborside International Golf Center is an urban original, built within the city limits just 16 minutes from downtown, with stirring views of the skyline. Harborside consists of two municipal courses, the Port and the Starboard, built on 458 acres of industrial landfill and inorganic sludge near Lake Calumet on Chicago's gritty South Side. The transformation of urban wasteland into two verdant links courses was the work of Illinois golf course architect Dick Nugent and his son Tim. The entire site was capped with a thick layer of clay, dirt, and sand, which prevented the growth of trees. The Nugents then applied the same principles used to grow grass on the lava fields of Hawaii. The result is broad, exposed shelves of curvilinear fairways. The signature hole on the Port, named "Anchor," is the par-three 15th with an island of green in the shape of a ship's anchor surrounded by sand. Lake Calumet comes into play on the final three holes. Former President Bill Clinton made his first and only hole-in-one on the par-three sixth hole at the Port Course. Harborside also has a red-roofed prairie-style clubhouse that echoes the designs of Frank Lloyd Wright. *Right: Port Course*

▷ JUNE 19   ▷ SKOKIE COUNTRY CLUB   ▷ ILLINOIS, U.S.A.

Skokie Country Club is not one of the better-known courses in the Chicago area, but it is one of the most interesting, both from an historical perspective and as an example of the restoration of classic design features. The course was started in the 1890s and expanded from nine to 18 holes in 1905. Donald Ross then thoroughly revised the course in 1914 and Skokie went on to host the 1922 U.S. Open, won by a 20-year-old Gene Sarazen. In the 1930s, the club sold some of its land for housing and acquired additional property south of the existing course. This led to the design of seven new holes in 1938 by the Midwest design firm of William Langford and Theodore Moreau, a very gifted team whose work is little-known today. Among the holes they fashioned were the third, 11th, and 12th, which incorporate the stream and lake at the south end of the property. Over the next 60 years, many of the distinctive features of the Langford/Ross design were lost or softened, but in 1999 the members adopted a bold plan to restore the course to the way it played in 1938. The back-to-the-future plan was created by Ron Prichard, an architect who specializes in classical course restoration. Prichard brought back cross bunkers that had been removed, angled the fairway bunkers to increase the strategic options, and restored the exaggerated grass bunker walls, which are the hallmark of Langford's design, and give the course its sense of dimension. With its old-fashioned vitality restored, Skokie looks new again.

▷ JUNE 20   ▷ THE GENERAL AT EAGLE RIDGE RESORT   ▷ ILLINOIS, U.S.A.

The General is the newest of the three 18-hole courses at the Eagle Ridge Resort in Galena. Designed by Roger Packard and two-time U.S. Open winner Andy North, the General opened in 1997. The course is located on the edge of the Mississippi in northwest Illinois, set among limestone cliffs, valleys of wildflowers, and rolling hills dotted with oak and walnut trees, a sharp contrast to the flat terrain of Chicagoland. On the short par-four 14th, with the tee perched on a limestone cliff 200 feet above the fairway, there are eagle-eye views of three States—Iowa, Wisconsin, and Illinois. The General is named for General Ulysses S. Grant, who lived in Galena, an old lead-mining town with an historic main street, before the Civil War.

Lawsonia's two public courses, the Links and the Woodlands, are located in the town of Green Lake on what was once the country estate of Victor Lawson, publisher of the *Chicago Daily News* and co-founder of the Associated Press. In 1887, while boating on Green Lake, Lawson and his wife Jessie were forced to find shelter from an approaching storm at what they called "Lone Tree Point." Captivated by the beauty of the site, they acquired 10 acres that were eventually developed into a thousand-acre estate called Lone Tree Farm, which included Tarvia-tarred roads, white-enameled brick barns, and boulder-faced bridges, as well as a private nine-hole course for the use of the Lawsons' guests. In 1943, the estate was purchased by the Northern Baptist Convention, which developed it as a national religious center, and continues to own the property. The Links Course, designed by William B. Langford in 1930, is modeled after the classic holes of the great British links courses and has endured as an American original. Langford, who took up golf as part of his regimen to recover from childhood polio, played on three Yale championship golf teams from 1906 to 1908. He became a golf architect after studying mining engineering at Columbia University.

▷ JUNE 22   ▷ BLACKWOLF RUN   ▷ WISCONSIN, U.S.A.

The American Club is a resplendent golf resort founded by Herb Kohler, the paterfamilias of the Kohler Company, now featuring four remarkable, distinct, and challenging Pete Dye courses. Located an hour's drive north of Milwaukee, Kohler was a company town, and the American Club, which is now a hotel with deluxe bathroom fixtures, was originally built in 1918 as a sturdy red-brick and blue-slate dormitory for immigrant workers. In 1988, Dye created Blackwolf Run, named for a Winnebago Indian chief, with two pastoral 18-hole layouts consisting of the River Course, with the shallow silver and blue Sheboygan River curling through an ultra-demanding layout, and the Meadow Valleys Course, which is no pushover itself. The 1998 U.S. Women's Open, won by Se Ri Pak in a playoff over amateur Jenny Chuasiriporn, was played on a composite of the two courses. *Above and right: River Course*

▷ JUNE 23   ▷ WHISTLING STRAITS   ▷ WISCONSIN, U.S.A.

Ten years after he designed Blackwolf Run, Pete Dye returned to the Kohler Resort to design the Straits Course at Whistling Straits in 1998, which earned such rapid acclaim that it was named the site of the 2004 PGA Championship. Whistling Straits, which also includes Dye's Irish Course, is located nine miles east of Kohler in the village of Haven. Dye took a pancake-flat, 560-acre site adjoining Lake Michigan that had been a military encampment and proceeded to create a rock 'em sock 'em seaside links. Dye built huge drifting dunes nubbed with colorful grasses by literally moving mountains of earth, topped off with a liberal dusting of 800,000 cubic yards of sand. The 2004 PGA proved to be a rousing success, with the pros managing to fire sub-par rounds notwithstanding the course's unprecedented visual intimidation, some 1,300 bunkers give or take a hundred or two, and over 7,500 yards in length from the back tees. When it was all over, Vijay Singh took away the Wanamaker Trophy after a playoff with Justin Leonard and Chris DiMarco. *Right: Straits Course*

▷ JUNE 24   ▷ ARCADIA BLUFFS GOLF CLUB   ▷ MICHIGAN, U.S.A.

Arcadia Bluffs Golf Club is a true links—that is, a course next to the sea routed through sandhills—overlooking Lake Michigan. Opened in 1998, the course is in the remote town of Arcadia, and it is an arcadia for golfers, laid out across 245 windswept acres of sand dunes. The dunes drop 225 feet from the highest point down to the bluff above Lake Michigan, with 3,100 feet of shore frontage. Designed by Warren Henderson and renowned teaching professional Rick Smith, Arcadia Bluffs emulates the great seaside Irish courses. There are wide fairways framed by tall fescue grasses that sway along the lake, 50 sod-walled bunkers, and big rippling greens. The flagsticks are short, three-foot wooden poles specially designed to resist the fierce winds off the lake.

The Treetops Resort in Gaylord is in a rural area of northern Michigan that has become chockablock with outstanding courses by well-known designers. Treetops alone boasts courses designed by Tom Fazio and Robert Trent Jones, but it is the Rick Smith Signature Course that has garnered the most plaudits. Smith earned his reputation as a top teaching pro, whose pupils include Jack Nicklaus, Phil Mickelson, and Lee Janzen. His course at Treetops was his first foray into design, and yet it is an outstanding course. There is nothing souped-up about the layout, but Smith took advantage of the hilly natural terrain to route the course through secluded dales surrounded by northern hardwoods, using traditional bunkering to create a look reminiscent of some of the great English inland courses. The par threes are unforgettable, playing from low-lying tees over great tangled webs of bracken ferns to natural green sites. *Right: Rick Smith Signature Course*

▷ JUNE 26   ▷ CRYSTAL DOWNS COUNTRY CLUB   ▷ MICHIGAN, U.S.A.

Crystal Downs Country Club, located in the town of Frankfort, and routed around a bluff overlooking Lake Michigan with views of Crystal Lake in the distance, is an almost mythic shrine for worshippers of American golf course architecture. The private course was designed by Dr. Alister MacKenzie, who visited the site in 1926, on his way from Cypress Point in California to his native Scotland, with construction supervised by his design consultant Perry Maxwell, the great architect of the lower plains states. The course is original in many respects. The rolling fairways framed by birch and pine are expansive, providing multiple lines of approach, and the bunkers are strategically placed seams of sand. The most striking feature of the course is the steeply pitched and exceptionally intimidating green surfaces, exemplified by the seventh green, which is shaped like a boomerang.

▷ JUNE 27   ▷ OAKLAND HILLS COUNTRY CLUB   ▷ MICHIGAN, U.S.A.

Oakland Hills Country Club's South Course is one of the landmark, quintessentially American courses. Located in Bloomfield Hills, a suburb of Detroit, the course was originally designed by Donald Ross in 1918, but the Oakland Hills of today reflects the heroic style of Robert Trent Jones. Jones was called in to redesign the course in 1950 so that it would humble the game's best players in the 1951 U.S. Open. Ben Hogan shot a final-round 67 to win the Open that year, and famously declared that he had brought "this monster to its knees." Oakland Hills has one of the most arduous and lovely finishing stretches of parkland holes, with the 16th hole playing along and then across the willow-lined pond to the green. In the 1996 U.S. Open, Tom Lehman and Steve Jones came to the final hole on Sunday in a dead heat. Lehman's tee shot kicked into the bunker at the corner of the pinched fairway, and Jones hit a brilliant second shot to the massive, tiered green to earn his victory. In 2004, Oakland Hills was the site of the European team's drubbing of the U.S. squad in the Ryder Cup.

▷ JUNE 28   ▷ TOURNAMENT PLAYERS CLUB OF MICHIGAN   ▷ MICHIGAN, U.S.A.

The Tournament Players Club of Michigan is located in Dearborn, a suburb of Detroit, near the headquarters of Ford Motor Company. Built on 210 acres of land along the Rouge River that had originally been purchased by Henry Ford in 1915, the area had fallen into disrepair over the years and become an industrial dump site. Enter Jack Nicklaus, who was commissioned by the PGA Tour, and Harold Poling, then CEO of Ford, to reclaim the land as a golf course. Opened in 1990, the transformation was complete, as Nicklaus unveiled a tapestry of fairways through the wetlands that come into play on virtually every hole. Since 1991, the course has hosted the Ford Senior Players Championship, one of five majors on the Champions Tour. The 12th hole, a 166-yard par three that plays across the marsh, is particularly difficult.

▷ JUNE 29   ▷ INVERNESS CLUB   ▷ OHIO, U.S.A.

Inverness in Toledo is one of America's most historic championship courses. The club dates back to a nine-hole course built in 1903, when S.P. Jermain, the club's first president, received permission from the Scottish village of Inverness to use its name and crest. In 1919, the club hired Donald Ross to rework those nine holes and add nine more. Several architects have tinkered with Ross's handiwork over the years, most notably George and Tom Fazio, who built four new holes before the 1979 U.S. Open, a change much decried by architectural purists. The club held its first U.S. Open in 1920 when Harry Vardon, almost 50, was on his way to winning until a fierce windstorm descended as he was playing the back nine, causing him to lose the tournament. Jack Nicklaus made his U.S. Open debut at Inverness in 1957, when Dick Mayer defeated Cary Middlecoff in a playoff, and Hale Irwin was the winner of the 1979 Open. The most memorable major tournaments at Inverness, however, have been the 1986 and 1993 PGA Championships. In 1986, Bob Tway unforgettably holed his bunker shot on the final hole to beat Greg Norman. Norman was again the agonizingly hard-luck runner-up in 1993, losing to Paul Azinger on the second extra hole of their sudden-death playoff.

Rock Hollow Golf Club is located in the town of Peru, 70 miles north of Indianapolis. Designed by Indiana native Tim Liddy, a long-time associate of Pete Dye, and opened in 1994, the public course is terraced through an abandoned sand and gravel quarry. The course was developed by Terry Smith, the president of Rock Industries, on land that his company had mined out 40 years earlier. For Smith, building a golf course was also a family affair, since his son Chris plays on the PGA Tour, and another son, Terry, is the professional at Rock Hollow, and holds the course record. The course's Flinstonian name is entirely self-descriptive, since the holes are laid out 50 feet below ground level, between the quarry walls. One of the toughest holes on the course that captures the essence of Rock Hollow is No. 14, a 228-yard par-three where the huge elevated green is guarded on the right by a rocky pond.

▷ JULY 1   ▷ CROOKED STICK GOLF CLUB   ▷ INDIANA, U.S.A.

Crooked Stick Golf Club, located outside Indianapolis, was the first course to reflect the emerging style of Pete Dye, who would go on to revolutionize golf course architecture and create the courses that defined target-style golf in the 1980s. Dye, who had been a successful insurance salesman in Indiana, designed Crooked Stick in 1964, shortly after he returned from a tour of the great courses of Scotland with his wife Alice that would have a profound effect on his approach to design. Laid out on a flat cornfield, Crooked Stick features the waste bunkers, sculpted hazards, and imaginative shaping that were to become Dye's hallmark and it remains one of his best courses. Dye returned to Crooked Stick to lengthen the course prior to the 1991 PGA Championship, when the prodigiously long-hitting John Daly burst onto the scene to win the title and begin his tempestuous legend. Dye named the course for a stick found in the cornfield, based on the belief that the game began when a boy tending his flock used his shepherd's crook to hit a rock in the field.

▷ JULY 2   ▷ MUIRFIELD VILLAGE GOLF CLUB   ▷ OHIO, U.S.A.

Muirfield Village Golf Club in Dublin, just north of Columbus, had its genesis in a conversation that Jack Nicklaus had with his old friend, Ivor Young, while they were sitting on the clubhouse veranda at Augusta National during the 1966 Masters. Nicklaus suggested that it would be wonderful to have a course in his hometown of Columbus that would convey the same type of golfing ambience as Augusta. Young was in the real estate business and when he returned to Columbus he found 10 or 11 potential sites for a course. Nicklaus and he ended up buying the first one they had visited—a 160-acre parcel that Jack used to hunt on when he was growing up. Construction began in 1972, Nicklaus working with his design partner at the time, the late Desmond Muirhead. Muirfield Village, named for the course in Scotland where Nicklaus won the 1966 British Open, is an impeccably manicured tableau of pasture and woodlands, with three inter-secting streams on the property trilling through the fairways and coming into play on 11 of the holes. Nicklaus fulfilled his dream of building a great course specifically designed for tournament golf, as Muirfield Village hosts the annual Memorial Tournament, dedicated each year to an individual honoree.

▷ JULY 3 ▷ LONGABERGER GOLF CLUB ▷ OHIO, U.S.A.

The Longaberger Company earned its reputation as the leading maker of handmade baskets in the United States, but since the Longaberger Golf Club opened in 2000, it has also become known as the purveyor of some of the best golf in the Midwest. The course is located in the town of Nashport, to the east of Columbus, not far from Longaberger's corporate headquarters—a building in the shape of a seven-story basket, right down to windows woven into the sides and two 100-foot-high handles. Designed by Arthur Hills, the sylvan course is carved through a variety of hardwoods, with a signature walnut tree on the 18th hole and rustic streams guarding six of the greens. Longaberger employees and its 70,000 independent sales associates have first crack at tee times, but the course is public and the pro shop in the capacious clubhouse does indeed feature collectible baskets. A second course, designed by Columbus native Tom Weiskopf, is also planned.

▷ JULY 4 ▷ PHILADELPHIA COUNTRY CLUB (SPRING MILL COURSE) ▷ PENNSYLVANIA, U.S.A.

Philadelphia Country Club was founded in 1890 and golf was introduced one year later, with three holes laid out on the club's lawn. In 1895, the club became the seventh member of the newly formed USGA. By 1925 the club's original 18-hole course had become overcrowded, and 210 acres were acquired for a new course in Gladwyne, six miles away. The club hired the leading Philadelphia firm of Toomey & Flynn, consisting of course architect William Flynn and civil engineer Howard Toomey, to design the new Spring Mill Course. Flynn crafted a classic and elegant parkland course, which features strategic use of bunkers to define the landing areas and deep tongues of sand lashed into the greensides. In 1939, Sam Snead was on his way to winning the U.S. Open at Spring Mill when a calamitous triple-bogey eight on the final hole cost him the championship. The next day saw a playoff between the three leaders after regulation, Byron Nelson, Craig Wood, and Denny Shute. At the end of the round, Nelson and Shute were still tied, necessitating a second 18-hole playoff. On the fourth hole, which now plays as the 17th, Nelson holed a one-iron from 215 yards for an eagle, and went on to capture the crown.

▷ JULY 5   ▷ MERION GOLF CLUB   ▷ PENNSYLVANIA, U.S.A.

Merion Golf Club in Ardmore, outside Philadelphia, is a classic American course and a hallmark of the Philadelphia school of design. The Merion Cricket Club was founded in 1865, and golf was introduced with a nine-hole course in 1896. The East Course was designed by Hugh Wilson, a member of Merion and Princeton graduate who was born in Scotland. Wilson was not a professional course architect, but showed an aptitude for design, and was selected by the club to spend seven months studying the great courses of Scotland and England in preparation for his work at Merion, which was completed in 1912. Wilson created a course that is still ranked in the top ten in the United States. He molded 128 bunkers—"the white faces of Merion"—as they were famously described by Chick Evans when he won the 1916 U.S. Amateur Championship at Merion. Merion, with its distinctive red wicker flagsticks, has hosted a number of historic tournaments. Ben Hogan won the U.S. Open there in 1950 in a remarkable comeback after his near-fatal car accident in 1949. Lee Trevino won his second U.S. Open at Merion in 1971, defeating Jack Nicklaus in a playoff.

▷ JULY 6 ▷ THE GOLF COURSE AT GLEN MILLS ▷ PENNSYLVANIA, U.S.A.

The Golf Course at Glen Mills, outside Philadelphia in rural Delaware County, is a daily-fee course that is part of the 800-acre campus of the Glen Mills School. Glen Mills is not any old school. Founded in 1826, it is the oldest residential facility in the United States for troubled youths, with a current enrollment of 900 boys from age 14 to 18 who have been sent to the school by court systems in 28 states. About 75 of the boys, who have been involved in crimes ranging from petty theft to murder, are getting a first-class education in the golf business by working in the clubhouse, pro shop, and maintaining the course. The course, opened in 2000 and designed by Bobby Weed, who worked for Pete Dye and has designed courses for the PGA Tour, is superb and demanding. The first four holes are routed through rolling cornfields before the course saunters through dense woodlands, ribbons of wetlands, and craggy rocks and streams, with more than 200 feet of elevation change. The massive main school building, with its narrow fluted brick chimneys and clock tower, looms above the 17th hole.

Huntsville Golf Club, located in the Pocono Mountains region near Wilkes-Barre, was completed in 1995. The course is testament to the perseverance of Brooklyn-born Dick Maslow, the founder and owner of Huntsville, who moved his factory to the Wilkes-Barre area in 1958. Maslow acquired a total of 560 acres of rolling farmland and hired Rees Jones to design the private course. When Jones saw the land, he told him that he needed to purchase a dramatic 180-acre adjoining parcel to create a great golf course. Maslow did just that, and the property Jones recommended is now the site of holes 11 through 14. With so much land to work with, Jones wove together a tapestry of heathland, hardwoods, streams, and wetlands. The course takes its name from the nearby Huntsville Reservoir.

▷ JULY 8   ▷ SAUCON VALLEY COUNTRY CLUB   ▷ PENNSYLVANIA, U.S.A.

Saucon Valley Country Club in Bethlehem has three championship courses—the Old Course, the Grace Course, and the Weyhill Course—plus a six-hole short course, giving it a nifty 60 holes altogether. The history of the club is closely tied to that of the Bethlehem Steel Company. The Old Course, which opened in 1922 and hosted the 1992 and 2000 U.S. Senior Opens, is a classic parkland layout designed by the English architect Herbert Strong on softly sloping terrain that once had been a farm. The Grace Course is named for Eugene Grace, the founder of the club, who after graduating from Lehigh University in 1899, became president of Bethlehem Steel in 1916 and served as president and chairman until his retirement in 1957. The Grace Course, designed by William Gordon and his son David in the 1950s, circles around the Old Course without returning to the clubhouse, pausing at the halfway house named "Villa Pazzetti" after another Bethlehem Steel executive. The Weyhill Course, also designed by the Gordons and opened in 1968, is the most dramatic of the three, with more severe and sudden changes of elevation. Laid out over what had been a dairy farm named Weyhill Farms, the 14th and 15th play over an abandoned quarry, and Saucon Creek snakes through the property. *Right: Weyhill Course*

▷ JULY 9   ▷ STONEWALL GOLF CLUB   ▷ PENNSYLVANIA, U.S.A.

The aptly named Stonewall Golf Club is in the town of Elverson in rural Lancaster County, an hour's drive west of Philadelphia. The impetus for building the course, completed in 1992, came from A. John May, the managing partner of a prominent Philadelphia law firm. The founders originally hired Tom Fazio to design the course, but he was unable to take the project beyond the initial stages because of other commitments. The club then turned to young architect Tom Doak, who has since made a big splash in the design world, but was relatively unknown at the time. Collaborating with Gil Hanse, Doak found Stonewall, with its mix of rolling pasture, woodlands, and pockets of wetlands on what once had been a dairy farm, to be an ideal site for his naturalistic, Scottish-influenced style of design. The layout features chipping areas around the greens and tall fescue grasses flanking the fairways. There are indeed half a dozen old stone walls on the property, while the 18th fairway sweeps down to the sunken green in front of an old stone dairy building that now serves as the clubhouse. In 2003, Doak completed a second 18-hole course at Stonewall.

▷ JULY 10   ▷ OAKMONT COUNTRY CLUB   ▷ PENNSYLVANIA, U.S.A.

Oakmont is the singular vision of its founder, Henry Clay Fownes, the Pittsburgh industrialist, and his son William C. Fownes, Jr. (who was given the "Jr." despite being named after his uncle). Located a dozen miles north of Pittsburgh, the course was planned by Fownes *père* and built by 150 men and 25 mule teams, beginning September 15, 1903, and opening a year later. The Fownes took a strict Calvinist view of golf as a game that was meant to be difficult and Oakmont reflects the credo of William Fownes that "a shot poorly played should be a shot irrevocably lost." Oakmont's penal bunkers are legendary, particularly the eight rows of the "Church Pews" that separate the third and fourth fairways. The clay soil did not allow for building deep bunkers, so Oakmont's were filled with heavy river sand and then, starting in 1920, furrowed with specially built heavy metal rakes with two-inch-long teeth. The Fownes had the greens rolled with a 1,500-pound roller that required eight men to pull. The Oakmont rakes are gone nowadays, but Oakmont's greens remain the fastest and wickedest in all of golf, where four-putts are not out of the ordinary and putts have been known to fall backwards into the cup. Oakmont has figured prominently on the stage of championship golf, with Ben Hogan winning the U.S. Open there during his epic season of 1953. In 1973, Johnny Miller fired a blistering 63, which remains the lowest final round in the history of the championship, to win the Open. In 1994, Ernie Els took the title by outlasting Colin Montgomerie and Loren Roberts in an 18-hole playoff that ended in sudden-death.

▷ JULY 11   ▷ OLD COURSE AT ST. ANDREWS   ▷ SCOTLAND

The "auld gray toon" of St. Andrews on the east coast of Scotland in the Kingdom of Fife is the home of golf, and no course is more closely identified with the history of the game than the Old Course at St. Andrews. The course is laid out along St. Andrews Bay in the shape of a shepherd's crook, with the first seven holes running out to Eden Estuary, followed by a four-hole loop, and then returning to the world's most recognized clubhouse. St. Andrews is a course that golfers learn to love but it is somewhat unprepossessing and strange at first sight, with broad fairways as rumpled as dirty laundry, lurking bunkers seemingly scattered randomly across the field of play, and immense double greens with rollercoaster surfaces. The earliest documented evidence of golf at St. Andrews dates from January 25, 1552, although no doubt golf had been played there for some time earlier. The Royal and Ancient Golf Club of St. Andrews was founded in 1754, and eventually became the governing body of the game outside of the United States. Many of the early Scottish pros, including Old and Young Tom Morris, hailed from St. Andrews, where they began as caddies. The Old Course has hosted 25 British Opens since 1873, with Tiger Woods winning the claret jug there in 2000, when he was at the peak of his invincibility.

▷ JULY 12   ▷ KINGSBARNS GOLF LINKS   ▷ SCOTLAND

Kingsbarns, a new links in the backyard of some of the world's oldest, has taken the golfing world by storm. Lying just five miles up the road from the Old Course at St. Andrews, Kingsbarns opened in 1998 and was instantly acclaimed as a links of the highest echelon. Even more unusual is that the course was designed by an American architect, Californian Kyle Phillips, with input from the course's American co-owner, Mark Parsinen. Phillips moved a great deal of earth, 400,000 cubic yards altogether, to create the broad, rolling fairways along the sea that look so natural. In the process, workers discovered graves and dwellings dating back 2,500 years. An old stone bridge from the early 19th century was also unearthed during construction; it now leads across the burn to the 18th green. The name of the course comes from a former castle near the fourth green, which once guarded the grain stored in the "King's barns."

▷ JULY 13   ▷ CARNOUSTIE GOLF LINKS   ▷ SCOTLAND

Carnoustie is a small and rather remote village that lies on the other side of the Firth of Forth from St. Andrews, but the 1999 British Open left no doubt that is the fiercest and most unrelenting of all the championship courses of Great Britain. Before 1999, Carnoustie was best known as the site of Ben Hogan's historic triumph at the British Open in 1953, the year the "wee ice mon" won all three of the majors he entered. Even in ordinary circumstances, Carnoustie is a tough track, but with the rough allowed to grow like the giant's beanstalk and the fairways reduced to narrow corridors, the pros were left crying for mercy. No golfer can forget Jean Van de Velde's agonizing finish on the 18th hole that year. The Frenchman's pitch from the tall rough found Barry Burn on his way to a triple-bogey seven, sending him to a three-way playoff that ended with Paul Lawrie as the last man standing. As Patric Dickinson wrote so presciently of Carnoustie back in 1950: "The *dénouement* is like the climax of an Elizabethan drama: daggers are out by the 16th, a poisoned-cup filled from the Burn and drunk deeply at the 17th; and the eighteenth green is littered with dead bodies which Fortinbras (fresh from a 72 at St. Andrews) arrives to clear up and cart off, on trolleys … but is it really a grand tragedy finish; or is it *grand guignol*? Or a bit of both?"

Royal Aberdeen is not one of the better known, but it is one of the best links in Scotland. The Society of Golfers of Aberdeen was founded in 1780, making it the sixth-oldest golf club in the world, and moved to its present home at Balgownie, a mile north of the city across the River Don, in 1888. The fairways run out and back through gentle valleys in the dunes overlooking Aberdeen Bay, touching the neighboring course of Murcar on the ninth green. Scottish golf writer Sam McKinlay wrote of Aberdeen: "I would go so far as to say that there are few courses in these islands with a better, more testing, more picturesque outward nine than Balgownie . . . What adds enormously to the charm of the first half of the course is that the player is never out of sight or sound of the sea except when he is in the valley. Some of the tees stand high on the dunes overlooking Aberdeen Bay, and if you have an eye for the beauties of nature you may see and hear a raft of eider duck mewing just off the shore or a flight of whooper swans heading north for the Ythan sanctuary."

▷ JULY 15   ▷ CRUDEN BAY GOLF CLUB   ▷ SCOTLAND

Cruden Bay runs over and through the saucers in the giant sandhills of the Aberdeen coast of northeast Scotland, next to the small fishing village of Port Errol. The course, originally designed by Old Tom Morris, underwent a substantial redesign in 1926 by Tom Simpson. It was perhaps Simpson's crowning achievement, and he included the first, eighth, and 18th among his selection of the finest 18 holes in Great Britain and Ireland. Before World War II, Cruden Bay was one of the great golf resorts of the north and the rival of Turnberry and Gleneagles. The truly grandiose Cruden Bay Hotel, owned and operated by the Great North of Scotland Railway and built of pink Peterhead granite, opened in 1899, the same year as the course. This "palace in the sandhills" never reopened after the war and was eventually demolished. Not far from the course on a high dune ridge is another palace, known as Slains Castle. The magnificent ruin provided the inspiration for Dracula's castle to author Bram Stoker, who frequently wandered the beach at Cruden Bay.

▷ JULY 16   ▷ ROYAL DORNOCH GOLF CLUB   ▷ SCOTLAND

Royal Dornoch is the farthest north of the great championship courses of Scotland, located by the village of Dornoch 60 miles north of Inverness on the east coast of Sutherland, and 600 miles north of London. A classic links course festooned with gorse, Dornoch runs out and back along Embo Bay, with seven miles of creamy beach leading to Littleferry and Loch Fleet to the north and out to the pale blue mountains beyond. The golf club was founded in 1877, although golf has been played in Dornoch since 1616, with Sir Robert Gordon writing in his *History of Sutherland*, published in 1630: "About this toun there are the fairest and largest links of any pairt of Scotland, fit for archery, Golfing, Ryding, and all other exercise; they do surpass the fields of Montrose or St Andrews." Dornoch's most famous native son was Donald Ross, born in a house on St. Gilbert Street in 1873. In 1898, Ross emigrated to Boston, and was eventually hired by James Tufts to design Pinehurst No. 2, where the crowned and exquisitely sculpted greens reflect Dornoch's influence. Dornoch was a popular resort for the upper crust of English golfers in the early years of the 20th century but then settled into relative anonymity. It has been rediscovered in recent years, with many golfers making the pilgrimage that Herbert Warren Wind described in his 1964 *New Yorker* article, "North to the Links of Dornoch."

▷ JULY 17   ▷ NAIRN GOLF CLUB   ▷ SCOTLAND

Nairn is one of the finest and most picturesque courses in the Scottish highlands, located on the stretch of coast between Fraserburgh and Inverness on the southern shores of Moray Firth. The Club was founded in 1877, when Nairn was a fashionable summer resort known as "the Brighton of the North." The course was laid out by Archie Simpson, the professional at Royal Aberdeen, with subsequent revisions by Old Tom Morris and James Braid. The first seven holes follow along the sweep of the firth, with views across the sea to Black Isle and westward to the mountains. The inland holes are plusher, with rings of gorse, heather, and dark green pines. In 1999, Nairn hosted the Walker Cup, with the amateur team from Great Britain and Ireland winning a decisive victory over the U.S.

Above: Clynelish distillery in the Scottish highlands

▷ JULY 18 ▷ GLENEAGLES RESORT ▷ SCOTLAND

Gleneagles is golf's version of Brigadoon, although, fortunately for golfers, this pleasure palace created in the Scottish moors is not imaginary. Located between Blackford and Auchterarder, with the Ochil Hills to the south and the foothills of the Grampians to the north, Gleneagles had its genesis in the rivalry between the various British railways before the First World War. Donald A. Matheson, the general manager of the Caledonian Railway, devised the brilliant plan to build the ultimate luxury hotel and two championship courses in the beautiful bower of the highlands. The famous King's and Queen's Courses were both designed by the great Scottish professional James Braid, with work beginning in 1913. Both courses opened in 1919, after construction was halted by the war, and the hotel was finally completed in June 1924. In 1993, Jack Nicklaus unveiled a third course, the PGA Centenary Course, which has been selected to host the 2014 Ryder Cup. *Right: Kings Course*

▷ JULY 19   ▷ GULLANE GOLF CLUB (NO. 1 COURSE)   ▷ SCOTLAND

Gullane is one of the great golfing centers of Scotland, with three courses wheeling around Gullane Hill in East Lothian. From the seventh tee of Gullane No. 1, the high point on the course, there are sumptuous views out to the Firth of Forth and the hills of Fife and across Aberlady Bay to Edinburgh in the west. Gullane No. 1 was founded in 1884, with Gullane No. 2, or the New Course, following in 1898. Gullane has hosted the British Ladies Championship four times, most recently in 2004. Babe Didrikson Zaharias became the first American to win the championship when she prevailed at Gullane No. 1 in 1947. The sense of boundless links, with flagsticks fluttering in every direction, was captured by Bernard Darwin when he wrote: "From Gullane Hill to the Luffness Club-house is one huge stretch of turf, and such turf! the finest, smoothest, and most delicate that ever was seen."

▷ JULY 20　　▷ NORTH BERWICK GOLF CLUB　▷ SCOTLAND

North Berwick is a venerable and much venerated course, full of historic charm, set in the midst of the golfing pageantry of East Lothian. At the turn of the 20th century, North Berwick was the most fashionable of all the Scottish resorts—the place for members of English society to see and be seen. Arthur Balfour, the future prime minister, was a regular on the links, and was captain in 1891-92. The original club was founded in 1832, but the New Club dates from 1879. North Berwick is particularly famed for its scenery, with views from the front nine over the Firth of Forth to the brooding Bass Rock with its colony of gannets and the small craggy islands of the forth, including Lamb and Fidra. To the west lie Dirleton and Archerfield Wood, with Muirfield beyond. The first and 17th holes both run out to Point Garry, while the green of the seventh hole is guarded by Eel Burn. The 15th is the famous par-three Redan hole, which takes its name from a Crimean War fortification, and has been copied all over the world, including at the National Golf Links of America and Shinnecock Hills.

▷ JULY 21   ▷ MUIRFIELD   ▷ SCOTLAND

Muirfield is the home of the Honourable Company of Edinburgh Golfers, founded in 1744, ten years before the Royal and Ancient Golf Club of St. Andrews, making it the oldest golf club in the world. The members originally played at the links of Leith but in 1836 the club moved six miles east to Musselburgh. The course eventually became overcrowded and in 1891 the club moved further east to Muirfield, where it has been ever since. Muirfield is the blueblood of Scottish golf, not only in its lineage and membership, but in the elegance and fairness of its design. The course is famous for its routing, with the clockwise outward nine encircling the counterclockwise inner nine. Many great champions have won the British Open at Muirfield, beginning with Harold Hilton in 1892, and including Jack Nicklaus in 1966, Lee Trevino in 1972, Tom Watson in 1980, Nick Faldo in 1987 and 1992, and, most recently, Ernie Els in 2002.

▷ JULY 22   ▷ PORTMARNOCK GOLF CLUB   ▷ IRELAND

Portmarnock is the golfing pride of Dublin, located across an estuary on a two-mile-long peninsula that juts into Dublin Bay. Like many other early Irish courses, Portmarnock was founded by Protestant businessmen, in this case a Scottish insurance executive named William Chalmers Pickeman, who rowed over to survey the site on Christmas Eve in 1893 with his friend George Ross. The first nine holes opened in 1894, on land owned by the Jameson distillery family, with an outhouse belonging to local resident Maggie Leonard serving as the first clubhouse. The course, which evolved over time, is a low-lying, somewhat understated, and strategic links compared to its more rambunctious cousins on the west coast. The 185-yard par-three 15th that runs hard along the shore of Dublin Bay, with a sprig of palm tree to the front right of the green, features views across the sea to Ireland's Eye and the Lambay Islands. Portmarnock has hosted more championships than any other Irish course, including the 1991 Walker Cup and many Irish Opens.

▷ JULY 23 ▷ THE ISLAND GOLF CLUB ▷ IRELAND

The Island is actually located on a peninsula, but for much of the club's long history the only way to reach the links was by a large rowboat from the village of Malahide across Broadmeadow Estuary. The first golfers at the Island were four bachelors from prominent Dublin families, who rode across the channel in 1887 to be able to play golf on a Sunday, which was prohibited at Royal Dublin Golf Club. They persuaded six of their friends, also all bachelors, to form a syndicate to secure the pristine linksland and build a course. For many years, the course could only be played by ticketholders invited by the syndicate, all members of the Protestant establishment. In the 1960s and '70s, The Island fell on hard times, but the members went forward with a successful plan to redesign the course, a 15-year project overseen by architects Fred Hawtree and Eddie Hackett (also during that time a bridge was built to the peninsula). The Island is now recognized as one of Ireland's greatest golfing treasures, with 11 old holes and seven new ones that run through the craggy sandhills with their colorful bunting of gorse, cotton lavender, and wild orchids. The front nine is shorter and tighter than the back, with the 14th featuring the narrowest fairway in Ireland threading along the estuary.

▷ JULY 24   ▷ THE EUROPEAN CLUB   ▷ IRELAND

The European Club owes its conception, design, and realization to the vision and determination of Pat Ruddy. Ruddy, who grew up in County Sligo in the west of Ireland, has been something of a one-man band for Irish golf, starting out as the golf writer for the *Evening Herald* in Dublin as a young man and becoming a leading course architect. The European Club is located about 35 miles south of Dublin, overlooking Brittas Bay. In 1987, Ruddy saw an advertisement in the real estate section of a Dublin newspaper for a stretch of seaside property suitable for a golf course. He arranged for a helicopter ride down the east coast to inspect the site from the air, discovering an Elysium of enormous sand dunes that cried out for a golf course. Ruddy was able to raise the funds to buy the property and then essentially built the course himself, with the help of his children, over a five-year period, completing it in 1992. Ruddy created a true blue, natural links that he has continued to refine over the years, but without the blind holes and quirkiness of some of the older links courses.

▷ JULY 25   ▷ OLD HEAD GOLF LINKS   ▷ IRELAND

Old Head Golf Links, opened in 1997, is located seven miles south of the harbor town of Kinsale in County Cork. The course occupies a 220-acre dragon's tongue of land lashed across high sea cliffs above the Atlantic. Old Head, declared Joseph Passov in *Links Magazine*, "is the most spectacular course on earth." Until 1978, the rocky promontory was farmland, but brothers John and Patrick O'Connor, both successful real estate developers, recognized that the site would make for a magical golf course. The O'Connors hired American course architect Ron Kirby, who teamed up with Ireland's leading architect Eddie Hackett, Waterville pro Liam Higgins, and the legendary Irish amateur Joe Carr. No less than nine of the holes rollick and rumble across the rocky cliffs, which rise 300 feet above the ocean, not far from where the *Lusitania* was torpedoed by a German U-boat in 1915. The symbol of Old Head is the lighthouse at the tip of the promontory built in 1853. *Above: Fishing boats along Kinsale peninsula*

▷ JULY 26 ▷ WATERVILLE GOLF LINKS ▷ IRELAND

Waterville Golf Links is located at the western tip of the Ring of Kerry, on a promontory overlooking Ballinskelligs Bay with the estuary of the River Inny on one side and the mountains of Kerry as a backdrop. Waterville was founded and built by the late Irish-American multimillionaire Jack Mulcahy in 1973, at a time when there were virtually no new courses being built in Ireland. Mulcahy, who returned to Ireland in the 1960s after making his fortune in the U.S., also built Waterville House, a charming golf and fishing hotel—Waterville having long been renowned for its salmon fishing. The golf course is the masterwork of Irish architect Eddie Hackett, one of the few projects in which he actually worked on a big budget. After a comparatively tame stretch of opening holes, the course gathers force as it climbs and winds through the dunes. Two of the now legendary holes are the Mass, the par-three 12th situated where Mass was secretly celebrated in the deep hollow in front of the green in the days when Catholic worship was persecuted, and the par-three 17th, Mulcahy's Peak. The 17th tee is the highest point on the course, playing across the wild broken dunes, and was the favorite vista of Waterville's founder, whose ashes are buried beneath the tee box.

Above: Waterville House

▷ JULY 27   ▷ LAHINCH GOLF CLUB   ▷ IRELAND

Lahinch is one of Ireland's most venerable links, named for the seaside village in County Clare overlooking Liscannor Bay and the famed razor-sheer Cliffs of Moher. The club was founded in 1892 by a group of well-to-do merchants from Limerick and in its early years the members came from the Protestant upper class. Lahinch quickly became a leading Irish golf resort, with fashionable golfers arriving from London by ferry and then railway from Dublin. The original course was designed by Old Tom Morris for a fee of £1 plus travel expenses, even less than he charged for his design at County Down in Newcastle. The course was reshaped by Charles Gibson, the professional from Westward Ho! in 1907, and then redesigned by Alister MacKenzie in 1927, just before his work on Cypress Point and Augusta National. While MacKenzie modernized the course, he did not tamper with two of Lahinch's most famous holes, the Klondyke and the Dell, described by Herbert Warren Wind as "two living museum pieces." The Dell is the par-three sixth, an original from Old Tom's design that requires a blind shot over a dune to a featherbed of green. Lahinch is also famous for its weather-forecasting goats, which huddle near the clubhouse when rain is on the way.

Above: the Strand at Lahinch

▷ JULY 28   ▷ DOONBEG GOLF CLUB   ▷ IRELAND

Doonbeg immediately leapt into the ranks of the great links of western Ireland when it opened in 2002. This much ballyhooed course set in the pleated dunes and piled stone walls along Doughmore Bay in County Clare lives up to its billing. Located near the wee village of Doonbeg, the course was developed by Kiawah Development Partners, making Doonbeg the Irish cousin of the Ocean Course at South Carolina's Kiawah Island. Greg Norman made the most of the rare opportunity to lay out a course on sacred golfing ground, making 22 visits over a three-year period to find the holes in the natural folds of the dunes and farmland. A 51-acre portion of the dunes was fenced off as a habitat preserve for the *vertigo anguistor*, a small snail, but that still left Norman with plenty of choice golfing ground. From the very first hole, Doonbeg captures the rustic, windswept flavor of Irish seaside golf, with the par-four fifth running out to the beach, and the shoreline hugging the right side of the 18th hole. Doonbeg can rightfully take its place alongside its famous golfing neighbors, Lahinch, Waterville, and Ballybunion.

▷ JULY 29   ▷ BALLYBUNION GOLF CLUB (OLD COURSE)   ▷ IRELAND

Ballybunion Old is the best-known course in Ireland and one of the most famous in the world, although its fame is relatively recent. Like many of the world's most resplendent links, Ballybunion was shaped as much by nature as by an architect, though Irish professional James McKenna was probably responsible for laying out the original course in the immense sand ridges that flank the encroaching Atlantic in County Kerry. Ballybunion traces its origin to 1893, starting out as a 12-hole course that was not fully extended to 18 until 1927. Tom Simpson was given free rein to alter the course in 1936, but recognizing that one should not attempt to repaint the Mona Lisa, he chose only to move three greens and add one fairway bunker, known as Mrs. Simpson. The first hole runs past a graveyard just off the right side of the fairway, while the 18th traverses a vast sandy waste area known as the Sahara. In between, the holes clamber and clatter through the sand dunes. Herbert Warren Wind wrote of his visit in 1971: "Very simply, Ballybunion revealed itself to be nothing less than the finest seaside course I have ever seen." That article and the enthusiasm for Ballybunion of Tom Watson, who first visited the course in 1981 and made it a staple of his British Open preparations, brought the links to the attention of the world. Ballybunion added a second course, the Cashen Course, in 1980. Designed by Robert Trent Jones, it is a creative, controversial, and taxing links of the first order.

▷ JULY 30　▷ CARNE GOLF LINKS　▷ IRELAND

    Carne is one of the wonderful, storm-tossed, remote, and not particularly well-known links of northwest Ireland, lying at the tip of the Belmullet Peninsula past the small village of Belmullet and overlooking Blacksod Bay. Opened in 1995, Carne owes its formation to Michael Mangan, who upon returning to County Mayo from London in the early 1980s, purchased a small farm, including a one-seventeenth share of a commonage—that is, shared grazing rights on agricultur-ally poor land. A couple of years later, when Mangan actually saw the grazing land, he recognized that the magnificent dunescape would make the ideal site for a golf course. Then came the difficult job of persuading each of the farmers who had a stake in the commonage to sell their share and raising the necessary funds to buy them out. Eddie Hackett, the foremost Irish course architect, was brought in when he was nearly 80 years old to design the course, walking the dunes and making drawings each night in his B & B. The result is a bodacious and boisterous links, laid out on a small budget through the cul de sacs and crannies of the massive dunes. *Above: Blacksod Bay*

▷ JULY 31   ▷ COUNTY SLIGO GOLF CLUB   ▷ IRELAND

County Sligo Golf Club, or Rosses Point, is the unsurpassed links of northwest Ireland, running through the lyrical landscape made famous in the poetry of William Butler Yeats. The course lies at the tip of Rosses Point, the five-mile sliver of land that runs out to the sea and along the channel that leads to Sligo Town and its harbor. Across from the quaint, black and white Tudor clubhouse lies the original Coney Island. The club was founded in 1894 by British army officers, with the original nine holes laid out by George Combe, who played a leading role at Royal County Down. The present design owes much to a week-long visit by the great English architect, Harry Colt, in June 1927. Rosses Point has been described as "golf's magic stepladder" and from the high ground there are sweeping panoramas over Sligo Bay and to the interior mountains, with the green summit of Knocknarea where the mythic warrior Queen Maeve is reputed to be buried. Above the course as it loops inland looms "bare Ben Bulben's head," the flat-topped mountain for which the 10th hole is named, with Drumcliff Estuary running below. Yeats is buried in the Drumcliff churchyard, its steeple visible from the course, under the plain limestone tombstone that bears his epitaph:

Cast a cold Eye
On Life, on Death.
Horseman, pass by!

▷ AUGUST 1   ▷ ROSAPENNA GOLF LINKS (SANDY HILLS)   ▷ IRELAND

Rosapenna Golf Links is located in the far northwest of Ireland's County Donegal, in the open swatch of duneland past the quaint 19th-century village of Carrigart, overlooking Sheephaven Bay. Rosapenna is a fascinating tale of bygone golfing glory and contemporary revival. The original course at Rosapenna was founded by the Earl of Leitrim, who brought Old Tom Morris over from St. Andrews to design the course in 1891, and built a grand resort hotel of Swedish timber. In 1962, the old hotel was destroyed by fire, but in 1980 the 800-acre property was acquired by Frank Casey, whose father had been the headwaiter at the hotel and who had worked there himself as a youngster. Casey hired Pat Ruddy in 1994 to design a brand new links course in the high ridge of untouched dunes above the original course. The splendid new links, opened in 2003 and christened Sandy Hills, bounds through the secluded valleys of the restless dunes, with magnificent views across the arc of the bay to the massive rock face of Horn Head meeting the Atlantic and south to Muckish Mountain and the wild steppes of Donegal. Casey has also built a new, comfortable hotel adjoining the two courses.

▷ AUGUST 2　▷ ROYAL PORTRUSH GOLF CLUB　▷ NORTHERN IRELAND

Royal Portrush is one of the most historic links in Ireland, unraveling through the shaggy dunes of Northern Ireland's Antrim Coast, not far from the Giant's Causeway, the thousands of stone pillars that form a natural esplanade to the sea. Founded in 1888, Portrush was a fashionable seaside resort drawing droves of golfers by the turn of the century. The present course is the inspired work of the English master Harry Colt in the early 1930s. Portrush is inevitably compared to Royal County Down, the other great links of Northern Ireland, but the temperaments of the courses are quite different. Portrush's narrow, angled fairways ripple through the dunes on the white chalky cliffs high above the Atlantic, while County Down lies at sea level beneath the Mourne Mountains. Instead of the yellow gorse that blankets County Down, Portrush is famous for its thick rough of sea grasses adorned with wildflowers and thickets of sea roses. The championship course at Portrush is named Dunluce after Dunluce Castle, the 16th-century fortress of the warrior chieftain Sorley Boy MacDonnell, its ruined shell tottering on the seaside cliff in view from the course. The Dunluce Course has the distinction of being the only course outside of Scotland and England to have ever hosted the British Open, with Max Faulkner winning the championship there in 1951. *Above: ruins of Dunluce Castle*

▷ AUGUST 3   ▷ PORTSTEWART GOLF CLUB   ▷ NORTHERN IRELAND

Portstewart Golf Club has a long pedigree, having been founded in 1894, but for almost a century it was overshadowed by Royal Portrush, its neighbor just three miles east along Northern Ireland's Antrim Coast. Then in 1990 Portstewart unveiled seven new holes, carved out of 60 acres of giant brambled and this-tled sandhills that the members had long coveted for their course. Now Portstewart no longer takes a backseat to any links in Ireland. The dramatic new holes, molded through the steep, saw-toothed dunes piled high with blankets of buckthorn and marram, were designed not by a big-name architect but by member Des Giffin, a math teacher at the local grammar school. The first hole, with its crow's nest tee, was unchanged and remains one of the best in Irish golf, looking down at Portstewart Strand out to the dome of Mussenden Temple in the distance, built by the Earl of Bristol on his 19th-century estate overlooking the Atlantic. The newer holes then race through the dunes, playing as Nos. 2 through 8. The back nine is quite different from but complements the front, with lower-lying holes straddling the banks of the River Bann as it arches its way slowly out to the sea and inland through green quilted fields.

▷ AUGUST 4   ▷ ROYAL COUNTY DOWN GOLF CLUB   ▷ NORTHERN IRELAND

Many knowledgeable golfers consider Royal County Down in Newcastle, Northern Ireland, to be the greatest golf course in the world. It is certainly one of the most surpassingly beautiful, with the course following the crescent of Dundrum Bay and looking across the spire of the Slieve Donard Hotel and the town to the Mountains of Mourne, with their chameleon's coloring of smoky purples, blues, and greens. The fairways glide through galleons of yellow-flowering gorse and clusters of "eyebrow" or bushy-topped bunkers. County Down was founded in a meeting at Mr. Lawrence's Dining Rooms, Newcastle, in 1889, and Old Tom Morris was brought over from St. Andrews, Scotland, to design the course for a fee of £ 4. By 1902, only six of the original holes remained, with George Combe, an early captain, carrying out the alterations, and further refinements were overseen by Harry Colt in the 1920s. The splendor of Royal County Down was best summed up by Bernard Darwin: "It is perhaps superfluous to say that it is a course of big and glorious carries, nestling greens, entertainingly blind shots, local knowledge, and beautiful turf . . . the kind of golf that people play in their most ecstatic dreams." *Above: Slieve Donard Hotel*

▷ AUGUST 5   ▷ TURNBERRY RESORT (AILSA COURSE)   ▷ SCOTLAND

Turnberry's Ailsa Course is one of extravagant and unforgettable beauty, with a sweeping view across the links from the terraced lawns of the grandiose, red-roofed hotel. The hotel and the two original courses were developed by the Glasgow & South Western Railway, which took over the private 13-hole course of the third Marquis of Ailsa in 1907. During World War II, the Ailsa Course and its sister course, the Arran, were turned into concrete runways used by the RAF. It seemed like golf might be finished at Turnberrry, but eventually, through the perseverance of Frank Hole, the managing director of the hotel, the Scottish course architect Philip Mackenzie Ross was commissioned to resurrect and redesign a new Ailsa Course, completed in 1951. In 1977, Turnberry hosted its first British Open, won by Tom Watson by one stroke over Jack Nicklaus in their famous "duel in the sun," and the glory of Ross's design was revealed to the golf world. The ninth hole, with the tee perched precariously on a promontory and with the emblematic whitewashed lighthouse to the left, vaults over and along the cliffs, with views across the Firth of Clyde to the Isle of Arran with its steep, slumbering mountains, the Ailsa Craig bubbling out of the sea, and all the way west to the Mull of Kintyre in the distance.

▷ AUGUST 6   ▷ PRESTWICK GOLF CLUB   ▷ SCOTLAND

Prestwick by contemporary standards is a particularly eccentric links, but one that exults in its unusualness. The course is located on the Ayrshire coast of western Scotland, separated from Troon by the Pow Burn that dominates the fourth hole. Prestwick is inextricably tied to the history of British golf, for the first 12 Open championships were held there beginning in 1860, when the course consisted of only 12 holes. The last Open to be held at Prestwick was in 1925, but the famous old links remains full of vitality. The third hole features the vast Cardinal bunker, fortified by an irregular ridge of wooden sleepers or railroad ties. The blind, par-three fifth is played over the sandhills known as the "Himalayas." The drive at the 16th must avoid the bunker named Willie Campbell's Grave, with the second shot over the "Alps" to the green guarded by the Sahara bunker. The railway line runs hard along the right side of the first hole, another distinctive feature of many of the old Scottish courses that is present at Prestwick.   *Above: clubhouse interior*

▷ AUGUST 7   ▷ ROYAL TROON GOLF CLUB   ▷ SCOTLAND

Royal Troon is one of the most highly acclaimed of the daisy-chain of fine links courses that stretch along the Ayrshire coast south of Glasgow. The first six holes straddle the shoreline before the course climbs into the sandhills at the seventh, with the next six holes running through the higher ground. The sixth is the longest hole in British championship golf at 601 yards while the eighth, the famous and fiendish "Postage Stamp Hole," with its tiny green, is the shortest at 123 yards. In the 1973 British Open, Gene Sarazen hit a punched 5-iron into the cup for a hole-in-one on the Postage Stamp, 50 years after he missed the cut at the Open at Troon. Founded in 1878, the course was added to the Open "rota" in 1923, when Sarazen made his maiden voyage and Arthur Havers won the championship. The course is known for its unrelenting back nine, which can become a torture track when it plays into the wind. Arnold Palmer won the Open at Troon in 1962, while underdog Todd Hamilton took home the claret jug in 2004 in a playoff with Ernie Els.

▷ AUGUST 8　▷ MACHRIHANISH GOLF CLUB　▷ SCOTLAND

Machrihanish Golf Club is one of Scottish golf's last undiscovered treasures, spread out on the dunes below the green mantle of the Mull of Kintyre at the tip of the long Kintyre Peninsula. A long trip by car from the mainland, Machrihanish is as Siegfried Sassoon once wrote a "rather ungetatable golf course" but this makes getting to Machrihanish something of a holy pilgrimage. It is a pilgrimage that inspired Michael Bamberger's book *To the Linksland*. The front nine gives the course its essential charm, with the holes ducking through the dunes overlooking the distant Hebridean islands of Islay and Jura, and Gigha, or "God's Island," closer to shore. The course dates from 1876, and five years later Old Tom Morris arrived from St. Andrews to recommend improvements, declaring the land "specially designed by the Almighty for playing golf." Old Tom apparently was responsible for the design of the famous first hole, with the tee shot over the broad bow of the Atlantic beach, though one version of events perhaps unfairly attributes Tom's placement of the tee in that particular spot to the fact that it was near the local pub.

▷ AUGUST 9 ▷ MACHRIE GOLF CLUB ▷ SCOTLAND

Machrie Golf Club is a wild and wonderful links, full of old-fashioned blind holes and wind-lashed sand dunes, located on the Isle of Islay in the Hebrides, a two-hour ferry ride from the west coast of Scotland. To one side of the links are the peat bogs with their palette of somber browns and purples that give Islay's world-famous single malt whiskys their distinctive flavor, leading out to the green hills that form the backbone of the island. To the other side are the towering dunes overlooking Laggan Bay and the Atlantic that frame the seventh, eighth, and ninth holes. The course dates to 1891, when Willie Campbell of Prestwick laid out the original 18, shortly before embarking for Boston to become the first pro at The Country Club. British architect Donald Steel created five new holes in the late 1980s, the second and 10th through 13th. Few courses can boast such overpowering and haunting isolation, with the only building in sight the white-washed hotel adjoining the course that was once an old farmhouse. The main village of Bowmore lies 20 minutes down the road, with its brightly painted houses running down to the sea from the church built in the round so that the devil would have no place to hide.

▷ AUGUST 10   ▷ RUNGSTED GOLF CLUB   ▷ DENMARK

Rungsted Golf Club, one of the most highly regarded courses in Denmark, is located 17 miles north of Copenhagen and within a mile of the coast. Rungsted opened in 1937, making it a relative newcomer compared to Copenhagen Golf Club, which was founded in an area known as Faelled in 1898, while the links at Fano dates from 1901. Designed by Major C.A. Mackenzie, Rungsted runs through groves of large beech trees and features small greens. The former home of Karen von Blixen, who wrote *Out of Africa* under the pen name Isak Dinesen, stands just a wedge shot away from the 13th hole and is now a museum dedicated to the author.

▷ AUGUST 11   ▷ FALSTERBO GOLF CLUB   ▷ SWEDEN

Falsterbo Golf Club is one of the great links of Europe, located by the little seaside resort of Falsterbo, 21 miles south of Malmö, Sweden's third city. The course, which dates from 1909, is spread over a small spear of ground that forms Land's End—the southernmost point of Sweden—with the Baltic on one side and the North Sea on the other. While a true links, with the fairways angled at different directions against the wind, several of the holes play over ponds and wetlands. The green of the demanding 427-yard fourth is tucked behind the marsh and the par-three 11th plays across a pond to an island green. The back nine sweeps around the somber, old domed lighthouse. The green of the 16th hole marks the tip of Sweden, with the view over the Oresund to Denmark and of the second-longest suspension bridge in the world that links Malmö to Copenhagen. The 17th and 18th run along the narrow ridge of dune separating the course from the Baltic and back to the clubhouse. *Above: Falsterbo lighthouse*

▷ AUGUST 12   ▷ BARSEBÄCK GOLF AND COUNTRY CLUB (OLD COURSE)   ▷ SWEDEN

Barsebäck Golf and Country Club, located about 30 miles up the western coast of Sweden from Malmö, has two superb 18-hole courses. The Old Course, designed by the late Ture Bruce, opened in 1969, while the New Course designed by the English architect Donald Steel opened in 1989. The heart and soul of Barsebäck is the stretch of holes on the Old Course that play along the leaden sea through the rushy grasses and offer links golf at its finest. The New Course is sculpted through an imposing forest of pines. Barsebäck hosted the 2003 Solheim Cup, in which the European team led by Annika Sorenstam soundly defeated the US. Barsebäck has been selected to host the Solheim Cup again when the competition returns to Europe in 2007.

Oslo Golf Club, the oldest course in Norway, is situated in the parkland of Bogstad. The course borders Bogstad Lake with a backdrop of the hills that are home to the Holmennkollen ski jump arena. The signature 16th hole plays across the watery tongue of the lake. Opened in 1924, Oslo started as a nine-hole course with sand greens. The club was originally named Kristiania Golf Club, but changed its name when the city changed its name to Oslo.

▷ AUGUST 14   ▷ ULLNA GOLF CLUB   ▷ SWEDEN

Ullna Golf Club is about an hour's drive outside of Stockholm, carved through the birch trees and wrapped around Lake Ullna. Founded in 1981, the course was designed by Sven Tumba, Sweden's greatest all-around sportsman, who played in four Olympics for the Swedish national hockey team during the 1950s and '60s. The course was created as a target-style design on the model of the American TPC courses with spectator mounds for viewing during tournaments (it has hosted events on both the men's and women's European Tours). Lake Ullna comes into play on many of the holes, starting with the island green on the par-three third and running the length of the 17th to a peninsula green at the finish. The lake is used in the winter by the ice yacht club of Stockholm as well as for skating, and across the lake is a man-made hill built for skiing.

▷ AUGUST 15 ▷ PALTAMO GOLF CLUB (MIDNIGHT SUN) ▷ FINLAND

Paltamo Golf Club, also known as Midnight Sun, is located in the small village of Paltamo, overlooking Oulu Lake in northern Finland. Designed by Americans Ronald Fream and David Dale of Golfplan, the course opened in 1991, with the final five holes completed in 2000. The course is girded by the lake, one of the largest in Finland, and ringed with Arctic birch. The town of Oulu, 100 miles to the west, is the capital of northern Finland, and is the home of the Oulu Golf Club founded in 1962. The current 27-hole Oulu Course, also designed by Golfplan, opened in 1992, with the third nine completed in 2004. From the beginning of June to the middle of July, the midnight sun allows golfers to play all night long.

▷ AUGUST 16   ▷ OZO GOLF CLUB   ▷ LATVIA

Ozo Golf Club, the only golf course in the Baltic Republic of Latvia, was founded by its namesake, National Hockey League star Sandis Ozolinsh, the greatest player to come out of Latvia. Ozolinsh took up golf shortly after he was traded from the San Jose Sharks to the Colorado Avalanche during the 1995-96 season, when the Avalanche won the Stanley Cup. After the Avalanche were eliminated from the playoffs in 1999, Ozolinsh took Latvia's leading sports journalist Armands Puce to play a round at Castle Pines in Denver. Afterwards, a casual conversation in the backyard of Ozolinsh's home about how nice it would be to have something similar back in Latvia hatched the idea for what was to become Ozo. When Puce returned to Latvia, he began looking for land for the course and found a site that had been used as a dumping ground just 10 minutes from the center of Riga. Ozolinsh hired Denver-based architect Rob Swedberg to design the course and Puce became the club's general manager. Ozo Golf Club opened on May 29, 2002, two years after construction began, and hosted its first professional tournament in the summer of 2003, the Hansabank Baltic Open.

▷ AUGUST 17   ▷ KRAKOW VALLEY GOLF CLUB   ▷ POLAND

Krakow Valley is located at the village of Paczoltowice, 45 minutes west of Krakow in the direction of Katowice, in a rural area where farmers with horse-drawn wagons are still the order of the day. Opened in 2004 and developed and owned by Zbigniew Lis, the site was previously a Communist collective farm growing wheat and barley. American golf architect Ron Fream created an open, prairie links-style look, taking advantage of the native grasses and wildflowers. The groves of trees around the perimeter of the course have been protected, with tall beech bordering some holes. Krakow itself offers the contrast of the 500-year-old town center with the Soviet-style architecture of the outer ring. The old barn adjoining the course has been refurbished into the 16-room Hotel Villa Pacoldi with a restaurant and bar.

Golf began in Czechoslovakia at the famous spa town of Karlovy Vary (better known by its German name, Carlsbad) in western Bohemia, which attracted aristocracy from throughout Europe. The town bears the name of Charles IV of Bohemia, who founded the spa in around 1360. In 1904, a nine-hole course was organized by members of the Gentlemen's Fencing Club in the Imperial Park in the valley of the River Teplá. In 1935, Czechoslovakia's first 18-hole course was completed at a new site in a splendid setting overlooking the Doupovské hills, the forests of Slavkov, and the Krusné Hory or Ore Mountains. After it was destroyed during World War II, the course was restored by a small group of dedicated enthusiasts. Since the fall of Communism, golf has blossomed again in the Czech Republic and Karlovy Vary and Mariánské Lazné (Marienbad) remain two of the leading courses.

▷ AUGUST 19   ▷ GOLF AND COUNTRY CLUB GUT ALTENTANN   ▷ AUSTRIA

Gut Altentann, Austria's top-rated course, lies in Henndorf am Wallersee, just six miles north of Salzburg, the hometown of Mozart. Founded in 1986, the course was Jack Nicklaus's first design foray into Europe. Like many of his designs, Gut Altentann is a robust layout, spread out over rustic, rumpled pastures and glades of alpine trees, with rock-laden lakes and streams coming into play. The property is one of historic interest, occupied by the Mondsee Monastery as far back as 785. The present-day clubhouse occupies the site of the manor house in which the archbishop and curates once lived, which was expanded over the years into the imposing Gut Altentann castle. The castle was destroyed by fire in 1680. In 1990, Gut Altentann hosted the inaugural Austrian Open, won by Bernhard Langer in a playoff with Lanny Wadkins.

▷ AUGUST 20   ▷ DACHSTEIN-TAUERN GOLF AND COUNTRY CLUB   ▷ AUSTRIA

Dachstein-Tauern Golf and Country Club is located outside the attractive old town of Schladming in the Austrian Alps. Designed by Bernhard Langer and opened in 1988, the course has an almost Floridian flavor, with fairways curving around a shimmering, fountain-filled lagoon. There are commanding views of the Dachstein peaks to distract the golfer. Better known as a ski resort, the four separate mountains have now been linked by lifts and trails.

▷ AUGUST 21　▷ GOLF CLUB CRANS-SUR-SIERRE　▷ SWITZERLAND

Crans-Sur-Sierre is synonymous with golf in the Swiss Alps. The original course was laid out in 1905 by Sir Arnold Lunn, an early pioneer of downhill skiing and the proprietor of the famed Palace Hotel at nearby Montana. When the English golfers who formed the course's clientele disappeared during World War I, the course was abandoned. After the war, two local hoteliers, Elysée and Albert Bonvin, took the initiative in creating a new course, with the full 18 holes completed in 1929. The present course covers a gently contoured plateau 5,000 feet above the fir-clad Rhône Valley. There are breathtakingly sublime views across the valley to the snow-covered majesty of the Matterhorn and Monte Rosa. Crans-Sur-Sierre has hosted the Swiss Open, now known as the European Masters, since 1939 and it is a favorite stop for the players on the European Tour and their families.

▷ AUGUST 22   ▷ WITTELSBACHER GOLF CLUB   ▷ GERMANY

Wittelsbacher Golf Club is located near the historic town of Neuberg on the Danube, some 40 or so miles northwest of Munich in Bavaria. Designed by Joan Dudok van Heel and opened in 1988, the course is one of understated elegance and subtle challenges, laid out over an estate that has been in the hands of the Wittelsbacher family, the former Royal House of Bavaria, for over 500 years. While the landscape is flat, the course is defended by more than 200 venerable oaks and lindens, as well as tentacled fairway bunkers and three water holes. From the course there are views of the 16th-century Grünau Castle. The president and paterfamilias of Wittelsbacher is His Royal Highness Prince Max of Bavaria, a keen golfer who is also a member of the Royal & Ancient, Pine Valley, Muirfield, and Royal St. George's. There are 26 elegantly furnished guestrooms in the modern clubhouse as well as a dormy house run by the club.

▷ AUGUST 23　▷ FRANKFURTER GOLF CLUB　▷ GERMANY

Frankfurter Golf Club has long been the gold standard of golf in Germany, located just three miles from the city center and near the Frankfurt airport. The club was founded in 1913, but the current course designed by Harry Colt, the greatest of English course architects, dates from 1928. Colt mastered the art of designing elegant, strategic parkland courses, and his understated genius is on display at Frankfurter as well as Falkenstein in Hamburg. Frankfurter is a heavily wooded and fairly hilly course, with eight particularly testing and on average lengthy par-fours. The course has staged the German Open on many occasions, although it is now considered too short for championship play. Henry Cotton won the first German Open held here in 1938 and Seve Ballesteros, Tony Jacklin, Graham Marsh, and Wayne Grady have all been winners at Frankfurter.

▷ AUGUST 24   ▷ BERLIN SPORTING CLUB (NICK FALDO COURSE)   ▷ GERMANY

Berlin Sporting Club is 150 miles from the Baltic Sea, but the Nick Faldo Course has the features and feel of a seaside links. The club is located outside the town of Bad Saarow near the shore of the Scharmützelsee lake. Working with Stan Eby, Faldo took great care in creating subtle drapes of fairway on a flat site. The strategic challenge comes from the sunken, grass-walled bunkers—130 in total—that are folded into the land. The course, which opened in 1997, hosted the 2000 World Amateur Team Championship to great acclaim and was the site of the 1999 and 2000 German Open. The Sporting Club Berlin also has a fine course designed by Arnold Palmer, opened in 1995, with the back nine playing through a forest, and a shorter course designed by Eby, opened in 2002.

▷ AUGUST 25   ▷ GOLF & COUNTRY CLUB SEDDINER SEE (SOUTH COURSE)   ▷ GERMANY

Seddiner See's South Course is one of the premier new courses in Germany, located along the shores of Seddiner Lake some 25 minutes south of Berlin, near the towns of Neuseddin and Wildenbruch. The only course in Germany designed by Robert Trent Jones, Jr., the South Course opened in 1994, followed by the North Course in 1997. Built at a cost of over 20 million Euros, no expense was spared, with a lavish clubhouse and impeccably conditioned fairways and greens. The course is relatively flat, but Jones defined the fairways with curved water hazards, hives of large swirling bunkers, and borders of birch and tall flaxen grasses.

▷ AUGUST 26   ▷ HAMBURGER GOLF CLUB   ▷ GERMANY

Hamburger Golf Club, generally known as Falkenstein, remains one of the very best German courses, even though in recent years the ranks have been considerably strengthened by such newcomers as Berlin Sporting Club and Seddiner See. While the club traces its history back to 1906, the present course was completed in 1930, and is located six miles from Hamburg near the Elbe River. Designed by the outstanding English team of Colt, Alison, and Morrison, the course would be right at home in the heathbelt of Surrey outside London. The fairways are carved from stands of pine and silver birch over moderately rolling terrain banded with heather. When the German Open was held at Hamburger in 1981, Bernhard Langer thrilled the crowd by becoming the first native German to win the event since its inception in 1912.

▷ AUGUST 27   ▷ CLUB ZUR VAHR   ▷ GERMANY

Club zur Vahr's championship course is situated 12 miles north of the Hanseatic city of Bremen in Garlstedt, on the road to Bremerhaven. Golf has been played in Bremen since 1895, when the Freudenberg family brought the game back with them from Ceylon to start a course on the city's race course in the suburb of Vahr. The Garlstedter Heide Course, part of Club zur Vahr's extensive sports complex, opened in 1970. August Weyhausen, the driving force behind the course, brought in Germany's foremost course architect, Bernhard von Limberger, who had won the German Amateur Championship at the nine-hole Vahr course in 1921, to design the new layout. A notably tough test, the numerous doglegs running through large pines and thick rough, with fairways punctuated by patches of heather, left little need for bunkers. The course is renowned for its six par fives, particularly the second and sixth, both of which offer alternative routes around the trees and over a stream to the green. *Above: rain shelter*

Gut Lärchenhof, located near Cologne, is the home each September of the Linde German Masters. Designed by Jack Nicklaus and completed in 1997, it is very much a modern, American-style target golf course, shaped through open countryside. One of the top events on the European Tour, the German Masters draws a strong field each year and is managed by Bernhard Langer, captain of Europe's victorious 2004 Ryder Cup team. In the tournament's first seven years the distinguished list of winners consists of Colin Montgomerie, Sergio Garcia, Michael Campbell, Langer, Stephen Leaney, K.J. Choi, and Padraig Harrington. The restaurant Gut Lärchenhof at the course has received a one-star rating from the Michelin Guide.

▷ AUGUST 29 ▷ NOORDWIJKSE GOLF CLUB ▷ NETHERLANDS

The Netherlands is known as a land of dikes and pancake-flat terrain, but the Dutch coast sports three links courses—Kennemer, Royal Hague, and Noordwijkse—that are every bit the equal of their cousins on the English side of the North Sea. Of the three, Noordwijkse has the most distinctively seaside character. After a stretch of holes on the front nine that funnel through a forest of pines, the holes positively prance through the dunes. Designed by the English architect Frank Pennink in 1972, the course is near the elegant seaside resort of Noordwijk aan Zee, just across from the brilliant bands of tulip bulbs that paint the countryside. Every spring the dizzying kaleidoscope of colored tulips is on display at the Keukenhof, or "kitchen garden," where Countess Jacoba of Bavaria grew vegetables for her kitchen when she lived on the property in the 15th century.

▷ AUGUST 30   ▷ ROYAL HAGUE GOLF CLUB   ▷ NETHERLANDS

The Royal Hague Golf Club, or Haagsche, located in the beautiful old wooded suburb of Wassenaar, is the oldest golf club in the Netherlands, having been founded in 1893. Like several other Dutch courses, the original course was badly damaged by the German army during World War II and had to be rebuilt. Haagsche has an aristocratic air about it and it shares the pedigree with several of the fine heathland courses outside London of having been designed by Harry Colt. The course is an entrancing hybrid, for it is not literally a seaside course and yet it is hard to imagine more billowing fairways, with rolling green waves of turf that crest so high it is impossible to see over them from the troughs. The holes are artfully arranged and framed by a palette of greens that range from the yellowy-green river birch to the bottle-green firs. The clubhouse has a traditional thatched roof and red-and-white shutters with a grass patio that runs out to the 18th green.

▷ AUGUST 31   ▷ ROYAL ZOUTE GOLF CLUB   ▷ BELGIUM

Golf was first played by a few retired Englishmen in the dunes at Knocke-sur-Mer on the Belgian coast, 30 miles from Ostend, in 1899. Count Maurice Lippens, who was chairman of the Compagnie Immobilière du Zoute, took the lead in building a regulation course, designed by Scottish architect Seymour Dunn, in 1908. The course received royal designation in 1925, and 13 years later King Leopold III met his future second wife while playing golf at Royal Zoute. The course was destroyed by the Germans in World War II, but at the end of the war the club enlisted the aid of British and Canadian military officers and a new course, designed by English architect Harry Colt, was built. Nowadays, Royal Zoute is one of the finest seaside courses in Europe and has hosted the Belgacom Open on the European PGA Tour.

▷ SEPTEMBER 1 ▷ ROYAL GOLF CLUB DE BELGIQUE ▷ BELGIUM

Golf in Belgium has long enjoyed royal patronage, with royal status conferred on each of Belgium's leading courses, including Royal Antwerp, Royal Zoute, Royal Waterloo, and Royal Golf des Fagnes. Royal Golf de Belgique, known as Ravenstein, is located at Tervuren, six miles from Brussels. Ravenstein was built in 1905 by order of King Leopold II to enable visiting British businessmen to play golf in Belgium. The course was designed by the English architect Tom Simpson, who was also responsible for the revision of Royal Antwerp. Château de Ravenstein, which serves as the clubhouse, is a national monument, and was built by the Infanta Isabella of Spain in the 17th century after the 15th-century hunting lodge of Philip of Cleves that originally occupied the site burned down. The Château is also the headquarters of the Fédération Royale Belge de Golf.

▷ SEPTEMBER 2   ▷ WALTON HEATH GOLF CLUB (OLD COURSE)   ▷ ENGLAND

Walton Heath's Old Course is one of the earliest and certainly one of the finest of the heathland courses around London, located less than 20 miles from the city center. The course, site of the 1981 Ryder Cup Matches, is laid out over a vast and solitary expanse of heath and gorse, and is renowned for its crisp turf and purple mounds of heather. The club largely owes its inception to Henry Cosmo Bonsor, chairman of the South Eastern Railway Company, who also happened to be the brother-in-law of William Herbert Fowler, a scratch competitive golfer and keen student of golf course design. Given the commission to create the course, Fowler explored the site on horseback in 1902 and his design was completed by the spring of 1904. An inventive and daring architect, Fowler went on to design such notable courses as Saunton East and The Berkshire, as well as the New Course at Walton Heath that opened in 1907, and was expanded to 18 holes in 1913. The club was particularly popular with politicians and members of the press from the outset. David Lloyd George and Winston Churchill were not only political rivals, but played matches against each other at Walton Heath, where Lloyd George was a member from 1907-1945 and Churchill from 1910-1965. James Braid, a towering figure in the history of the game, was enlisted as the first professional, and the "Sage of Walton Heath" held the position for 45 years until his death in 1950.

▷ SEPTEMBER 3   ▷ STOKE PARK CLUB   ▷ ENGLAND

Stoke Park Club, formerly known as Stoke Poges Golf Club, is a first-rate parkland course designed by Harry Colt that abounds in historical, architectural, and cinematic interest. The Stoke Park estate is first mentioned in the Domesday Book in 1086, with the village of Stoke Poges taking its name from the marriage of Amicia de Stoke to Sir Robert de Poges in 1291. Centuries later, John Penn, son of William Penn, spent a large share of the compensation he received from the new United States government for the family's 26 million acres in Pennsylvania to build the mansion, starting in 1789, that today serves as golf's grandest club- house and also houses a five-star hotel. The Penn mansion, designed by James Wyatt, architect to George III, influenced the design of the White House, while the monument built by Penn to Lord Coke, Chancellor of the Exchequer, stands in the practice range. In 1908, "Pa" Lane Jackson, founder of the Corinthian Sporting Club, purchased the estate and hired Colt to design the course. The most famous of movie golf scenes, the match between James Bond and Goldfinger, was filmed at Stoke Park, with the mansion serving as the backdrop. Sean Connery, a keen golfer, hit his own shots in the movie. Incidentally, when Bond drives off in his Aston Martin he is going down a driveway that is actually a dead end.

▷ SEPTEMBER 4   ▷ ST. GEORGE'S HILL GOLF CLUB   ▷ ENGLAND

St. George's Hill is one of the outstanding, although not one of the best known, of the heath-belt masterpieces of Harry Colt outside London. Laid out in 1913, St. George's Hill is also one of the earliest examples of building a golf course as part of a private residential estate, with a castellated clubhouse of red brick. The course is reminiscent of Pine Valley, which is not altogether surprising, since Colt was also a consultant to George Crump on his design there. The golf connoisseur Sir Peter Allen wrote of St. George's Hill: "Of all the inland courses of Britain, I think I like this one best and I believe that Colt said that this was his favourite work. It is not the toughest inland course—Walton Heath is that—or as well known as Sunningdale, but for variety and beauty to my mind it has no equal."

▷ SEPTEMBER 5   ▷ SUNNINGDALE GOLF CLUB (OLD COURSE)   ▷ ENGLAND

Sunningdale's Old Course is the grand dame of the great heathland courses built in the sand belt southwest of London at the turn of the last century. Twenty-five miles from London, the course occupies land that had once been part of the Benedictine nunnery of Broomhall, abolished by Henry VIII, and since 1524 the site has been owned by St. John's College, Cambridge. The course, designed in 1901 by Willie Park, Jr., and revised by Harry Colt, two of the greatest luminaries of British golf course architecture, is enchantingly beautiful. The fairways are lapped and crossed by pools of heather and each hole is encased by burly conifers. The Old Course has hosted the 1987 Walker Cup, the 1992 European Open (won by Nick Faldo), and three Women's British Opens in the past decade. The New Course, designed by Colt in 1922, is more open and a truly outstanding course in its own right. There is a picturesque clubhouse and the halfway house is famous for its sausage sandwiches.

▷ SEPTEMBER 6   ▷ KEILIR GOLF CLUB   ▷ ICELAND

Golf in Iceland is a sort of Nordic version of golf in Hawaii, with treeless courses laid out through floes of black lava. Keilir Golf Club, in the little fishing village of Hafnarfjordur, about a 15-minute drive from Reykjavik, is one of the finest of the lava courses. Established in 1967, the course was built on rolling farmland along the ocean. In 1994, nine holes were added which play as the front nine, through the 1,000-year-old Kapelluhraun, or Chapel Lava Fields. A new clubhouse was also built overlooking the Atlantic in 1993. Across the bay is the Snaefellsjokull volcano and the Snaefells Glacier, the site of Jules Verne's *Journey to the Centre of the Earth*.

▷ SEPTEMBER 7   ▷ SHINNECOCK HILLS GOLF CLUB   ▷ NEW YORK, U.S.A.

Shinnecock Hills Golf Club owes its founding to a visit to the Biarritz golf course in southwest France by William Vanderbilt and his party in the winter of 1890-91. Vanderbilt witnessed an exhibition by the Scottish pro Young Willie Dunn at the famous "Chasm Hole" and decided then and there that the game should be introduced in the United States. Shortly thereafter, Vanderbilt and his friends enlisted the aid of Samuel Parrish, another member of their wealthy Southampton circle and the founder of the Parrish Art Museum. That summer, Parrish brought another Scottish pro, Willie Davis of Royal Montreal, to design a 12-hole course through the sandhills and underbrush overlooking Shinnecock Bay, using a crew of 150 Shinnecock Indians from the nearby reservation. The original course underwent a couple of redesigns, the second by C.B. Macdonald, who did the neighboring National Golf Links, but an almost entirely new course was created in 1931 by William Flynn and Howard Toomey (with a young Dick Wilson as construction engineer) after a highway was routed through the old course. The course has a striking links look, with its soaring and swooping ribbons of fairway spread out through the windblown sierras of wild fescue grasses. Shinnecock hosted the second U.S. Open in 1896 and the event did not return again for 90 years. The 1986 Open at Shinnecock was an immense success, with Ray Floyd the winner, and the Open returned again in 1995 and most recently in 2004, when Retief Goosen was the victor. The understated and symmetrical shingled clubhouse, designed by the legendary Stanford White, was completed in 1892. The first clubhouse in America, it is a landmark in its own right.

▷ SEPTEMBER 8   ▷ THE NATIONAL GOLF LINKS OF AMERICA   ▷ NEW YORK, U.S.A.

The National Golf Links of America, located in Southampton, was the first great American golf course and the enduring masterpiece of Charles Blair Macdonald, the patriarch of golf in the United States. A native of Chicago, Macdonald attended St. Andrews University in Scotland as a teenager in the 1870s and fell passionately in love with the game. Macdonald, who is credited with inventing the term "golf course architect," was determined to build a course in the United States that would be the equal of the great courses of Scotland. He combed the Eastern seaboard in search of ideal terrain, and found it on Long Island in the 200 acres of sandy scrub knitted with bayberry and blackberry bushes adjoining Shinnecock Hills and overlooking Peconic Bay. Macdonald studied first-hand and also obtained detailed maps of famous holes in Scotland, after which he modeled several holes at the National. He also created originals that showed great ingenuity. Macdonald and his protégé, local engineer Seth Raynor, went on to design many superb courses, but the National, opened in 1909, remained his most treasured creation and he continued to dominate the club and refine his design through the rest of his life. The National is a very private club and has hosted only one prominent event in its history, the first Walker Cup competition in 1922.

▷ SEPTEMBER 9   ▷ ATLANTIC GOLF CLUB   ▷ NEW YORK, U.S.A.

Atlantic Golf Club owes its genesis to a weekend visit to the Hamptons by Westchester real estate developer Lowell Schulman in 1988. Schulman decided then and there that he would build a golf course, recognizing that there were limited options for affluent golfers in the Hamptons. Schulman set out to find a suitable piece of property, and that same weekend he looked at the 203-acre Equinox Farm off Scuttlehole Road in Bridgehampton. The site was not ideal for growing potatoes, but was made to order for a golf course—a rolling property with glacially created kettle ponds and a sunken spine of wetlands that is home to the eastern tiger salamander. Schulman hired Rees Jones to design a course that could stand head-to-head with the East End's Big Three of Shinnecock Hills, National, and Maidstone. Jones created a rigorous but traditional links course, with fairways terraced through the elevation changes, sinewy grass-walled bunkers, and borders of native maritime grasses. Opened in 1992, the course was an immediate success. There are long views over the surrounding fields and from the high point on the course the Atlantic Ocean can be seen four miles to the south.

The Maidstone Club in East Hampton, on Long Island's fashionable East End, is not considered a particularly tough or long course by modern standards, but there is no course that packs more enchantment within its 18 holes. Founded in 1891 as a tennis and bathing club for old-line society members, the grass courts and cabanas along the Atlantic continue as defining features. Golf was introduced in 1894, expanding to 18 holes by 1899. Impressionist Childe Hassam painted early golfers at Maidstone playing along the dunes next to the Atlantic, not far from East Hampton's elm-lined Main Street. The Scottish pro Willie Park, Jr., who was closely involved in the original design, was brought back in the early 1920s to reconfigure the course after additional land was acquired in the dunes between Hook Pond and the ocean. Park's design is an intoxicating procession across and around Hook Pond on the fourth through seventh holes and back again on the 16th and 17th. In between is a stretch of the most authentic sand-riddled seaside holes in the United States. The par-three eighth plays across a bulwark of dune that was created by the terrible hurricane of 1938, while the ninth runs through a valley in the dunes, with a slice leaving the golfer to play before a small gallery of gawking sunbathers on the beach.

▷ SEPTEMBER 11   ▷ BETHPAGE STATE PARK (BLACK COURSE)   ▷ NEW YORK, U.S.A.

Bethpage State Park's Black Course on Long Island is the crown jewel of public golf in the United States. The Black, and its sister courses, the Red and Blue, were built beginning in 1934, during the height of the Depression, as a Work Relief project, employing as many as 1,800 men (at the same time, an existing course was redesigned to become the Green Course). The entire project was overseen by the legendary golf course architect A.W. Tillinghast, who would shortly move to California to become an antiques dealer in Beverly Hills, having been driven out of business by the Depression. Tillinghast intended the Black to be a "man-eater" and he designed some of the biggest, baddest, and most carnivorous bunkers in captivity on the rolling, sandy site, with fescue grasses rippling through the waste areas. In 1996, the USGA selected the Black Course to host the 2002 U.S. Open, the first municipal course ever to stage the event. Rees Jones, the "Open Doctor," was called in to restore the course, and burnished it into a glorious test for the game's best. Tiger Woods won the Open at Bethpage, and the event proved such a success that it will return in 2009. Bethpage can trace its history back to 1695, when an Englishman named Thomas Powell purchased a large tract of land on the road near Jericho and named his property based on the passage from the book of Matthew (21:1): "And as they departed from Jericho, a great multitude followed Him, and when they drew nigh unto Jerusalem and were come to Beth'phage unto the Mount of Olives."

▷ SEPTEMBER 12   ▷ FRIAR'S HEAD GOLF CLUB   ▷ NEW YORK, U.S.A.

Friar's Head opened in 2003 near Riverhead on Long Island's North Fork. From the road that runs by the course, the site appears to be an unprepossessing piece of farmland that was sold by the Talmadge family, who were among the first settlers of the East End, to the course developer, Ken Bakst. The far end of the 350-acre property, however, opens on the sand dunes above Long Island Sound, which are anchored by a dwarf maritime beech-oak forest that dates back 10,000 years. Bakst, a leading amateur golfer who won the 1997 U.S. Mid-Amateur, hired the team of Bill Coore and Ben Crenshaw to design the course. Crenshaw and Coore quickly recognized the need to meld the very disparate topography of the site. Over time, they did just that, developing an ingenious routing in which Nos. 2, 7, 11, and 14 serve as transition holes between the sandy moraine and the former potato farm. The coastal holes feature great swirling ridges of sand freckled with sea grasses and the broad fairways of the farmland holes are punctuated by the irregularly edged bunkers that have become a hallmark of Coore and Crenshaw's work.

The Creek Club in Locust Valley on Long Island's tony North Shore holds back its pleasures for a few holes and then, on the sixth tee, all is revealed. The fairway plunges steeply downhill to a butterflied green, with a broad view of the skeins of fairways and sea grasses that sweep down to Long Island Sound and across to the Connecticut coast. Members are still able to arrive via the sound by boat near the 10th hole, with the fairway squeezed between a tidal lagoon and a strip of sandy beach. The 11th requires a brave carry to a pontoon of green in the lagoon. The club was founded in 1922 by a committee of 11 leading Long Island sportsmen, including Vincent Astor, Marshall Field, J.P. Morgan, Harry Payne Whitney, and Charles Blair Macdonald, who was enlisted to design the course with Seth Raynor. They named their club after Frost Creek, an inlet of the sound that loops around the 13th and 14th holes.

▷ SEPTEMBER 14   ▷ GARDEN CITY GOLF CLUB   ▷ NEW YORK, U.S.A.

Garden City Golf Club on Long Island is *sui generis*, for it is neither a parkland course nor a seaside links but is laid out over sandy soil on the wide expanse of the Hempstead Plain. The course was originally designed in 1899 by Devereux Emmet, a man of independent means who moved in high society. In 1902, Garden City hosted the U.S. Open, with Walter Travis, a member of the club, finishing second. The curmudgeonly Travis was a man of deep principle, who believed that American courses lacked the character and challenge of their British counterparts. In 1906, Travis wrote an article describing how the course could be improved through deeper bunkering and more movement within the greens, and the club's board decided to engage him to carry out his plan. Over the next two years, Travis added 50 bunkers, deepened others, and reworked all 18 greens, creating remarkable configurations of greenside bunkers and hives of cross-bunkers. Travis's redesign led to friction between him and Emmet, but the course remains a testament to their vision. Each spring, the club holds the Travis Memorial Tournament, a leading amateur invitational event that was named in Travis's honor after his death in 1927. *Above: tee marker*

▷ SEPTEMBER 15   ▷ OAK HILL COUNTRY CLUB   ▷ NEW YORK, U.S.A.

Oak Hill Country Club's East Course in Rochester is one of America's most classic and demanding parkland courses, and has hosted many major championships over the years, including three U.S. Opens, the 1995 Ryder Cup, and the 2003 PGA Championship won by unsung Shaun Micheel. Designed by Donald Ross in the 1920s, and revised and lengthened by Rochester native son Robert Trent Jones, the central design feature is Allen's Creek, which comes into play on seven holes. The fairways are pinched by more than 15,000 majestic trees, most of which were planted under the direction of member Dr. John R. Williams, who gave up his medical practice to become Oak Hill's arborist. In 1989, Curtis Strange won his second consecutive U.S. Open at Oak Hill, withstanding the brutally long three par-four finishing holes and aided by Tom Kite's triple bogey on the fifth hole, where he put his tee shot in Allen's Creek. Oak Hill's "Hill of Fame" over-looks the 13th green and is composed of oak trees, each of which is dedicated to an outstanding golfer.

Glen Abbey Golf Club, located in Oakville, 35 minutes west of Toronto, is Ontario's premier public course and was commissioned by the Royal Canadian Golf Association to serve as the host course of the Canadian Open. Opened in 1976, Glen Abbey was the first solo design of Jack Nicklaus, assisted by Jay Morrish and Bob Cupp. Nicklaus describes the layout as a "spoke-and-wheel" design around the clubhouse, conceived to allow optimal viewing of Canada's national championship. The front nine is wider than the back, which features a particularly demanding stretch of five holes that run through the valley, beginning on the 11th. Tiger Woods played one of the most spectacular shots of his career to win the 2000 Canadian Open at Glen Abbey, a six-iron second shot from 218 yards from the right fairway bunker over the lake guarding the par-five 18th hole. The Canadian Golf Hall of Fame is located in the Leonard E. Shore building attached to the clubhouse.

St. George's Golf and Country Club, tucked away in a residential neighborhood of Toronto, is rated the top golf course in Canada by the Canadian magazine *Score Golf* and is the second-highest ranking Canadian course on *Golf Magazine's* Top 100 in the World, behind Highland Links. The course was conceived by Robert Home Smith, a builder and developer who began acquiring the land near the Humber River in 1909. Smith persuaded his friend Sir Edward Beatty, the head of the Canadian Pacific Railway, to support the project, and leading architect Stanley Thompson was hired to design the course. Known as "the Toronto Terror," Thompson was coming off his brilliant successes at Banff Springs and Jasper Park Lodge in Alberta. Completed in 1929, the course was associated with the Royal York Hotel in Toronto, which was owned by the Canadian Pacific. Indeed, the course was originally called the Royal York Golf Club until the name was changed in 1946 when the arrangement with the railway ended. At St. George's, Thompson made the most of the nicely undulating terrain with valleys, ridges, and a stream that defends the 14th green. The club is also notable for its Tudor clubhouse on Islington Avenue, with its wood shake roof and large steeple, reflecting Home Smith's personal philosophy and the motto of his company: "A little bit of England far from England."

▷ SEPTEMBER 18   ▷ DEVIL'S PULPIT GOLF ASSOCIATION   ▷ CANADA

Devil's Pulpit Golf Association consists of two courses—the Devil's Pulpit and the Devil's Paintbrush—built in the Caledon Hills 35 miles northwest of Toronto. Both courses were developed by Chris Haney and Scott Abbott, the inventors of the Trivial Pursuit board game. Although only three miles apart and both designed by Michael Hurzdan and Dana Fry, the courses have entirely different characters, representing the yin and yang of golf course architecture. The Devil's Pulpit, opened in 1990, is a highly sculpted, more traditional parkland course. Hurzdan and Fry moved 1.7 million cubic yards of earth to create the course, including 300,000 cubic yards on the first hole alone, where a pond was built to create a dramatic tee shot from the elevated tee. The Paintbrush, on the other hand, opened in 1992, is laid out on an exposed, treeless bluff, its rumpled fairways fringed with brown native fescue grasses. An authentic Scottish-style links, there are plenty of blind shots, sprawling, shapeless bunkers lined with wooden slats, and an eighth hole that features the stone ruins of an old barn and a 17-foot-high sod wall bunker. The Devil's Pulpit is named after a rock formation seen from the seventh tee. The Devil's Paintbrush is a small flower found on the course, commonly named orange hawkweed. *Right: Devil's Paintbrush*

▷ SEPTEMBER 19   ▷ MONT TREMBLANT GOLF RESORT   ▷ CANADA

The Mont Tremblant Resort is set in the Laurentian Mountains of Quebec. While the resort is best known for skiing, it has two superb golf courses, Le Géant (the Giant) and Le Diable (the Devil). Le Diable, opened in 1998, was designed by Michael Hurzdan and Dana Fry, and features flamboyant red-tinged waste bunkers on the course carved from the pine forest. In 1999, Le Diable hosted the Canadian Skins Game with Mike Weir, Fred Couples, John Daly, and David Duval competing. Opened in 1995, Le Géant was designed by Canadian architect Thomas McBroom, with fairways cradled by the surrounding Laurentians.

Above: Le Géant   Right: Le Diable

The Links at Crowbush Cove is the premier course on Prince Edward Island, Canada's small Maritime Province that is earning a reputation as a big-time golf destination. Altogether, there are 26 courses on the island. PEI is also the home of LPGA Tour player Lori Kane. Designed by Thomas McBroom and opened in 1994, Crowbush Cove is set in the coastal dunes on the north central shore of the saddle-shaped island. There are nine water holes and eight holes that wind through the dunes and wetlands along the Gulf of St. Lawrence. Another fine layout on Prince Edward Island is the Green Gables Golf Course, located in the PEI National Park, designed by Stanley Thompson and built in 1939. Just to the left of the 11th fairway is Green Gables, the home of Anne Shirley in Lucy Maud Montgomery's classic novel set on Prince Edward Island, *Anne of Green Gables*.

▷ SEPTEMBER 21   ▷ HIGHLANDS LINKS   ▷ CANADA

Highlands Links is a natural wonderland situated in the Cape Breton Highlands National Park on the northern extreme of Nova Scotia's 4,000-square-mile Cape Breton Island. The course was built by the National Park Service of Canada in 1939 as a public works project with the goal of stimulating tourism. Stanley Thompson, the great Canadian architect, who had triumphed over difficult terrain at Banff Springs and Jasper Park in Alberta, was brought in to design the course. Thompson wove the holes through a variety of spellbinding scenery, all the while maintaining the broad, rolling character of the course. Carved through virgin forests of fir, spruce, and birch, the massive swales on several of the fairways were created by piling up rocks and boulders and covering them with soil from river silt. The course overlooks Ingonish Bay and the Atlantic with Whale Island across the channel, while holes such as the 10th and 14th that run inland face the green cloak of Mount Franey. The Clyburn River runs through the middle holes, accompanying the golfer on the 480-yard stroll from the 12th green to the 13th tee. Some of the most notable holes, each of which has a Gaelic name, are the back-to-back par fives Mucklemouth Meg and Killiecrankie. The white clapboard Keltic Lodge, famed for its lobster dinners, was built at the same time as the Highlands Links to provide visiting golfers with first-rate accommodations.

The Bell Bay Golf Club is located by the charming village of Baddeck on Cape Breton Island. Opened in 1997, the course was designed by leading Canadian architect Thomas McBroom. Bell Bay runs through the woods high above the saltwater Bras d'Or Lake, Cape Breton's inland sea, with splendid views across the bay named for Alexander Graham Bell. Bell and his wife Mabel Hubbard Bell had their summer estate, named Beinn Bhreagh or "beautiful mountain" in Gaelic, on the shore of Bras d'Or Lake. Built in an area with a long history of shipbuilding, each of the holes at Bell Bay is named for a particular ship. The first hole is named Alexander after the area's most famous resident and for the first brigantine built in Baddeck in 1833. The third hole is named Scupper, after the ship built at Bell's outdoor laboratories at Beinn Bhreagh, where he conducted many of his experiments, and which are visible from the fairway.

▷ SEPTEMBER 23   ▷ SUGARLOAF GOLF CLUB   ▷ MAINE, U.S.A.

Ever since it opened in 1985, Sugarloaf Golf Club at the well-known ski resort has been the picture postcard for golf in Maine. Part of Sugarloaf's attraction is its remoteness. The course is carved out of the pristine forest that cloaks the western mountains of Maine and which radiates with spectral crimson and gold in the autumn. It was designed by Robert Trent Jones, Jr., who selected the land split by the Carrabbasset River at the base of the mountains as the site for the course. The fairways at Sugarloaf are engulfed with white birch and pines, making accuracy a necessity. The front nine is full of doglegs, with views of the Bigelow Range and 4,237-foot-high Mt. Sugarloaf. The back nine begins with a short par four, with the tee set 110 feet above the fairway in the valley below. The next five holes each play along or across the rocky gauntlet of the Carrabbasset River.

Lake Sunapee Country Club is located in New London, in the western part of the Granite State, southeast of Hanover, sitting at an elevation of 1,125 feet facing Mt. Kearsarge. The course is a very fine but not very well-known example of the understated brilliance of architect Donald Ross. Ross was brought to the area in 1927 by E.J. Poor, a founder of the club and a prominent member of Salem Country Club outside Boston, another vintage Ross design. Ross selected the site for the course and Lake Sunapee opened in 1928 as a public course, but changed to a private club sixty years later. At more than 6,700 yards with a par of 70, the course is no pushover, with eight of the 12 par-fours playing over 400 yards. Henry J. Homan, Lake Sunapee's first professional, manager, and greenkeeper, acquired the course in 1945, and it has remained in the family ever since. Nowadays the course is owned by Homan's grandson Doug Homan. In 1999, Doug hired architect Ron Forse to undertake a gradual but extensive restoration of the original Ross features that had been lost over time. Gene Sarazen summered in the area for many years and was a regular player at Lake Sunapee.

▷ SEPTEMBER 25   ▷ EQUINOX RESORT   ▷ VERMONT, U.S.A.

The Gleneagles Golf Course at the Equinox Resort lies at the base of the Green Mountains in Manchester and has long been a New England beauty. The rugged layout with steeply canted greens and panoramic views across the valley and over the steeple of the First Congregational Church to 3,816-foot Mount Equinox was designed by Walter Travis in 1926. In the early 1990s, Rees Jones, who has distinguished himself with his sensitive restorations of a number of classic American courses in preparation for the U.S. Open, reworked and revitalized the course. Guinness, the Irish brewery that acquired the Equinox Resort in 1992, also refurbished and upgraded the historic hotel, which dates to 1769. Ethan Allen and the Green Mountain Boys were regulars at the hotel's Marsh Tavern. Several presidents have been guests at the Equinox, and Mary Todd Lincoln spent summers at the resort with her two sons both before and after the assassination of President Lincoln.

▷ SEPTEMBER 26   ▷ EKWANOK COUNTRY CLUB   ▷ VERMONT, U.S.A.

Ekwanok Country Club in Manchester is the first and one of the most treasured creations of Walter Travis. When it opened in 1900, it was the first American course that could stand head-to-head with the great courses of the British Isles in the sophistication of its design. Travis took up golf late in life, but won both the U.S. and British Amateur Championships in the early 1900s. Travis had very decided views on course design, which reflected his own abilities as an unerringly straight but not particularly long driver and a crackerjack putter. Ekwanok's narrow fairways careen beneath the broad peaks of the Taconic Mountains and there are large dollops of bunkers protecting the pitched greens. Many of the bunkers have recently been restored to bring them closer to Travis's original intention. After Ekwanok, Travis went on to design a handful other fine courses, such as Garden City and Westchester, but Ekwanok remained the course nearest to his heart. He is buried nearby and the famous Schenectady putter that he used to win the British Amateur in 1904 is displayed in the clubhouse library.

▷ SEPTEMBER 27   ▷ CRUMPIN-FOX CLUB   ▷ MASSACHUSETTS, U.S.A.

Crumpin-Fox Club is located in Bernardston in north central Massachusetts, set in the Pioneer Valley on the eastern edge of the Berkshires. Over 20 years in the making, this public course reached its ultimate fruition through the dedication of three successive owners. The course owes its conception to the late David Berelson, who hired Roger Rulewich, Robert Trent Jones's right-hand man for many years, to locate a site and design the course. Financial considerations forced Berelson to sell the project in 1977 to Bernardston resident Andy St. Hilaire, who completed nine holes. In 1987, he sold the course to his friend Bill Sandri, who acquired additional land enabling Rulewich to complete the other nine, and the course reopened in June 1990. Each hole of Crumpin-Fox is isolated from the others, hewn from the dense forest that makes the course a festival of fall foliage. Ponds and streams figure on several holes, with a large lake running down the entire left side of the signature 592-yard par-five eighth hole. Crumpin-Fox takes its name from the Bernardston-based Crump Soda Company, which was sold in 1853 to Eli Fox, becoming the Crump & Fox Soda Company.

▷ SEPTEMBER 28   ▷ MYOPIA HUNT CLUB   ▷ MASSACHUSETTS, U.S.A.

Myopia Hunt Club, like such other classic courses as Merion and Garden City, owes its distinctive design to a gifted and determined member of the club. The man behind Myopia was Herbert Corey Leeds, a skilled all-around athlete, who starred as the shortstop on the Harvard baseball team during the 1870s, and was severely bitten by the golf bug when he was 40 years old. Leeds set about overhauling Myopia's basic nine-hole course, completing the remodeling of the existing nine in 1896 and adding a second nine in 1902. Between 1898 and 1908, Leeds's course hosted four U.S. Opens. Myopia dates all the way back to 1879, having been originally founded mainly as a club for amateur baseball. The founding members all wore glasses and so the club acquired its unusual appellation. The club was incorporated as the Myopia Hunt Club in 1892, with fox hunting the dominant activity, but golf soon came to the fore. Leeds believed strongly that a stray shot should be penalized and built about 200 deep, curly grass-walled bunkers around sloping, natural greens. Leeds also created small sugarloaf mounds by covering old stone boundary walls with earth. One hazard to be avoided at Myopia is the Taft bunker, 15 yards short of the 10th green. Leeds had a dispute with President Taft, who was a member at Myopia, and so he kept making the bunker deeper each time Taft landed in it, until at one point caddies had to be supplied with ropes to hoist the rotund First Golfer from the sand.

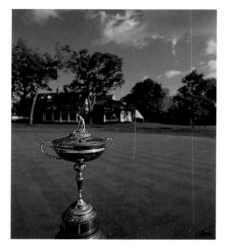

▷ SEPTEMBER 29   ▷ THE COUNTRY CLUB   ▷ MASSACHUSETTS, U.S.A.

The Country Club in Brookline, Massachusetts, just outside downtown Boston, is the original American country club. With its canary yellow and white clap-board clubhouse, it remains a beautiful enclave of rolling fairways with rocky outcroppings through the stately oaks and maples. The Country Club has been the site of some of golf's most epic battles, beginning in 1913, when Francis Ouimet, a 20-year-old unknown amateur who grew up on Clyde Street across from the club, won the U.S. Open by defeating the English stars Harry Vardon and Ted Ray in a playoff. In 1999, the course was the setting for the historic come-from-behind win by the U.S. squad in the Ryder Cup Matches. The Country Club began as a retreat for pursuits like riding, shooting, and horse racing before golf was introduced thanks to a figure described as "a young girl from Pau." The girl in question was Florence Boit, the daughter of wealthy Boston expatriates, who brought her clubs from France on a visit to her uncle Arthur Hunnewell's estate in Wellesley in 1892. Hunnewell, together with Laurence Curtis and Robert Bacon, then took the lead in establishing golf at The Country Club. Florence Boit and her three sisters are the subject of John Singer Sargent's masterpiece in the Boston Museum of Fine Arts. *Above: Ryder Cup*

▷ SEPTEMBER 30   ▷ KITTANSETT CLUB   ▷ MASSACHUSETTS, U.S.A.

The Kittansett Club lies across from Cape Cod on the mainland side of Buzzard's Bay, ten miles northeast of New Bedford. Laid out on a hook of ground where English settlers landed in 1639, the course has a links-like feel because of the views across the sea grasses and the sandy coast but is routed through scrub oak. Built in 1922, Kittansett was designed on paper by the great architect William Flynn, but the course's design also owes a great deal to the owner of the property, Fred Hood, who closely supervised the construction. One of the interesting features Hood was responsible for was grassing over rock formations and piles of debris to form mounds. Many of the original design features were lost over the years, so the club hired architect Gil Hanse to carry out a restoration. Hanse removed hundreds of trees that had covered over the original mounds, rebuilt the bunkers to their original large size, and opened up the dramatic view across Buzzard's Bay from the 16th green.

▷ OCTOBER 1   ▷ NEWPORT COUNTRY CLUB   ▷ RHODE ISLAND, U.S.A.

Newport Golf Club was founded in 1893 by Theodore A. Havemeyer—the "Sugar King"—head of American Sugar Refining Company and one of the founders of the United States Golf Association. When the club opened on July 4, 1893, the cream of American society was on hand, with more than 300 members of the Social Register present. On October 2, 1895, Newport held the first USGA-sponsored Amateur Championship, won by Charles Blair Macdonald. Two days later, it hosted the first U.S. Open, won by Horace Rawlins, but the Amateur was considered a bigger deal in those days. In 1995, the U.S. Amateur returned to what is now Newport Country Club for its centennial, with Tiger Woods winning the Havemeyer Cup that is still awarded to the Amateur champion. The original Newport course was laid out on Rocky Hill Farm by the Scottish pro Willie Davis, with more work done by Donald Ross in 1915. The current course, however, is the creation of A.W. Tillinghast, who redesigned nine of the existing holes and added nine new ones in 1923-24. The clubhouse, overlooking Hazard's Beach and opened in 1895, was designed by the young Whitney Warren in the French beaux-arts style. Warren later founded the firm of Warren & Wetmore, which designed New York's Grand Central Station.

Wannamoisett Country Club in Rumsford, Rhode Island is one of the most remarkable courses designed by the legendary Donald Ross. Ross is best known for his work at Pinehurst, where he had his headquarters, but some of his finest courses are in Rhode Island, where he spent the summers at Little Compton. Ross was the master of understated elegance and subtle treachery and nowhere is this more evident than at Wannamoisett, completed in 1914. Ross had to wedge the course into a square parcel of 104 acres that lacked much in the way of natural features, and yet the holes are extremely demanding. Forced carries were created through clever routing over gullies and cross-bunkers, and Ross made the most of a pond and a small stream that runs through the property. The slick greens are among Ross's finest and, unlike many of his designs, remain true to the original conception. As Ross himself summed it up: "This is the best layout I ever made; a fine course on 100 acres of land, no congestion, fine variety." Since 1962, Wannamoisett has hosted the Northeast Amateur, with the list of champions including Ben Crenshaw and David Duval.

▷ OCTOBER 3   ▷ FISHERS ISLAND CLUB   ▷ NEW YORK, U.S.A.

Fishers Island Club is a golfing nirvana on the exclusive summer colony that lies off the Connecticut coast in Long Island Sound. Fishers Island is part of New York, although it is reached by ferry from New London, Connecticut. There is no more charming setting in golf than Fishers Island, with the fairways pirouetting around the western tip of the island overlooking East Harbor out to the sound and across to Block Island. The course itself is a vintage design of Seth Raynor, opened in 1926, with big squared-off plateau greens. Raynor came to golf course architecture working as the engineer for C.B. Macdonald on his design of the National Golf Links. Raynor learned from Macdonald the art of emulating the strategic designs of the great Scottish holes, and he thereafter adopted several of these classics in each of his designs. The fifth at Fishers is a long par-three Biarritz hole, based on the long-lost shot across the chasm at Biarritz in France, with Raynor's version playing to an elevated green across a nook of sandy beach. After Raynor died in January 1926, the course was completed by his assistants, Charles Banks and Ralph Barton.

▷ OCTOBER 4   ▷ COUNTRY CLUB OF FAIRFIELD   ▷ CONNECTICUT, U.S.A.

The Country Club of Fairfield was founded by Oliver G. Jennings in 1914, after he decided that Brooklawn Country Club was becoming too crowded for his liking. Jennings acquired a parcel of land for his new course along Long Island Sound consisting of onion fields, salt meadow, and wetlands surrounding the tidal marsh adjacent to Southport Harbor. Jennings also had the good sense to hire Seth Raynor to design the course, with construction beginning in 1916 and not completed for five years. Raynor had to overcome the swampy nature of the site while preserving its alluvial beauty, obtaining landfill from the bottom of Southport Harbor and transporting topsoil from Long Island by barge. The course is speckled with wetlands and ponds, and the sixth plays across the inlet of Southport Harbor known as the Lagoon.

▷ OCTOBER 5   ▷ WINTONBURY HILLS GOLF COURSE   ▷ CONNECTICUT, U.S.A.

In 1995, the residents of Bloomfield, a suburb close to Hartford, decided to build a first-rate municipal course. One of the town residents happened to be Brad Klein, a well-known writer and authority on golf architecture. Klein persuaded Pete Dye and his associate Tim Liddy to design the course for a fee of $1, which Dye never actually kept since the bill is framed in the clubhouse. Wintonbury Hills Golf Course finally opened in September 2003 on an uncluttered, 290-acre site of gently rolling farmland hemmed in by wetlands to the west. The 14th hole is a tough par four running along the reservoir that opens out to the east. On several holes, there are long views out to the hills and the century-old Heublein Tower in the distance.

▷ OCTOBER 6   ▷ BULL'S BRIDGE GOLF CLUB   ▷ CONNECTICUT, U.S.A.

Bull's Bridge Golf Club is a private course located in northwest Connecticut's Litchfield County, straddling the borders of South Kent and New Milford. The course, opened in 2003 and facing the Berkshires to the north, was designed by Tom Fazio and developed by Tom Plant, who also worked with Fazio on Hudson National Golf Club. The course rambles through a rolling 360-acre site with a mantle of mountain laurel, yellow birch, and maples, studded with stony outcroppings. The course takes its name from historic Bull's Bridge, the covered bridge crossing the Housatonic River in Kent that was operated in the 18th century by Jacob and Mary Bull, proprietors of the local inn. The existing bridge dates from 1842.

▷ OCTOBER 7   ▷ HUDSON NATIONAL GOLF CLUB   ▷ NEW YORK, U.S.A.

Hudson National Golf Club in Croton-on-Hudson occupies a lofty 260-acre eyrie above the Hudson River on the second-highest elevation in Westchester County. When Henry Hudson sailed up the river in 1609, the land was occupied by the Kitchawank Indians. During the Revolutionary War, the 450-foot-high bluffs provided a key lookout for Washington's army as the British fleet sailed north. The golf course, designed by Tom Fazio, opened in June 1996. Fazio made the most of the rugged topography by not overdoing it, laying out a straightforward, big-boned course with commanding views and old stone walls sprinkled around the fairways. In the 1920s, a nine-hole course named Hessian Hills was built on the property, but when the clubhouse burned down in 1932, the course was disbanded and allowed to return to nature. The ruins of the old clubhouse overlook the fifth tee. Hudson National's new clubhouse is an imposing four-story stone manor house.

▷ OCTOBER 8   ▷ SLEEPY HOLLOW COUNTRY CLUB   ▷ NEW YORK, U.S.A.

Sleepy Hollow Country Club is located in Scarborough-on-Hudson in the hills of Westchester made famous by Washington Irving in *The Legend of Sleepy Hollow*. Irving's headless horseman, supposedly the ghost of a Hessian soldier, threw his head at Ichabod Crane at the foot of the "haunted bridge" that now links tee to green on Sleepy Hollow's third hole. The club was very much a millionaire's playground, founded in 1911 by the likes of William Rockefeller, John Jacob Astor, and Oliver Harriman. The clubhouse is one of the most impressive in the world, having originally been built as the estate of Colonel Elliott Fitch Shepard and his wife, who was from the Vanderbilt family. Designed by Stanford White, it is a 75-room Italianate villa constructed of limestone and orange brick with a rococo interior of marble and mahogany. The golf course was designed by Charles Blair Macdonald during the summer of 1911, with A.W. Tillinghast contributing seven holes—the first, the 18th, and the eighth through 12th, in the late 1920s. The par threes at Sleepy Hollow are particularly outstanding. The 10th plays to a low-lying green lapped by a pond, while the 16th plays across a gully to an elevated green perched triumphantly above the Hudson River.

▷ OCTOBER 9   ▷ TRUMP NATIONAL GOLF CLUB   ▷ NEW YORK, U.S.A.

Trump National Golf Club in Westchester County officially opened on July 27, 2002, with owner Donald Trump, a five-handicapper, hitting the opening ceremonial drive. In typical Trump style, no expense was spared in building the course and the Donald has proclaimed the course the best in New York State, predicting that it will outrank nearby Winged Foot, where Trump himself is a member. Designer Jim Fazio ripped up the old Briar Hall Country Club and began from scratch, moving three million cubic yards of dirt and rock in what was the largest excavation project in Westchester's history. A series of man-made lakes were constructed that dominate the front nine, and granite walls were built to run across the property. The trophy piece of the course is the par-three 13th hole, where a 101-foot tall waterfall built of black granite pumps 5,000 gallons a minute into the frothy pool that encircles the green.

▷ OCTOBER 10　▷ WESTCHESTER COUNTRY CLUB　▷ NEW YORK, U.S.A.

Westchester Country Club's West Course in Harrison since 1967 has been the site of the PGA Tour's Westchester Classic, now known as the Buick Classic, a tournament that typically precedes the U.S. Open by one week and draws a strong field. Westchester is in many respects the archetypal Westchester County course, with its tight, hilly fairways, small animated greens, and stony ledges that give the course some of the flinty personality of its designer, the early leading amateur golfer Walter Travis. This old-fashioned course is a favorite of the pros, and four of the holes are rated among the most difficult on Tour. Westchester is an interesting amalgam of Travis's rigorous school of design, the tranquil beauty of the mature oaks, pines, and maples, and the opulence created by Westchester's founder, John McEntee Bowman. Bowman, who was president of the Bowman-Biltmore Hotel chain, purchased 583 acres from the Hobart J. Park estate in 1919. He began developing a lavish resort known as the Westchester Biltmore Country Club which, in addition to the golf course that opened in 1922, included polo fields and a beach club on Manursing Island in Long Island Sound. The centerpiece of the resort was a towering hotel, built in the style of an Italian palazzo. By 1929, Bowman had run into financial trouble, and the members purchased the property from him, with the hotel becoming the present-day clubhouse.

▷ OCTOBER 11 ▷ WINGED FOOT GOLF CLUB (WEST COURSE) ▷ NEW YORK, U.S.A.

The West Course of Winged Foot Golf Club in Mamaroneck is Westchester's great championship course, although the club actually boasts another excellent course in the East Course. Both were designed by the incomparable A.W. Tillinghast at the peak of his career. Winged Foot was founded by members of the New York Athletic Club in Manhattan, who adopted the NYAC's winged foot symbol as their name. In 1922, the club acquired 280 acres of land that once was home to the Mohican Indians and adjoined the house of James Fenimore Cooper, author of *The Last of the Mohicans*. Both courses were completed by June 1923, with Tillinghast overseeing a massive construction project that included removal of 7,200 tons of rock, which was used to build the distinctive clubhouse designed by Clifford Wendehack. The West Course is considered Tillinghast's greatest masterpiece. Even though Tillinghast worked with more dramatic sites, the combination of deep, steeply banked bunkers built into the tiered, pear-shaped greens makes the course an immensely arduous challenge. As Tillinghast put it: "A controlled shot to a closely guarded green is the severest test of a man's golf." Trees are a defining element of the Winged Foot experience, though the club recently removed some that encroached too much on play. The property is a magnificent arboretum with more than 20,000 trees from 50 different species, including flowering magnolias, dogwoods, crab apples, and Kwanzan cherries. Winged Foot has hosted four U.S. Opens, beginning with Bobby Jones's win in 1929, and the 1997 PGA Championship won by Davis Love III.

▷ OCTOBER 12   ▷ BALTUSROL GOLF CLUB (LOWER COURSE)   ▷ NEW JERSEY, U.S.A.

Baltusrol Golf Club's Lower Course has been one of the USGA's favorite venues for the U.S. Open, although the hillier, heavily wooded Upper Course is an outstanding layout in its own right. Both courses were designed after the First World War by A.W. Tillinghast, two of Tillinghast's earliest and greatest in a line of great courses. The club had been founded in 1895 by Louis Keller, the reclusive publisher of New York City's *Social Register*. Keller had acquired 500 acres at the foot of Baltusrol Mountain in Springfield, named after Baltus Roll, a farmer who lived in a small house on the mountain where he was murdered by thieves on the night of February 27, 1831. Among the memorable tournaments hosted by Baltusrol, including a record seven U.S. Opens, were the 1967 and 1980 U.S. Opens, both won by Jack Nicklaus. Robert Trent Jones was brought in to strengthen the course before the 1954 U.S. Open, when he designed the famous par-three fourth hole that plays across a pond to a double-tiered green. When some of the members criticized the hole, Jones took them to the tee and played a four-iron shot that rolled in the cup for a hole-in-one. "Gentlemen," he remarked, "I think the hole is eminently fair." Baltusrol's majestic Tudor clubhouse, one of the grandest in golf, faces the fourth hole.

▷ OCTOBER 13   ▷ PLAINFIELD COUNTRY CLUB   ▷ NEW JERSEY, U.S.A.

Plainfield Country Club is one of the landmark courses designed by Donald Ross, located 25 miles from New York City. The club was organized in 1890 by a group of Wall Street brokers as the Hillside Tennis Club. Five years later, a nine-hole course was introduced, and in December 1897, the club moved to its present setting on rolling countryside that was the site of a battle during the American Revolution. The club changed its name to Plainfield in 1904. In 1916, Ross was engaged to build a completely new 18-hole course, which, because of the advent of World War I, was not completed until 1921. Plainfield is widely acknowledged as a Ross masterpiece, where he was able to take full advantage of the gentle ridges in the property. There are six water hazards, nests of cross bunkers, and many of the greens are crafted on knolls, creating the shelves and knobs for which Ross is famous. In recent years, the club hired architect Gil Hanse to restore many of the subtle design features that had been lost over time, including restoring the original grass-faced bunkers, enlarging the greens, and eliminating trees that had obscured the angles of play. In 2005, Plainfield will host the U.S. Senior Open.

▷ OCTOBER 14   ▷ MORRIS COUNTY GOLF CLUB   ▷ NEW JERSEY, U.S.A.

Morris County Golf Club in the town of Convent Station has the rare distinction of having been founded as a women's-only club in 1894. By that summer, there was a seven-hole course designed by John Brinley, the landscape architect for the New York Botanical Garden in the Bronx. The club hosted the second U.S. Women's Amateur in 1896, won by 16-year-old Beatrix Hoyt of Shinnecock Hills. The women members made the fatal mistake of allowing 200 men, mainly husbands and fathers, to become associate members. By 1896, the men had seized control of the club with Paul Revere, the great-grandson of the midnight rider, elected president. The current course, designed by Seth Raynor, opened in 1920 and is laid out on a rolling, hilly site with rocky outcroppings. There are a number of short par fours that require accurate pitches to small, tightly trapped greens set in punchbowls and on knolls. The 18th hole swings around a pond that guards the left side of the green. The course opened with a 36-hole exhibition match between the barnstorming British duo of Harry Vardon and Ted Ray and the American amateurs Bobby Jones and Chick Evans.

▷ OCTOBER 15 ▷ SOMERSET HILLS COUNTRY CLUB ▷ NEW JERSEY, U.S.A.

Somerset Hills Country Club is in Bernardsville, not far from the USGA's headquarters in Far Hills. The club dates to 1896, when it was formed as the Ravine Land and Game Association with an early nine-hole course. In 1916, the club purchased 194 acres from the estate of Frederic P. Olcott, which included a private racetrack, and the great architect A. W. Tillinghast was hired to create what turned out to be one of his more unusual designs. Completed at the end of 1917, the course does not bear much resemblance to Tillinghast's other famous layouts, such as Winged Foot and Bethpage Black, but instead the holes reflect the variety and subtlety of the terrain. The front nine is laid out over the old Olcott racetrack on open ground with large, odd-shaped mounds created by Tillinghast known as "the Dolomites." The back nine runs through wooded terrain with a rocky stream and a pond that guards the peninsula green on the par-three 12th. Somerset Hills is an exclusive club, but it has hosted various USGA events over the years, including the 1990 Curtis Cup.

▷ OCTOBER 16   ▷ ATLANTIC CITY COUNTRY CLUB   ▷ NEW JERSEY, U.S.A.

Atlantic City Country Club is actually in the town of Northfield, a few miles away from the famous Atlantic City boardwalk. The club dates from 1897, but the present course was designed by the leading Philadelphia architect William Flynn in 1923. Set in marshland, the course is relatively flat, with views from the front nine across Lakes Bay and to the skyline of Atlantic City. The term "birdie" is supposed to have originated at Atlantic City at the turn of the last century when a member named Ab Smith hit an approach shot within a few inches of the hole and called it a "bird of a shot," the word "bird" often being used at that time to refer to anything great. The members of the foursome, and soon all the members of the club, agreed to pay double for a score of one under par on a hole and began to refer to it as a "birdie." Atlantic City was owned and operated for many years by Leo Fraser, who was president of the PGA of America. The current owners hired Tom Doak in 2000 to carry out a restoration of the course. He opened up the views over the marsh and created the new 14th and 15th holes.

▷ OCTOBER 17   ▷ PINE VALLEY GOLF CLUB   ▷ NEW JERSEY, U.S.A.

Pine Valley Golf Club is perennially ranked and is generally considered the greatest golf course in the world. There are many incongruities in Pine Valley's lofty stature. The course is located in the pine barrens of southwestern New Jersey near Clementon, which would not spring to mind as the site for the world's greatest course, and Pine Valley was designed not by a well-known professional architect, but by a dedicated—some would say crazed—amateur. Pine Valley was the all-consuming passion of its founder and creator, George Crump, a Philadelphia hotelier and member of the Atlantic City Golf Club. Crump labored on the course from 1913 until his death in 1918, moving to the site and living first in a tent and then a bungalow. Crump died having finished 14 holes, with Hugh Wilson, the architect of Merion, completing the design. Crump received key advice regarding the routing from the leading English architect Harry Colt, but Crump created a novel course, in which the fairways are islands subsumed by sandy waste areas overgrown with Scotch broom, huckleberry, and wild grasses, and each hole is framed by the statuesque forest of pines, oak, larch, and hemlock. Legends of Pine Valley's difficulty are legion. There is a standing bet that no one can break 80 the first time he plays the course. Arnold Palmer won his bet when he shot 68 in 1954 as the U.S. Amateur Champion, and Jack Nicklaus stopped to play the course in 1960 while on his honeymoon, with his wife Barbara waiting for him in the car.

Wilmington Country Club is located in the Brandywine Valley, just a few miles to the west of Wilmington in an area of attractive stone houses, stone walls, and stone cisterns. The club was founded in 1901, moving to its current site in 1959 after it purchased 335 acres from Henry Francis DuPont that had been the orchards and vegetable gardens of Winterthur, the famous DuPont Estate that adjoins the club. First came the South Course, designed by Robert Trent Jones, and in 1962 the North Course, designed by Jones's rival Dick Wilson, was completed. The courses feature a series of small ponds, which are linked by an underground irrigation system to the reservoir that serves as a water hazard on both courses. H.F. DuPont, who expanded Winterthur and turned it into a world-renowned, 175-room museum of American period furniture with wooded gardens, was himself an avid golfer. He built a private nine-hole course at Winterthur that he and his guests would play while listening to opera music broadcast from speakers placed in the woods, and which is now part of the Bidermann Golf Course. *Right: South Course*

▷ OCTOBER 19   ▷ BULLE ROCK   ▷ MARYLAND, U.S.A.

Bulle Rock in Havre de Grace, a half-hour north of Baltimore, features a lustrously green Pete Dye-designed layout that opened in 1998. With views of the Chesapeake Bay, the sleek, contoured fairways of Bulle Rock's South Course are framed by hardwoods and tall golden grasses. There are three lakes that come into play, each replenished by a three-mile pipeline specifically constructed for the course that connects to the Susquehanna River. The course is named for Bulle Rock, the first thoroughbred racehorse in America, brought over from England by James Samuel Patton in the 1730s and known as the father of all thorough-breds in this country. Patton's granddaughter's husband owned the Blenheim horse farm that is now the site of the golf course. The golf course was founded by Ed Abel, who became hooked on the game after he sold his two construction companies in 1993. He then dedicated himself to building a course that would be open to the public but provide conditions and amenities comparable to the best private country clubs. Bulle Rock has been named the site of the McDonald's LPGA Championship starting in 2005.

▷ OCTOBER 20   ▷ MID OCEAN GOLF CLUB   ▷ BERMUDA

Mid Ocean Golf Club is the crown jewel of golf in Bermuda, designed by the first great American golf course architect, Charles Blair Macdonald, in 1924. Located in Tuckerstown, the course begins and ends by the ocean, but the character of Mid Ocean is that of a striking inland layout rather than a traditional Scottish links. The course is laid out through coral hills forested with cedars, casuarinas, pines, oleander, hibiscus, and bougainvillea, with forced carries over marshy wetlands. The most famous hole is the fifth, which is one of the world's great "Cape" holes, that is, a hole where the golfer is challenged to bite off as much of the diagonal carry across the hazard as he dares. In this case, the golfer drives from an elevated tee across Mangrove Lake, with the elongated green tucked back against the corner of the lake.

▷ OCTOBER 21   ▷ SILLOTH ON SOLWAY GOLF CLUB   ▷ ENGLAND

Bernard Darwin wrote of Silloth on Solway Golf Club that "I never fell more violently in love with a course at first sight." This sublime and remote links is located 20 miles west of Carlisle, and was founded by a group of Carlisle businessmen in 1892. The links, with its crisp Cumberland turf and wild, rushy marram grass, runs along Solway Firth. There are romantic views of the hills of the Scottish lowlands and Southerness Golf Club lying across the far shore, and the English Lake District to the south. The course will forever be associated with the exploits of Cecil Leitch, four-time winner of the British Ladies' Championship from 1914 to 1926, and her four golfing sisters, who grew up playing the course. The turf from Silloth has been used over the years for putting greens and bowling courts throughout England and for the lawn tennis courts at Wimbledon.

▷ OCTOBER 22   ▷ GANTON GOLF CLUB   ▷ ENGLAND

Ganton Golf Club is one of the great English inland courses, although it also possesses the most attractive attributes of a seaside links. Located nine miles from Scarborough and the coast, the course lies at the foot of the Yorkshire Wolds in the fertile valley of the River Derwent. Ganton is renowned for the deep green purity of its fairways and its seemingly bottomless bunkers of natural golden sand bearded with gorse. As Patric Dickinson described it: "There are grades of rough from *piano* to *fortissimo*, and a great deal of close-growing and not unobtrusive gorse: gold-red-gold of bunker, yellow-gold of gorse bloom, and olive-green of gorse prickle, and in between all shades and preciosities of green: jade, emerald, sea-green." Harry Vardon, who went on to win six British Opens, was hired as Ganton's professional in 1896, five years after the course was founded. It was here on July 22, 1899 that Vardon famously thrashed Willie Park, Jr. in the last 36 holes of their 72-hole home and away match at North Berwick and Ganton to win by 11 and 10. Ganton hosted the 1949 Ryder Cup, as well as the 2000 Curtis Cup and 2003 Walker Cup matches.

▷ OCTOBER 23   ▷ ROYAL LYTHAM AND ST. ANNES GOLF CLUB   ▷ ENGLAND

Royal Lytham and St. Annes is one of Britain's most incongruous championship courses, for it embodies all the characteristics of seaside golf, including odd bounces on the lumpy fairways and phalanxes of pot bunkers, but the links is surrounded by the red brick rowhouses of urban England. Lytham lies about a mile from the coast, with a railway line running along the course's seaward side and homes built by the St Annes-on-Sea Land Building Company, founded by a group of Lancashire businessmen in 1874, on the other. The club was founded in 1886 by Alexander Doleman of Musselburgh, Scotland, a talented golfer who had opened a school in the then fashionable resort of Blackpool. In 1897, the club moved to its present site, with the course laid out by George Low and subsequently refined by Herbert Fowler, Harry Colt, and C.K. Cotton. Bobby Jones won the first British Open held at Lytham in 1926, and the mashie he used for his miraculous escape from sandy perdition on the 17th hole hangs in the clubhouse. Seve Ballesteros was the winner in both 1979 and 1988, while Tom Lehman became the first American professional to win the Open at Lytham in 1996.

▷ OCTOBER 24   ▷ ROYAL BIRKDALE GOLF CLUB   ▷ ENGLAND

The Lancashire coast of northwest England running north from Liverpool to the town of Southport offers an abundance of outstanding links courses, including Southport & Ainsdale, Formby, Hillside, and West Lancashire, but none feature more majestic dunes than Royal Birkdale. Birkdale is also considered an exceptionally fair links, which helps to explain its popularity for championship events, having hosted eight British Opens since it became part of the "rota" in 1954, as well as two Ryder Cup Matches and the Walker Cup. The original course opened in 1889 but the club moved to its present site in 1897, and the course was revamped by Fred Hawtree and J.H. Taylor in 1931. The futuristic clubhouse, resembling a white, curvilinear ocean liner, was also built in 1931. The holes ripple through the sandhills, with the greens sequestered between the dunes. Birkdale has had an illustrious list of Open champions. Arnold Palmer won his first British Open title at Birkdale in 1961, overcoming a gale that ripped through the course on the second day of the tournament, while Peter Thomson, Lee Trevino, Johnny Miller, Tom Watson, Ian Baker-Finch, and Mark O'Meara have also won at Birkdale.

▷ OCTOBER 25 ▷ FORMBY GOLF CLUB ▷ ENGLAND

Formby Golf Club lies on the Lancashire coast, a course of rich turf nestled in the sandhills and piney woods, just 14 miles north of Liverpool and five miles south of Southport. The club was formed when 10 gentlemen met at the Reverend Lonsdale Formby's reading room on December 11, 1884, and resolved to name it the Formby Golf Club. Nine holes were then laid out over the rough, sandy terrain of a rabbit warren, expanded to 18 by 1893, with the imposing club-house opened by Lord Derby in 1901. The present course is largely the work of Willie Park, Jr., carried out in 1907. The opening holes are laid out on the flat ground, with the railway line running along the first, before the course begins to funnel through the formidable sandhills. Unlike most seaside links, Formby is bordered on three sides by forests of firs, creating a strong sense of seclusion. The threat of coastal erosion caused the club in the early 1980s to replace the old seventh through 10th holes with holes that run through the woodlands. Formby has hosted three British Amateurs, including 1984 when José Maria Olázabal beat Colin Montgomerie in a memorable final. As Frank Pennink once wrote: "It is easy to fall in love with Formby at first sight, for it has that rare trait of real charm to a very high degree."

▷ OCTOBER 26   ▷ ROYAL LIVERPOOL GOLF CLUB   ▷ ENGLAND

Royal Liverpool Golf Club, or Hoylake, as it is better known, is widely considered one of the sternest and truest of the great links courses. Golf at Hoylake dates all the way back to 1869, making it one of the oldest clubs in England. The existing course took shape in 1895 after the club moved from the now-defunct Royal Hotel to its present clubhouse, and was updated by Harry Colt in 1923. Laid out near the estuary of the River Dee, the course is famed for the knee-high banks of turf known as the Cops that serve as out of bounds, the quality of its greens, and fierce rough fretted with dwarf rose and blackberry. Sir Peter Allen described Hoylake as "the Final Honour School, together with Muirfield perhaps, of British golf, where luck enters into it to the minimum and justice is not only done but manifestly seen to be done." Hoylake has hosted 10 British Opens, the first in 1897, and was the site of Bobby Jones's victory in the 1930 Open on his way to the Grand Slam. After 1967, when Roberto de Vicenzo captured the claret jug, Hoylake was dropped from the Open "rota" because of logistical considerations, but it has been selected to host the championship again in 2006.

▷ OCTOBER 27   ▷ ALWOODLEY GOLF CLUB   ▷ ENGLAND

Alwoodley Golf Club is located five miles from the center of Leeds, an industrial city in Yorkshire in the north of England. The character of the course is defined by the Yorkshire moors, with the fairways stretching over Wigton Moor, which was part of Lord Harewood's estate. A small wood known as "Wigton Cover" flanks the back of the seventh green and runs alongside the eighth. Alwoodley has one of the most interesting architectural pedigrees of any course in England. When the club was founded in 1907, Harry Colt was hired for the design, but was asked to consult with the club's honorary secretary, a local physician named Dr. Alister MacKenzie, who had a keen interest in course design. MacKenzie, who went on to design Augusta National, Cypress Point, and Royal Melbourne, among others, took the lead, and his first design work already reflects his graceful, patterned bunkering and highly contoured greens. The course is a rich medley of colors with golden gorse in the spring, meadows of heather the color of plum pudding, and the deep auburns and reds of autumn leaves.

▷ OCTOBER 28   ▷ WOODHALL SPA (HOTCHKIN COURSE)   ▷ ENGLAND

Woodhall Spa is the exemplar of that particularly British genus of golf courses, the heathland links. Unlike the better-known seaside links of Scotland and England, Woodhall Spa is tucked away amidst the farmland of Lincolnshire in northern England. Its fairways are surrounded by fields of heather that burn like purple embers in the summer with accents of yellow gorse set against a layered backdrop of oak, fir, and silver birch. The Hotchkin Course takes its name from Stafford Hotchkin, or Col. S.V. Hotchkin, who came to own Woodhall Spa in the 1920s. Hotchkin substantially redesigned the existing course that had originally been laid out by Harry Vardon in 1905 and revised by Harry Colt, creating the cavernous bunkers carved from the sandy soil for which the course is known. Woodhall Spa itself is a resort village that owes its existence to the discovery of mineral waters in the early 19th century. The resort flourished in the early 1900s, with guests coming for the "bromo-iodine" waters, golf, and the summer pastoral of woodlands and rhododendrons. The tower on the moor, the emblem of the village, dates from the 1440s and is located behind the third green. In 1995, the English Golf Union acquired Woodhall Spa, where it has its headquarters, and built a second course named The Bracken.

Hunstanton and Brancaster are the two outstanding links courses of northeast England, located on the Norfolk coast seven miles apart from one another. Hunstanton had its origin in 1891 when the club's first president, Hamon le Strange, paid £30 for George Fernie of Troon to lay out nine holes. Additional funds were raised and, four years later, nine more holes were added. James Braid visited a few years later and "left a track of cunning bunkers behind him." Over the years, further revisions were made to create what today is a links of championship caliber. The course is divided by a natural grandstand of dunes between the shores of the Wash and the River Hun, described by Bernard Darwin as "a name of ominous sound, into which we may slice on the way out if we are not careful." The lower lying, marshy holes on the front nine run along the inland side, skirting the banks of the little river, while the back nine parades along the higher ground by the North Sea coastline.

Royal West Norfolk, better known as Brancaster, is often compared with Hunstanton, for they are the two superb links of East Anglia. Brancaster is the more uneven, old-fashioned, and romantic of the two, laid out on the narrow strip of land between the dunes of the Norfolk coast that run down to the harbor of Brancaster Staithe and the saltmarsh called Mow Creek. The eighth and ninth holes are the heart and soul of the course, renowned for what Bernard Darwin termed their "overpowering lonely gorgeousness." Both holes leapfrog with forced carries across the marsh, with a particularly menacing example of the many deep, sleepered bunkers strewn along the course guarding the ninth green. During unusually high tides, the marsh floods and the clubhouse is cut off from the rest of the course. With its haunting beauty, Brancaster has changed little over the years, and its distinguishing features remain, as Horace Hutchinson, the first great golf writer and captain of the club wrote in 1892: "the absence of all artificiality and the great variety to be found in the holes."

▷ OCTOBER 31   ▷ NOTTS GOLF CLUB   ▷ ENGLAND

Notts Golf Club is a fine and demanding moorland course located in Hollinwell in Nottinghamshire. The course owes its inception to a meeting called in 1887 by the Reverend A. Hamilton Baynes at his home, to which he invited all those in Nottingham interested in golf. Only five hardy souls answered the call, but that was enough to get things going, and the club settled at its present site in 1898. The course was designed by Willie Park, Jr. through a forest of oak, silver birch, and pine. A course of varied terrain, the fairways are surrounded by several varieties of gorse that bloom a bright yellow at different times throughout the year. A rock formation behind the second green is known as "Robin Hood's Chair," since it was here according to legend that Robin sat waiting for Maid Marian. Below the eighth fairway is the holy well or "Hollinwell" at the source of the River Leen from which the town takes its name, and which once supplied the drinking water for the monks in the nearby abbey. *Above: the Hollinwell*

▷ NOVEMBER 1   ▷ NEFYN & DISTRICT GOLF CLUB   ▷ WALES

Nefyn & District is the Welsh version of Pebble Beach, an old-fashioned course laid out on the sea cliffs of north Wales near the village of Nefyn. The course is unique in that it has 26 holes, a front 10 and two distinctive back eights. Three holes of the 10 used for both the Old Course and New Course cling to the cliffs, and all have the Irish Sea in view from every hole. The Old Course is short on yardage, but features four more cliffside holes in the closing eight, including the 12th, a blind, downhill par-five that overlooks the tiny fishing village of Porth Dinllaen at the sea's edge with the Ty Coch pub, built in 1823. The course was founded in 1907. Prime Minister David Lloyd George, who was Welsh by birth and an avid golfer, was invited to preside at the course's reopening in 1919 after World War I, but attended the Peace Conference at Versailles instead of coming to Nefyn. *Above: village of Porth Dinllaen*

Aberdovey Golf Club is one of the great courses of Wales but it is best known as being the beloved favorite of golf writer Bernard Darwin, for it was where Darwin learned to play the game while on his boyhood holidays. The course is situated at the mouth of the Dovey Estuary, in the dunes overlooking Cardigan Bay. Over the years, Harry Colt, Herbert Fowler, and James Braid each made revisions, but the course owes its beginning to Colonel Richard Ruck, Darwin's maternal uncle, who in 1886 borrowed nine flower pots from a woman in the village, which he cut into the greens for holes. Darwin wrote of Aberdovey: "It is the course that my soul loves best of all the courses in the world. Every golfer has a course for which he feels some such blind and unreasoning affection. When he is going to his golfing home he packs up his clubs with a peculiar delight and care; he anxiously counts the diminishing number of stations that divide him from it, and finally steps out on the platform, as excited as a schoolboy home for the holidays, to be claimed by his own familiar caddie. A golfer can only have one course towards which he feels quite in this way, and my one is Aberdovey."

▷ NOVEMBER 3   ▷ ROYAL ST. DAVID'S GOLF CLUB   ▷ WALES

Royal St. David's is located in Harlech on the Welsh coast. The course lies under the commanding gaze of Harlech Castle, a forbidding masterpiece of concentric fortification built beginning in 1283, during the reign of King Edward I, on the gray stone cliffs above the seaside plain that shelters the course. From the castle's battlements there is a bird's-eye view across the barrier dunes to the sweep of Tremadoc Bay and northeast to the mountains of Snowdonia, described by Patric Dickinson as looking like "the serrated back of some vast ancient saurian monster, which changes colour with every mood of the elements." The course had a whimsical beginning one day in 1893 when William Henry More, who would become the club's first secretary, spotted Harold Finch-Hatton, recently returned from Australia, throwing a boomerang on the "Morfa" or sheep-grazing plain below the castle. The two decided that the land would be perfect for a golf course and by the fall of 1894, 18 holes had been laid out. St. David's is a testing but not brutish course that flows through shallow dunes and meadowlands, finishing with a par three.

▷ NOVEMBER 4   ▷ BURNHAM AND BERROW GOLF CLUB   ▷ ENGLAND

Burnham and Berrow Golf Club is located by the little seaside resort of Burnham-on-Sea in Somerset in the southwest of England. The course dates from 1891, with J.H. Taylor, one of the great "Triumvirate," serving as the first professional. Over the years, the course was lengthened and holes added to make a full 18, so that it now stretches beyond the Berrow Church that is surrounded by the course. The most distinctive feature is the massive sandhills, with several of the blind shots eliminated over time, so that there is now a mix of holes over the sandhills and along the plain. From the peaks of the dunes around the course there are views across the Bristol Channel and the islands of Steep Holme and Flat Holme out to the Glamorganshire coastline, while turning inland the golfer gazes across the rolling green hills of Somerset with Cheddar Gorge beyond.

▷ NOVEMBER 5   ▷ ST. ENODOC GOLF CLUB   ▷ ENGLAND

St. Enodoc Golf Club is in north Cornwall, lying above the tiny village of Rock and overlooking the estuary of the River Camel, which is crossed by ferry from Padstow. This quaint seaside course features some of the most stupendous sandhills in all of golf with lyrical views across Daymer Bay. The sixth hole, named the Himalayas, requires a second shot over the mountain of dune with its cratered bunker that dwarfs even the "Alps" at Prestwick and the "Maiden" at St. George's. The 10th hole turns inland, hugging Brea Hill, with a series of holes around the ancient St. Enodoc Church. Sir John Betjeman, the poet laureate who wrote much verse about playing at St. Enodoc, lies buried in the little church. The club was founded about 1891, although golf had been played in the dunes even earlier, with the full 18-hole course laid out by James Braid in 1907.

Westward Ho! or Royal North Devon Golf Club was founded in 1864, making it the first links course in England, with the existing design largely the work of Herbert Fowler in 1908. This wild and entrancing links, a kind of golf time capsule, was laid out on the open land known as the Burrows just south of the Torridge estuary in the town of Westward Ho! Cattle, horses, and sheep freely graze over the course since it lies on common land. The course runs along the pebble ridge that protects the land from the waters of Bideford Bay, although in recent years the ridge has been breached by the sea. The middle holes play around giant sea rushes, up to six feet tall, with bayonet-like tips that are mildly poisonous. The highest point on the course is the sixth tee, which provides a stirring view across the estuary to the villages of Appledore and Northam up the hillside, where Westward Ho!'s most famous son, J.H. Taylor, the five-time British Open champion, was born and lived out his life. The club and the town both take their name from the popular 19th-century novel by Charles Kingsley.

▷ NOVEMBER 7 ▷ ROYAL ST. GEORGE'S GOLF CLUB ▷ ENGLAND

There are few more joyous places to play golf than Royal St. George's in Sandwich, with the larks trilling above the links overlooking Pegwell Bay. The course is on the Channel Coast, with Prince's adjoining to the north and Royal Cinque Ports in Deal just to the south. The overwhelming feature of St. George's is the immense sand dunes, with the fairways running through the cloistered valleys. St. George's was founded by Dr. Laidlaw Purves, an eye specialist from Edinburgh, who first gazed upon the chain of giant sandhills when he and some friends climbed to the top of St. Clement's Church in Sandwich. The course opened to great acclaim in 1887, was chosen as the site for the British Amateur in 1892, and then became the first course in England to host the Open Championship two years later. From 1894 to 1949, Sandwich held the Open nine times. The par-five fourth displays one of the most cavernous bunkers in the United Kingdom, while the par-five 14th is crossed by a small stream known as the "Suez Canal." St. George's again began hosting Opens in 1981, and has been the scene of two of the more remarkable recent Opens, with Greg Norman sailing to victory in 1993, and Ben Curtis, the darkhorse from Ohio, pulling off his stunning upset in 2003. *Above: starter's hut*

▷ NOVEMBER 8   ▷ ROYAL CINQUE PORTS GOLF CLUB   ▷ ENGLAND

Royal Cinque Ports, or Deal, as it is more commonly known, lies just a mile or so south of its more famous neighbor, Royal St. George's, on the Kent coast in southeast England. The course runs north and south along a narrow strip of dunes by the pebble ridge that drops abruptly to the English Channel, stretching from the outskirts of Deal Town to the south to the beginning of Sandwich Bay to the north. The spine of dunes that runs the entire length of the course reaches its apex on the fourth tee, creating classic linksland golf with a more exposed quality than the massive, sheltering sandhills of St. George's. Founded in 1892, Deal hosted the Open championship in 1909 and 1920, but it is better known in England as the home of the annual Halford Hewitt Challenge Cup, a team competition among the English Public Schools inaugurated in 1924. The insidious canal that runs through the first and 18th holes, reminiscent of the Swilcan Burn at St. Andrews, has figured prominently in the annals of golf at Royal Cinque Ports.

▷ NOVEMBER 9   ▷ GOLF DE HARDELOT   ▷ FRANCE

English golfers popularized golf at many of the fashionable French seaside resorts, but this was particularly true of the coast along the Pas de Calais and Picardy, which is home to Wimereux, Le Touquet, and Hardelot. Hardelot owes its birth to Sir John Whitley, who recognized the potential for golf of the dunescape along the stretch of coast from Berck to Cape Gris Nez, christened the "Opal Coast" by the painter Levêque. Whitley walked the entire length of the coast looking for an ideal site, and came across an old castle that had been restored in Gothic style by Sir John Hare in 1849. It was here that he founded the original nine-hole Hardelot course in the early 1900s, designed by Harry Vardon. The course that exists today, known as Hardelot Les Pins, was designed by the English architect Tom Simpson. Rebuilt after World War II, the course weaves its way through the sandy soil of the old pine forest.

▷ NOVEMBER 10　　▷ GOLF D'ETRETAT　　▷ FRANCE

Golf flourished in France at the turn of the 20th century at the famous seaside resorts of Normandy—Dieppe, Etretat, Cabourg, Grandville, and Deauville. Golf d'Etretat lies atop the spectacular white limestone cliffs that make this France's "Alabaster Coast." Like many of the courses along the Channel Coast, Etretat was started by visiting British golfers. Founded in 1908, the course was laid out by Monsieur Chantepie, the designer of La Boulie outside Paris, with advice from Arnaud Massy, the only French golfer ever to win the British Open (he did it in 1907). The white cliffs of Etretat and its harbor attracted many of the great Impressionist and landscape artists, including Corot, Boudin, and Monet. At the far end of the cliffs from the course is the monument to the aviators Charles Nungesser and François Coli, who were last seen over Etretat in 1927 during their unsuccessful attempt to fly from Paris to New York in their biplane "The White Bird."

▷ NOVEMBER 11   ▷ NEW GOLF DE DEAUVILLE   ▷ FRANCE

The famous seaside resort of Deauville first came into vogue when it was popularized by the Duc de Morny, the half-brother of Napoleon III and grandson of Talleyrand. By the beginning of the 20th century, grand hotels were flourishing, and the old course at Deauville was founded in 1899. The old course is no longer with us, but the New Golf de Deauville was laid out by the English course architect Tom Simpson in the 1920s. The Hotel du Golf, built by François André, overlooks the course and the putting green with a flower-covered old stone well at its center. With Deauville Bay in the distance, the course runs through oak, elm, ash, and the apple trees that have made the Auge countryside renowned for calvados, while the ruined wall of the Marquis de Lassay's castle looms above the 13th fairway. Over the years, Bobby Jones, Jimmy Demaret, and Roberto de Vicenzo all visited the New Golf de Deauville.

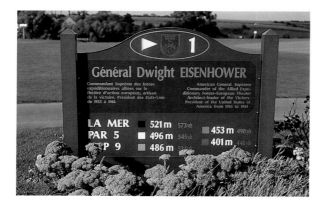

▷ NOVEMBER 12   ▷ GOLF D'OMAHA BEACH   ▷ FRANCE

Golf d'Omaha Beach is laid out above the fishing village of Port en Bessin, overlooking the D-Day beaches where the Allied forces landed at dawn on June 6, 1944, and near the Normandy American Cemetery where almost 10,000 U.S. servicemen are buried. Founded in 1985 by Guy Dupont, the course was designed by French architect Yves Bureau. There are three nines, La Mer (the Sea), Le Bocage (the Hedgerow), and L'Etang (the Pond), with each hole on La Mer and Le Bocage bearing a memorial plaque to a D-Day hero. From the sixth green of La Mer, there are views across the high sea cliffs to the constructed harbor of Port Winston at Arromanches, where the Allied fleet berthed. Several scenes in *Saving Private Ryan* were filmed on the golf course and at Port en Bessin, which was liberated by the American army on June 7, 1944.

Golf de la Bretesche is located in the little village of Missilac, on the road from Vannes to Nantes in western France. The course cuts through the woodlands and encircles the 14th-century La Bretesche castle. The castle with its crenellated ramparts sits on an island in a lake, its entrance guarded by a drawbridge over the moat. The golf course was developed by Gerard Métairie, one of the tenants living in the castle, which had been turned into flats. He consulted three-time British Open winner Henry Cotton about designing the course, but Cotton's fee estimate proved too expensive. Instead, another Englishman, Bill Baker, was chosen to design the course, which opened in 1969. The stone outbuildings and stables of the castle have been converted into a hotel.

▷ NOVEMBER 14   ▷ GOLF DE CHANTILLY   ▷ FRANCE

There are a passel of superb parkland courses in the environs of Paris, the first of which was La Boulie, opened in 1901, followed by Fontainebleau in 1908, and Chantilly a year later. These clubs, which also include Morfontaine and St. Germain, are frequently compared to the splendid and better-known courses around London, because they share similar terrain and several were also designed by the leading old-school English architects. In the early 1920s, the English architect Tom Simpson was engaged to redesign the existing holes at Chantilly to create the championship course known as Le Vineuil. The course is set in the great forest of the Ile de France, 25 miles north of Paris, and there is a serene spaciousness to many of the holes despite the dense woodlands. Near the course are the famous stables that make this the French thoroughbred country. Chantilly opened on September 28, 1909, with an exhibition match between French champions Arnaud Massy and Jean Gassiat, and five years later it hosted what was to be the first of many French Opens. Over the years, Henry Cotton, Roberto de Vicenzo, Peter Oosterhuis, and Nick Faldo all have won the French Open at Chantilly.

▷ NOVEMBER 15   ▷ LES BORDES   ▷ FRANCE

Les Bordes is an exquisite golfing mosaic set in the heart of the Sologne, a region of boggy, untrammeled forest near the Loire Valley that is known for its wild boar, wild mushrooms, and white asparagus. The course was established in 1986 by the late Baron Marcel Bich, inventor of the ballpoint pen that bears the Bic name, on his hunting estate. After the Baron's death in 1994, the course was taken over by his friend and co-founder Yoshiaki Sakurai. Designed by American Robert von Hagge, Les Bordes is the premier course in France and one of the finest in Europe. While its remoteness prevents the course from gaining more acclaim, it adds mightily to the overall ambiance. Von Hagge wove the fairways through the Sologne countryside and there are long rifts of waste bunkers, native grasses, large ponds, and patches of marshland that encroach on the fairways. The rustic clubhouse is very pleasant, and the putting green serves as a sculpture garden. Jean Van de Velde holds the course record of one under par. *Above: putting green sculpture garden*

▷ NOVEMBER 16 ▷ GOLF CLUB BIELLA ▷ ITALY

Golf Club Biella is without a doubt one of the finest courses in Italy, but it is not easy to get to, requiring a zigzagging drive up the mountain known as the Colina Serra above the small town of Magnano, 40 miles east of Turin. The course showcases the forests of birch that cover the mountains of northern Italy's Lake Country, creating thousands of frail, ghostly figures in the twilight. The course is popularly known as Le Betulle, or "the birch." Despite its elevated setting, the course has ample proportions, with water hazards, rocky outcroppings, and crowned greens. The par-fives are particularly strong, and there are five of them altogether.

▷ NOVEMBER 17 ▷ MILANO GOLF CLUB ▷ ITALY

Milano Golf Club is one of the quiet, unsung treasures of golf in Italy, set in the outskirts of Milan in the great Park of Monza. The Park was once the preserve of the Hapsburgs, rulers of the Austro-Hungarian Empire, but is now better known as the site of the famous Grand Prix racetrack. The course, like many of the rarefied courses of northern Italy's Lake Country, was designed by an Englishman, in this case Charles Blandford. The fairways are wonderfully secluded, weaving through the mature forest of oak and beech, and the bunkering is first-rate, with large islands of sand flashed up around the small greens. The clubhouse, built in the 1950s, has a distinctly Modernist influence with its rectilinear slabs of concrete. The original clubhouse behind the 13th green now serves as a restaurant, and was once the site of the royal pheasant house.

▷ NOVEMBER 18   ▷ OLGIATA GOLF CLUB   ▷ ITALY

Olgiata Golf Club is set in a rolling landscape of dense, overgrown woodlands 12 miles to the north of Rome off the Via Cassia, near the famous thoroughbred training center of Dormello-Olgiata. Like many of Italy's finest courses, Olgiata exudes elegance and is very much in the traditional English parkland style. The course was designed in 1961 by the English team of Ken Cotton and Frank Pennink, who were responsible for a number of stylish courses throughout Europe. Cotton, a graduate of Oxford and a scratch golfer, founded the firm in 1946. Pennink attended Oxford, was a two-time winner of the English Amateur Championship, and a successful golf journalist. The fairways at Olgiata are spread out from one another, creating a strong sense of isolation on each hole. Olgiata has twice hosted the World Cup, with the Canadian team of Al Balding and George Knudson upsetting the American pair of Lee Trevino and Julius Boros in 1968, and the Spanish duo of José Maria Canizares and José Rivero prevailing in 1984.

▷ NOVEMBER 19   ▷ THE NATIONAL GOLF CLUB   ▷ TURKEY

The resort town of Belek on the Turkish Riviera overlooking the eastern Mediterranean, some 30 miles east of Antalya, has become the center for golf in Turkey. The National Golf Club was the first course built in the Antalya area, and bills itself as still the best, although it now has competition from a number of other fine layouts, including Gloria Golf Club, the Nobilis, and Antalya Golf Club. Designed by David Feherty and opened in 1994, the course is carved out of eucalyptus and pines and straddles a series of natural lakes, against the backdrop of the purple Taurus Mountains. Of the 450 bird species known to inhabit Turkey, 109 have been identified at the National, including the Tyto Alba or barn owl that is the symbol of the Belek region. Antalya, the capital of southwest Turkey, was founded in 159 B.C. by Attalos II, king of Pergamon, and subsequently occupied by the Romans, Byzantines, Seljuks, and Ottomans, each of whom left their architectural stamp on the city.

▷ NOVEMBER 20 ▷ EMIRATES GOLF CLUB ▷ UNITED ARAB EMIRATES

The Emirates Golf Club hosts the Dubai Desert Classic, a popular event with pros on the European Tour. The original Majlis Course, with its lush green fairways, was the first grass course in the Arabian desert, and is now complemented by the Wadi Course. Designed by Karl Litten in 1987, the Majlis Course takes its
name from the Arabic for "meeting place." Large ponds were excavated and the fill used to create fairways lined with palms and casuarina trees, creating a golf
oasis in the bare desert that consumes nearly one million gallons of water a day. The Dubai Creek Golf Club, which opened in 1993, has a course that flows
through ship-mast high date and coconut palms along the shores of Dubai's saltwater inlet from the Arabian Sea. The clubhouse of the Emirates Golf Club is
designed to resemble a series of Bedouin tents, while Dubai Creek's clubhouse is modeled after an Arab dhow, with soaring white sails.

▷ NOVEMBER 21 ▷ DELHI GOLF CLUB ▷ INDIA

Not surprisingly, golf in India is rooted in the social history of the British Raj. Indeed, the Royal Calcutta Golf Club was founded in 1829, making it the oldest golf club in the world outside of Britain. Delhi Golf Club in New Delhi is a comparative youngster, tracing its origin to 1928, and it is one of the most interesting and exotic of the Indian courses because it is laid out among the 15th-century tombs of Moghul nobles. The unusual setting was selected by the chief of Delhi's horticulture department, a golfing Scotsman who headed a governmental committee entrusted with establishing a course for the capital city. An amateur archaeologist, he hoped to discover buried treasures while laying out what was originally known as the Lodhi Golf Club in the thick bush between the Moghul Emperor Humayun's tomb and the historic Babarpur *tehsil*, or estate. While no priceless artifacts were discovered, the course is one of the best in India, with the seventh green near the red sandstone Barah Khamba, or twelve pillars, a ruined mausoleum of the Afghan-Lodhi dynasty, and the Lal Bangla mausoleum beside the clubhouse. Expanded in 1950 and renamed the Delhi Golf Club, the Commonwealth War Graves Commission planted more than 200 trees and thousands of flowering shrubs, making the course a sanctuary for many species of Indian wildlife, including the peacocks that wander the fairways.

▷ NOVEMBER 22   ▷ VICTORIA GOLF CLUB   ▷ SRI LANKA

Like other former British colonies, Sri Lanka (Ceylon) has a long golfing tradition, with the English having founded Royal Colombo Club in 1882, followed by Nuwara Eliya Golf Club laid out in the hills amidst the tea plantations. The Sri Lanka Amateur Championship, begun in 1891, is the oldest national amateur championship in the world next to the British Amateur. Victoria Golf Club, flowing through 500 acres of farmland and jungle in Digana, just a few miles east of the former capital of Kandy, is the youngest of Sri Lanka's courses, having opened in 1999. Designed by English course architect and golf journalist Donald Steel, the narrow, rolling fairways ramble through coconut palms, Jak tree forests, majestic Mara trees, and pepper vines. The course overlooks the Victoria Dam and the Kandy Mountains.

Gokarna Forest Golf Resort is a few minutes from Kathmandu in the Kingdom of Nepal, laid out in a 500-acre remnant forest of medieval Kathmandu Valley. The Himalayas provide the ultimate mountain backdrop for this course at the rooftop of the world, set in the former Royal Hunting Preserve that was once the Forbidden Valley. Opened in 2000, Gokarna was designed by young Scottish architect David McLay Kidd, who captured the golf world's attention with his unabashedly throwback links course at Bandon Dunes in Oregon. Gokarna is routed through groves of silver oaks with creeks and carp-filled lakes coming into play on several holes and spotted deer wandering the fairways. Most of the course runs through hills and valleys, but the sixth hole opens to the plain of the holy Bhagmati River.

▷ NOVEMBER 24   ▷ HIMALAYAN GOLF COURSE   ▷ NEPAL

Pokhara, Nepal's second city 125 miles west of Kathmandu, boasts two nine-hole courses, the Yeti Course at the Fulbari Resort, and the Himalayan Golf Course. The courses lie in the fertile Pokhara Valley with its rice paddies, mustard fields, and wild geraniums under the immense peaks of the Annapurna Himalayan Range and Annapurna I, the tenth highest mountain in the world at 26,538 feet. The Himalayan Course, designed by ex-British army officer Major R.B. Garung, threads its way through a steep river canyon with the boulder-filled stream fed by the Himalayan snows providing a worthy hazard. The signature hole is the fifth, with the green set in the island formed by the forked stream, facing the razor-edged "fish tail" peak of Machhapuchhre.

▷ NOVEMBER 25　▷ ROYAL THIMPU　▷ BHUTAN

Royal Thimpu is located in Thimpu, the capital of the Buddhist kingdom of Bhutan, closed to the outside world until 1974. This land that time forgot is cradled in the ridges of the eastern Himalayas, surrounded by Tibet to the north and northwest and India to the east, south, and west. The nine-hole course was the first built in Bhutan, laid out by golf course architect Stephen Kay next to the Taschichho Dzong, Bhutan's main governmental building, which houses the royal throne room. A native New Yorker, Kay went to Bhutan in 1985 and constructed one hole working with a local civil engineer, and then sent back detailed drawings for the remaining holes. On a second visit in 1986, Kay met Carl Marinello, the golf pro who had been hired to train the Bhutanese national team, and who, like Kay, had grown up and played high school golf in Queens. Marinello's team of novice golfers but skilled archers achieved phenomenal success, finishing ahead of China in the Asian Games. The golf course may be basic but it is popular with Thimpu's residents, including the maroon-robed monks who can be found out on the course

▷ NOVEMBER 26　▷ BAGAN GOLF RESORT　▷ MYANMAR

Bagan Golf Resort, opened in 1999, is a few minutes from the ancient city of Bagan, lying along the east bank of the broad Ayeyarwady River on the plain of central Myanmar. The course plays through several of the ruined Buddhist temples, pagodas, and shrines built of brick, sandstone, and stucco that make Bagan a world historic landmark. It is estimated that some 13,000 religious structures were built around Bagan, beginning in 1057 during the rule of King Anawrahta, 42nd ruler of the Bagan dynasty, and continuing until Bagan was overrun by Kublai Khan and the Mongol Horde in 1287. Approximately 2,000 of the structures still remain. Marco Polo visited Bagan in the late 13th century, shortly before it was conquered by the Mongols, and wrote the following description: "The towers are built of fine stone, and one has been covered with gold a finger thick, so that the tower appears to be of solid gold . . . . The king caused these towers to be built as a monument to his magnificence and for the benefit of his soul. They make one of the finest sights in the world." *Above: Buddhist shrine*

▷ NOVEMBER 27   ▷ PUN HLAING GOLF CLUB   ▷ MYANMAR

As in India and Sri Lanka, golf was brought to colonial Burma, which is now Myanmar, by British administrators and army officers. Yangon Golf Club in the capital city of Yangon, formerly Rangoon, was founded in 1909 as the first club in Burma. In the past few years there has been a burst of new course activity in the area with the Yemon Island Golf Resort, the 36-hole Yangon City Golf Resort, and the Pun Hlaing Golf Club. Opened in 2000 and designed by Gary Player, Pun Hlaing is generally regarded as the finest course in Myanmar, built as part of a residential community on the 650-acre peninsula between the Hlaing and Pun Hlaing Rivers eight miles from downtown Yangon. The exposed course has long, tapered water hazards and canals with the greens guarded by pod-shaped red sand bunkers. *Above: Greenkeepers at Yangon Golf Club*

▷ NOVEMBER 28   ▷ SPRING CITY GOLF AND LAKE RESORT   ▷ CHINA

Spring City Golf and Lake Resort is situated some 30 miles east of Kunming City, the capital of Yunnan Province. The resort is home to courses designed by Jack Nicklaus and Robert Trent Jones, Jr. Jones's Lake Course stairsteps around the lake, echoing the neatly stacked ledges of agricultural fields that climb the slopes of the Yunnan hills. The area's attractions include the Buddhist Yuantong and Bamboo Temples, a mythical Stone Forest, Lake Dianchi, and the East and West Temple Pagodas. *Right: Lake Course*

▷ NOVEMBER 29   ▷ MISSION HILLS GOLF CLUB   ▷ CHINA

Mission Hills Golf Club & Resort is located just a few miles from Shenzen in Guangdong Province and offers a sumptuous golf feast of ten courses designed by Jack Nicklaus, Vijay Singh, Nick Faldo, Jumbo Ozaki, Ernie Els, Annika Sorenstam, David Duval, José Maria Olazábal, David Leadbetter, and Greg Norman. The granddaddy of them all is the Nicklaus Course, which hosted the 1995 World Cup won by the U.S. team of Fred Couples and Davis Love III.

Above: Ozaki Course. Right: Faldo Course

▷ NOVEMBER 30   ▷ MISSION HILLS GOLF CLUB   ▷ CHINA

With 10 different courses, Mission Hills can rightfully boast that it is the world's largest golf resort. The courses are varied, with an island green at the Faldo Stadium Course, the ziggurat tee boxes of the Ozaki Canyon Course, and the lush, riverine look of Els's Savannah Course among the many features. The hotel has 228 rooms overlooking the golf courses. *Above: Els Course. Right: Valley Course*

▷ DECEMBER 1   ▷ HARBOUR PLAZA GOLF CLUB   ▷ CHINA

Harbour Plaza Golf Club is located in Dongguan (Canton), almost midway between Shenzen and Guanzhou, and a 30-minute drive from the Fu Yong Pier, where the Turbo Cat ferry arrives from Hong Kong. Designed by Robert Trent Jones, Jr., the course consists of three nines, Lake, Valley, and Lychee. The Lake nine runs along the large Hwang Gang Reservoir, with the third, fourth, and fifth holes playing along the wetlands. The Valley and Lychee nines loop around a series of interlocking ponds and are framed by green mountains and terraced lychee nurseries.

▷ DECEMBER 2 ▷ CHUNG SHAN HOT SPRING GOLF CLUB ▷ CHINA

Chung Shan Hot Spring Golf Club opened in 1984, making it the first golf course built in China in the Communist era. It now boasts two of the most highly regarded courses in a booming Chinese golf market, the original course designed by Arnold Palmer, and the second by Jack Nicklaus, opened in 1993. The courses straddle the hills of Shenzen Province, a half-hour drive from the border near Macau. The Nicklaus course, the more challenging of the two, slopes across either side of a 1,000-foot high peak, and like many Nicklaus layouts, it has a roomy, full-cut feel to it, with more than 90 large, terraced bunkers. *Right: Palmer Course*

Given its long history as a British Crown Colony, it is no surprise that golf in Hong Kong dates back to the founding of the Royal Hong Kong Golf Club in 1889 in Happy Valley, after which the club moved to Deep Water Bay in 1898. The club now has three 18-hole courses at Fanling, in addition to the original nine-hole course at Deep Water Bay. Despite the steep terrain and small geographic area, other courses have followed, including Shek O Country Club, Discovery Bay Golf Club on Lantau Island designed by Robert Trent Jones, Jr., and 36 holes of public golf designed by Gary Player at the Jockey Club at Kau Sai Chau. Of all of Hong Kong's courses, however, none is more spectacular than Clearwater Bay Golf & Country Club, spread out over the serpent's tail of the Sai Kung Peninsula high above the South China Sea. Designed by the Japanese duo of T. Sawai and A. Furukawa, the course consists of the Ocean Nine, opened in 1982, and the Highland Nine, opened in 1987. The views overlooking the eastern approach to Hong Kong Harbor are stupendous, with the signature 14th hole playing across and along the seaside cliffs.

▷ DECEMBER 4   ▷ THE CLUB AT NINE BRIDGES   ▷ SOUTH KOREA

The Club at Nine Bridges is located on Jeju Island, or Jeju-Do, the egg-shaped island 60 miles south of the mainland that is referred to as South Korea's Hawaii. Named for the arched stone bridges on the property, the course opened to great fanfare in August 2001. The dazzling highland layout spreads through the piedmont near the volcanic Hallasan, South Korea's tallest mountain at 6,400 feet, which dominates the center of the island and is surrounded by a national forest preserve. Nine Bridges was designed by globetrotting California-based architect Ronald Fream, and developed by Jay Lee, CEO of the Cheil Jedang Group and the grandson of the founder of Samsung. Fream created broad fairways of bentgrass and wide belts of sand through the existing creek beds piled with volcanic stones and lined with oaks. Lakes were created on holes five and seven, and a 50,000-ton water hazard encircles the island 18th green. One bridge that was added connects the 18th green to the clubhouse. The surrounding mountains shelter the course from Jeju Island's fierce winds.

The glories of golf in Japan are in no small measure the product of a three-month visit by the English golf course architect Charles Hugh Alison, who arrived in Japan on December 1, 1930, aboard the liner *Asama Maru* sailing from California, accompanied by his construction supervisor George Penglase. Alison had served as the secretary of Stoke Poges Golf Club outside London, designed by the great English architect H.S. Colt, before becoming Colt's partner shortly after World War I. Komyo Otani, a member of Tokyo Golf Club who had been introduced to the game as a student in England, took the lead in hiring Colt to design a new course for the club. But Colt had second thoughts about the long voyage, and instead dispatched Alison. Alison proceeded to design Japan's first championship course, laid out on a flat plain at Asaka. Built by a vast army of workers, the course was completed in May 1932 with the characteristic deep, twirling bunkers that came to be known in Japan as "Alisons." In 1940, the course was taken over by the military and completely destroyed, but a new course was built by Otani after the war based closely on Alison's design.

▷ DECEMBER 6　▷ HIRONO GOLF CLUB　▷ JAPAN

Hirono Golf Club near Kobe was designed by the English course architect Charles Alison during his tour of Japan in 1930–31, on an idyllic site that was part of the large estate of Viscount Kuki, a former feudal warlord and avid golfer. Opened in June 1932, Hirono is generally regarded as Japan's finest course. While in Tokyo, Alison was approached by Seiichi Takahata, a member of The Addington in London, about the project he was involved with at Hirono. Alison visited the site, finding it tailor-made for golf with its lovely lakes and natural valleys, ravines, and rivulets. After studying the property, Alison retired to his room at the Oriental Hotel near the Kobe train station with notes and contour maps, and after seven days emerged with a detailed plan. Of his work at Hirono, Alison later wrote: "In 1930, wild boar were said to flourish there, but I am thankful to say that my acquaintance with them was made only at the dinner table. On 300 acres available for golf, there was no human habitation, nor view of one… A map of land was prepared by a Japanese surveyor showing the lakes and principal hills and dales. Notwithstanding the trees and in places the dense undergrowth, this proved to be an excellent guide."

In 1930, architect Charles Alison arrived on his historic visit to Japan to design the Tokyo Golf Club's new course. He then traveled with Komyo Otani to the retreat of Baron Kishichiro Akura at Kawana on the Izu Peninsula, famous for its hot springs, two to three hours south of Tokyo. The son of one of Japan's wealthiest industrialists, Akura had been educated at Cambridge and modeled his 500-acre estate after those he had admired in the English countryside. Akura then set about developing a world-class golf resort and hotel at Kawana. The first course at Kawana, the Oshima Course, was designed by Otani and completed in 1928. It is named for Oshima Island just off the coast, with its still smoldering volcano. Akura then hired Alison to design the Fuji Course, which opened in 1936. The course rises and plunges through the emerald green hills on a promontory above the sea, with cloud-covered Mt. Fuji in the distance rising above an inlet in the Pacific. *Right: Fuji Course*

▷ DECEMBER 8   ▷ BONARI KOGEN GOLF CLUB   ▷ JAPAN

Bonari Kogen Golf Club is a course of exceptional beauty crafted from an abandoned sulfur mine in Fukushima, Japan. Designed by American golf architect Ronald Fream and founded by Masanori Tsujita, it took 13 years to transform the mining wasteland, which didn't have a single blade of grass, into coiling green fairways scaled with cloverleaf bunkers and rock-lined pools through the ridges of maple and pine. The most spectacular hole is the par-five third, laid out above scarred, reddish-brown cliffs formed by a great gash in the earth with a creek running below. The course is located within the Bandai National Park and is framed by the serene steel-blue peaks of the Adatara Mountain Range, including Mount Bandai.

▷ DECEMBER 9   ▷ SEGOVIA GOLF CLUB   ▷ JAPAN

Segovia Golf Club, located in Chiyoda, Ibaraki, was built at the end of the 1980s. The course was designed by the late Desmond Muirhead, who was Jack Nicklaus's partner when the Golden Bear was getting started in course design. An urbane and controversial figure with eclectic tastes, Muirhead took a long hiatus from course architecture in 1975 to open an art gallery in California and pursue his interest in collecting Japanese Kakiemon and Oribe porcelain. Muirhead returned to golf in 1986 and began designing courses with literary and artistic motifs, his creations including a hole shaped like a mermaid with fish-shaped bunkers and an island green in the form of an ark. He did much of his work in Japan, building highly stylized, thematic courses. Segovia takes its inspiration from Spanish themes, with holes named Miro, Gazpacho, and Costa Brava.

▷ DECEMBER 10   ▷ DALAT PALACE GOLF CLUB   ▷ VIETNAM

Dalat Palace Golf Club is in the central highlands of Vietnam in Dalat, known as the "City of Eternal Spring" for its cool, crisp mountain air. The course was built in 1922 as a nine-hole layout. In the 1950s, the course was expanded to 18 holes and then redesigned in 1994. A four-and-a-half hour drive north of Ho Chi Minh City, through rice paddies and banana farms, the course is banked through the soft hills of Dalat sprinkled with pines. There are a number of ponds on the course, which sits above Xuan Huong Lake, named for an 18th-century woman poet. Dalat was a favorite summer retreat of French colonialists seeking an escape from the oppressive summer heat and attracted by the area's lakes and waterfalls. They built the Mediterranean villas which give the city its architectural distinction and also earned Dalat the title of "Le Petit Paris." The clubhouse, built in 1956 and recently restored, is in the French colonial style.

▷ DECEMBER 11   ▷ DRAGON HILLS GOLF AND COUNTRY CLUB   ▷ THAILAND

Dragon Hills Golf and Country Club is in Rachaburi in western Thailand, not far from Kanchanaburi and the infamous Bridge over the River Kwai, where there is a war cemetery and War Museum. Dragon Hills, set in the remote jade green Rachaburi hills, has three resplendently serene courses—Dragon Pearl, Dragon Green, and Dragon Lakes. The courses were designed by North Dakotan Jim Engh, Jack Nicklaus, and Nicklaus's rival at the 1980 U.S. Open at Baltusrol, Isao Aoki. Dragon Pearl, which opened in 1994, was Engh's first solo design. With features sculpted from the rugged terrain and man-made ponds, the course is a noteworthy precursor of the courses Engh went on to design on severe sites in the American West. *Right: Dragon Pearl Course*

▷ DECEMBER 12   ▷ SPRINGFIELD ROYAL COUNTRY CLUB   ▷ THAILAND

Springfield Royal Country Club is located in Cha-Am, two hours and twenty minutes west of Bangkok, not far from the royal seaside resort of Hua Hin. Designed by Jack Nicklaus and opened in 1993, the course is a demanding one, with undulating greens and plenty of water hazards, and is also one of the best maintained in Thailand. The golf club is ten miles from the Springfield Beach Resort, with an opulent, red-roofed clubhouse that occupies the high ground overlooking the course and the Gulf of Thailand. Nearby is Phetchaburi, a town known for its old temples. Above the town in the Khao Wang hills sits the summer palace and observatory of Phra Nakhon Khiri built by King Mongkut, which is now a national museum accessible by cable car.

▷ DECEMBER 13   ▷ ROYAL HUA HIN GOLF CLUB   ▷ THAILAND

Royal Hua Hin, opened in 1924, is Thailand's oldest golf course, located in the center of the royal seaside resort of Hua Hin, overlooking the Gulf of Thailand. The course winds through the hills behind the preserved Hua Hin railway station on the Bangkok-Singapore line. Popularly known as "The Railway," the course was designed by Scottish railway engineer O.A. Robins for King Vajiravudh and his golf partner, Queen Rhamphaibarni. The prayer tree between the first and 10th tees is a novel but much-welcomed feature. Just outside the town within the Rama 6 Army Camp is Maruekkataiyawan, the teak summer palace built for the king.

▷ DECEMBER 14   ▷ BLUE CANYON COUNTRY CLUB   ▷ THAILAND

Blue Canyon Country Club, considered Thailand's premier course, is located on the northern end of Phuket Island, Thailand's ultimate tropical getaway set in the Andaman Sea. Strangely shaped, sheer stalks of limestone sprout out of the aquamarine waters of Phang Nga Bay, including James Bond Island, which was featured in *The Man With the Golden Gun*, and Koh Pannyi with its floating fishing village. Blue Canyon, opened in 1991, was once an abandoned tin mine and rubber estate. Designed by Yoshikazo Kato, the course hosted the 1998 Johnnie Walker Classic, won by Tiger Woods in a playoff with Ernie Els. The best-known hole, the par-three 14th, plays to a tadpole-shaped island green set in the large lagoon.

▷ DECEMBER 15   ▷ THE MINES RESORT   ▷ MALAYSIA

Golf in Malaysia dates back to the founding of the Royal Selangor Golf Club outside Kuala Lumpur in 1893, and has flourished in recent years. In 1997, one of Malaysia's most spectacular courses opened at the Mines Resort City outside Kuala Lumpur, developed by Malaysian business mogul Tan Sri Lee Kim Yew. Designed by Robert Trent Jones, Jr., the course is a monumental environmental reclamation project, crafted out of an open-cast tin mine that had ceased operation. In 1999, the Mines hosted the World Cup won by the U.S. tandem of Tiger Woods and Mark O'Meara.

▷ DECEMBER 16 ▷ HORNBILL GOLF AND JUNGLE CLUB ▷ BORNEO, MALAYSIA

Tan Sri Lee Kim Yew, the obsessively eco-conscious developer of the Mines Resort outside Kuala Lumpur, followed up that development by creating the Highlands Resort and the Hornbill Golf and Jungle Club in the Malaysian Province of Sarawak on Borneo. The remote resort, built at an estimated cost of $100 million, is nestled in a 5,000-acre enclave of partially logged-out, ancient rain forest beneath the Penrissen Mountain Range, some 50 miles south of the Sarawak capital of Kuching. Designed by Australian Neil Crafter and opened in July 2000, the course tumbles through the lush highland jungle at 3,000 feet above sea level, with boulders left where they were found on the fairways, and river ravines and ponds coming into play. With its emphasis on environmental preservation, the resort uses solar power and serves only vegetarian food grown on its own organic farm. The course is named for the rhinoceros hornbills that are indigenous to the Borneo rain forest.

▷ DECEMBER 17   ▷ SINGAPORE ISLAND COUNTRY CLUB (BUKIT COURSE)   ▷ SINGAPORE

Singapore Island Country Club is the golf capital of the small, prosperous island nation founded in 1819 by Sir Stamford Raffles. The club is the result of the combination in 1963 of the Royal Singapore Golf Club and the Royal Island Golf Club, which in turn trace their origins to the Singapore Sporting Club. The club now has four courses, the Bukit ("Hill"), the Island, the New, and the Sime. In 1891, members of the Singapore Sporting Club formed a nine-hole golf club. By 1920, the club decided to build an 18-hole course, and a 250-acre site was obtained adjoining the MacRitchie Reservoir. Designed by the great Scottish professional James Braid, the original Bukit Course, opened in 1924, remains Singapore Island's showcase. Braid feared sea travel, and so, as with his other creations outside Britain, he designed the course by mail using topographical maps. The fairways were hacked from the dense jungle and English trees planted in addition to the native species, creating a traditional parkland look. The hilly Bukit Course with its Bermuda fairways hosted the 1969 World Cup, won by the U.S. team of Lee Trevino and Orville Moody.

▷ DECEMBER 18   ▷ LAGUNA BINTAN GOLF CLUB   ▷ INDONESIA

The Indonesian island of Bintan has become a major golf destination, with a string of tropical courses running along the north coast of the kidney-shaped island facing the South China Sea. Reached by a 45-minute ferry ride from Singapore aboard a high-speed catamaran, the Ria Bintan Golf Club (part of Club Med Ria Bintan) has two courses designed by Gary Player, the Ocean Course and Forest Course. Further east, the Laguna Bintan Golf Club, designed by Greg Norman, spans forest, wetlands, beachfront holes rimmed by boulders, and an abandoned quarry. It is part of the Banyan Tree Resort. The Bintan Lagoon Resort offers the Jack Nicklaus Sea View Course, with the lovely par-three 12th caressing the South China Sea and the green of the 13th actually split by a stream, as well as the hillier Woodlands Course designed by Ian Baker-Finch. *Above: Ria Bintan Golf Club (Ocean Course)*

Nirwana Bali Golf Club is located on the southwest coast of Bali, a 30-minute drive from Kuta. Opened in 1997 and designed by Aussie great Greg Norman and Bob Harrison, the course is the centerpiece of the Nirwana Bali Resort. The layout combines spectacular cliff holes running alongside the Indian Ocean with hazards formed by terraced rice paddies typical of the lush Balinese countryside, beginning with the seven rows of staggered rice paddies that descend down the hill to the left of the first tee. The fantasy hole par-three seventh plays across the inlet of the sea to a green mounted on a vine-draped cliff, facing the sacred Hindu sea temple of Tanah Lot that is perched on a rocky pedestal in the ocean 200 yards further down the coastline. Nirwana's female caddies come from the neighboring villages and receive an intensive three-month training program.

▷ DECEMBER 20   ▷ BALI HANDARA KOSAIDO COUNTRY CLUB   ▷ BALI, INDONESIA

Bali Handara has long been the holy grail of golf, a tantalizingly tropical course cloistered in the central highlands of Bali. The course is laid out in a lush volcanic crater 3,500 feet up the wooded mountainside of Mount Batukaru that rises to a cloud-covered 7,500-foot-high summit, making it a welcome escape from the coastal heat. Designed by Peter Thomson and Michael Wolveridge in 1974, construction was supervised by Guy Wolstenholme, who won the English Amateur. The course is routed through an old dairy farm and the subtropical jungle between two large lakes, near the village of Bedugal. It was built entirely by hand, with a workforce of more than a thousand local laborers, most of them women. The fairways are a mix of Kentucky bluegrass imported from the U.S. and native Bermuda, broken by jigsaw piece-shaped bunkers. There are ponds between the eighth and ninth and 16th and 17th fairways and a jungle stream that crosses the third, fifth, sixth, and seventh holes.

▷ DECEMBER 21   ▷ NEW SOUTH WALES GOLF CLUB   ▷ AUSTRALIA

New South Wales, outside Sydney, lies on the northern headland of Botany Bay, with commanding views over the Pacific and along the coastline. Captain James Cook landed on the south side of the bay in the *Endeavour* on April 29, 1770, dispatching a boat that found fresh water at "Captain Cook's Waterhole" just below what is now the 17th tee. The course, which was routed and planned by Alister MacKenzie in 1926, lies between Cape Banks, named after Joseph Banks, one of the botanists in Cook's party, and La Perouse, named for Jean-François Galaup de la Perouse, the commander of two French frigates that anchored on January 26, 1788. The course makes two loops along the coast, Nos. 5 through 7 on the front nine, and Nos. 13 through 16 on the back. The sixth hole presents a spectacular tee shot across the rocky ocean that is reminiscent of the 16th at California's Cypress Point, MacKenzie's masterpiece on the other side of the Pacific.

▷ DECEMBER 22   ▷ ROYAL MELBOURNE GOLF CLUB   ▷ AUSTRALIA

Royal Melbourne Golf Club, the top-ranked course in Australia, is the most illustrious of the series of masterpieces that stretch across Melbourne's famous sand belt, including Commonwealth, Victoria, Metropolitan, and Yarra Yarra. Founded in 1891, it is the oldest golf club in Australia with a continuous existence under the same name. In 1901, the course moved to a location in the rugged heathland by the racetrack in the suburb of Sandringham, marking the birth of golf in the sand belt. In the 1920s, the club moved slightly east to its present location in Black Rock, and hired Alister MacKenzie to oversee the design. MacKenzie arrived in 1926 to survey the site, the beginning of his historic tour of Australia, and entrusted the realization of his vision for what would become the West Course to Australian Open champion Alex Russell and greenkeeper Mick Morcom. MacKenzie created a wonderfully strategic design through thickets of ti tree and mimosa, while the scooped out, scalloped bunkering that blends into the shaved, rolling greens has never been surpassed.

▷ DECEMBER 23   ▷ THE DUNES GOLF LINKS   ▷ AUSTRALIA

The Dunes Golf Links is a public course on the Mornington Peninsula near Melbourne, with fairways splashed across ruddy native grasses and sandy wastes. The course owes its creation to the financial distress of the Limestone Valley Golf Club, a basic course that previously occupied the site. When that course was put up for sale, one of the creditors, Duncan Andrews, came to view the property on a whim. He was so taken by the natural beauty of the setting that he decided to purchase it himself. Andrews brought in Australian designer Tony Cashmore to undertake a complete overhaul of the site. Cashmore sculpted an authentic links with a bold palette of colors, creating many of the natural looking features from scratch. The Dunes is both visually striking and very playable, making it one of Australia's top public courses.

▷ DECEMBER 24   ▷ NATIONAL GOLF CLUB (MOONAH COURSE)   ▷ AUSTRALIA

The Moonah Course at the National Golf Club, which opened in 2000, is a breathtaking links that swoops across the sweeping folds of the seaside farmlands and sand dunes of Victoria's Mornington Peninsula. With its broad fairways and swaths of native grasses, framed by the jagged ridges of the Bass Strait Dunes near Gunamatta Beach, the course is an Australian original. Designed by golf's Great White Shark, Greg Norman, Moonah is one of three courses at the National Golf Club. The original Robert Trent Jones, Jr. course overlooks the Cape Schanck hills, and is now known as the Old Course. The Ocean Course, which also opened in 2000, was designed by Peter Thomson and Michael Wolveridge. The Moonah Course takes its name from the native moonah trees studded across the countryside, which can grow to be 1,000 years old.

▷ DECEMBER 25   ▷ ROYAL ADELAIDE GOLF CLUB   ▷ AUSTRALIA

Golf in Adelaide dates back to 1870, but the original Adelaide Golf Club dissolved in 1876 and was not revived until 1892. The club moved in 1906 to its present site in the suburb of Seaton, less than two miles from the coast, with the course designed by Harry Swift and H.L. Rymill. Alister MacKenzie advised on the redesign of the course in 1926 while on his whirlwind tour of Australia, having been engaged to redesign Royal Melbourne. MacKenzie wrote of Royal Adelaide: "One finds a most delightful combination of sand dunes and fir trees, a most unusual combination even at the best seaside courses. No seaside courses that I have seen possess such magnificent sand craters as those at Royal Adelaide." Not all of MacKenzie's suggestions were adopted but his rerouting did bring the dunes more into play and prevented holes from being played across the railroad tracks. The sand hills clotted with pines and swamp oaks are magnificent and the deep, loamy pot bunkers are multitudinous. Royal Adelaide has hosted the Australian Open nine times, most recently in 1998.

▷ DECEMBER 26   ▷ BROOKWATER GOLF CLUB   ▷ AUSTRALIA

Brookwater Golf Club, located in Queensland southwest of Brisbane, is a dazzling layout designed by Australian golfing legend Greg Norman and his design partner Bob Harrison. Opened in 2002, Brookwater has the rippling fairways of a links-style seaside course, but it is set in a dense forest of ironbarks and tall, spindly golden eucalypts that pinch the narrow corridors of green. The undulating nature of the site allowed the designers to create the bold, whorled bunkers that echo the creations of the great Alister MacKenzie in the Melbourne sand belt. The course is the centerpiece of a planned development, with housing set back from the holes.

▷ DECEMBER 27   ▷ ELLERSTON GOLF COURSE   ▷ AUSTRALIA

Ellerston Golf Course was designed by Greg Norman and Bob Harrison on the private estate of Australian media mogul and sportsman, Kerry Packer. Packer, reputed to be the wealthiest man in Australia and a passionate golfer, gave Norman free run of his 70,000-acre preserve in the wild, secluded high country of the Hunter Valley in New South Wales, north of Sydney. After two or three days of exploration, a 400-acre site was selected that features the sinewy Pages Creek, tousled native vegetation, and gum trees. This exacting course, which was completed in 2001, takes full advantage of the craggy bush, with long views over the hills, and shoals of white sand bristling with blond wiry grasses. The essential design feature of the course is the winding creek that comes into play on nine holes, including five where it runs directly in front of the green.

▷ DECEMBER 28　▷ KAURI CLIFFS GOLF COURSE　▷ NEW ZEALAND

Kauri Cliffs, on the northern tip of New Zealand in Matauri Bay, opened on February 1, 2000. The course and the luxurious 16-room Kauri Cliffs Lodge were developed by Julian Robertson, a New Yorker by way of South Carolina who founded Tiger Hedge Funds. During a family trip to New Zealand, Robertson became entranced with the prospect of building a golf course on the 4,000 acres of rolling coastal farmland above the ocean cliffs overlooking the Cavalli Islands, Waiaua Bay, and the outer reaches of the Bay of Islands. Robertson bought the land and hired Florida-based golf architect David Harman, who made more than 50 trips to the site in three years. The holes on the landward side play through sprawling meadows and stands of native puriri, totura, and the name-sake kauri trees. Robertson planted more than 300 kauri, among the world's strongest trees, which covered much of the top half of New Zealand's North Island before the arrival of European settlers. The coastal holes play across ravines above the ocean to stair-step fairways. The par-five fourth hole is named "Cambo" in honor of New Zealand golf star Michael Campbell; the sixth hole is "Waterfalls" as the footbridge over the ravine crosses directly over a waterfall; and the par-five 18th is named "Tane Mahuta" (Maori for "Lord of the Forest") after a particular kaui tree that is the largest such specimen in the world. *Above: bungee jumping*

▷ DECEMBER 29   ▷ PARAPARAUMU BEACH GOLF CLUB   ▷ NEW ZEALAND

Paraparaumu Beach Golf Club has long had the reputation of being New Zealand's finest course, and its only true seaside links, although it now has coastal rivals in the resort courses built at Kauri Cliffs and Cape Kidnappers. The course is situated in North Wellington, about an hour's drive from the center of the capital, on the west coast. The fairways billow and heave through shallow valleys beneath the green and auburn folds of the Tararua Range, with Mount Hector rising to 5,000 feet, and are sheltered by Kapiti Island, which lies offshore. In 1946, Douglas Whyte, a member of the Royal and Ancient Golf Club of St. Andrews, and Alex Russell came across a rudimentary course in the dunes of Paraparaumu Beach and realized the potential for a championship links. Russell, an Australian Open champion, had carried out Alister MacKenzie's vision for the West Course of Royal Melbourne in 1926 to brilliant effect, and went on to design the East Course in 1932. He used all of his skill and experience in his design for Paraparaumu, which opened in 1949.

▷ DECEMBER 30   ▷ CAPE KIDNAPPERS GOLF COURSE   ▷ NEW ZEALAND

Cape Kidnappers Golf Course near the town of Napier, on the east coast of the North Island, is the second course to be developed on the New Zealand coast by American financier Julian Robertson, whose Kauri Cliffs course 500 miles to the north has earned raves throughout the golf world. Robertson hired American golf architect Tom Doak for the project after playing Doak's acclaimed course at Pacific Dunes in Oregon the second day after it opened. Completed in 2003, Cape Kidnappers is Doak's first design outside the U.S. The setting is awe-inspiring, with the course laid out over a series of tilted ridges that spread like great green talons across the cliffs 500 feet above Hawke's Bay, with views stretching for 70 miles along the entire curvature of the bay. A pulled tee shot on the sixth or 15th holes will find the antipodean abyss, but it will take nearly ten seconds before the ball reaches the ocean below. Cape Kidnappers was named by Captain Cook in 1769 when Maori warriors attempted to "rescue" his Tahitian translator Tayeto by kidnapping him from the *Endeavour*. In Maori mythology, the point of land is the fish hook that the god Maui used to pull the South Island from the sea.

▷ DECEMBER 31   ▷ MANGILAO GOLF CLUB   ▷ GUAM

The American territory of Guam in the South Pacific is just 30 miles long and less than nine miles wide, but there are golf courses galore, including Mangilao, Hatsuho, Leopalace, and Talofofo. Mangilao, opened in 1992, is Guam's version of Pebble Beach. Designed by Robin Nelson and located on the island's east coast, the front nine is looped around three lakes. The back nine runs along the lower tier of the coastal plateau above the Pacific, with the fairways carved from the jungle. The spectacular 188-yard par-three 12th plays across a semicircle of the sapphire sea to a green resting above a flat ledge of rock.

INDEX OF COURSES

This index includes all of the courses in the book, listed with the date they appear, and arranged geographically by country and by state within the United States. Courses that are open to the public are marked with one star, and those that have limited access to the public are marked with two stars. For both categories, the course's website is listed when available. The limited-access courses are open to the public only during certain days or hours, may include other requirements such as a handicap card, and arrangements generally must be made in advance. Golfers should also note that some of the courses marked as public that are located at resorts might have restrictions on play for non-resort guests. Courses with no stars are private.

United States

LOUISIANA
Money Hill Golf & Country Club, 4/6

MAINE
*Sugarloaf Golf Club
www.sugarloaf.com, 9/23

MARYLAND
*Bulle Rock
www.bullerock.com, 10/19

MASSACHUSETTS
Country Club, The, 9/29
*Crumpin-Fox Club
www.sandri.com/crumpin.htm, 9/27
Kittansett Club, 9/30
Myopia Hunt Club, 9/28

MICHIGAN
*Arcadia Bluffs Golf Club
www.arcadiabluffs.com, 6/24
Crystal Downs Country Club, 6/26
Oakland Hills Country Club, 6/27
TPC of Michigan, 6/28
*Treetops Resort
www.treetops.com, 6/25

MINNESOTA
*Deacon's Lodge
www.grandviewlodge.com, 6/9
Hazeltine National Golf Club, 6/10

MISSISSIPPI
*Dancing Rabbit Golf Club
www.dancingrabbitgolf.com, 4/7

MISSOURI
Club at Porto Cima, The, 6/13
St. Louis Country Club, 6/14

MONTANA
*Old Works Golf Course
www.oldworks.org, 6/6

NEBRASKA
Sand Hills Golf Club, 5/16
*Wild Horse Golf Club, 5/17

NEVADA
Cascata Golf Club, 1/18
*Las Vegas Paiute Resort
www.lvpaiutegolf.com, 1/17
*Reflection Bay Golf Club
www.lakelasvegas.com, 1/19

NEW HAMPSHIRE
Lake Sunapee Country Club, 9/24

NEW JERSEY
Atlantic City Country Club, 10/16
Baltusrol Golf Club (Lower Course),
10/12
Morris County Golf Club, 10/14
Pine Valley Golf Club, 10/17
Plainfield Country Club, 10/13
Somerset Hills Country Club, 10/15

NEW MEXICO
*Black Mesa Golf Club
www.blackmesagolfclub.com, 5/9
*Paa-Ko Ridge Golf Club
www.paakoridge.com, 5/8

NEW YORK
Atlantic Golf Club, 9/9
*Bethpage State Park (Black Course)
www.nysparks.state.ny.us/golf, 9/11
Creek Club, The, 9/13
Fishers Island Club, 10/3
Friar's Head, 9/12
Garden City Golf Club, 9/14
Hudson National Golf Club, 10/7
Maidstone Club, 9/10
National Golf Links of America, The, 9/8
Oak Hill Country Club, 9/15
Shinnecock Hills Golf Club, 9/7
Sleepy Hollow Country Club, 10/8
Trump National Golf Club, 10/9
Westchester Country Club, 10/10
Winged Foot Golf Club (West Course), 10/11

NORTH CAROLINA
*Grove Park Inn, The
www.groveparkinn.com, 4/23
*Pinehurst Resort (No. 2 Course)
www.pinehurst.com, 4/20
*Pine Needles Lodge and Golf Club
www.pineneedles-midpines.com, 4/21
Wade Hampton Golf Club, 4/22

NORTH DAKOTA
*Hawktree Golf Club
www.hawktree.com, 6/8
*Links of North Dakota
www.redmike.com, 6/7

OHIO
Camargo Club, 5/1
Inverness Club, 6/29
*Longaberger Golf Club, 7/3
Muirfield Village Golf Club, 7/2

OKLAHOMA
*Karsten Creek Golf Club
www.karstencreek.net, 5/7
Southern Hills Country Club, 5/6

OREGON
Astoria Country Club, 5/25
*Bandon Dunes
www.bandondunesgolf.com, 5/23
*Pacific Dunes
www.bandondunesgolf.com, 5/24
*Running Y Ranch Resort
www.runningy.com, 5/22
*Sunriver Resort (Crosswater Course),
www.sunriver-resort.com, 5/21

PENNSYLVANIA
*Golf Course at Glen Mills, The
www.glenmillsgolf.com, 7/6
Huntsville Golf Club, 7/7
Merion Golf Club, 7/5
Oakmont Country Club, 7/10
Philadelphia Country Club (Spring Mill
Course), 7/4
Saucon Valley Country Club, 7/8
Stonewall Golf Club, 7/9

RHODE ISLAND
Newport Country Club, 10/1
Wannamoisett Country Club, 10/2

SOUTH CAROLINA
*Caledonia Golf & Fish Club
www.fishclub.com, 4/19
Cassique Golf Club, 4/18
Haig Point Golf Club, 4/15
*Harbour Town Golf Links
www.seapines.com, 4/14

★Ocean Course at Kiawah Island, The
www.kiawahresort.com, 4/17
Yeamans Hall Club, 4/16

SOUTH DAKOTA
Sutton Bay Club, 5/18

TENNESSEE
Honors Course, The, 4/24
★Springhouse Links at Gaylord
Opryland Resort
www.gaylordhotels.com/
gaylordopryland, 5/4

TEXAS
★Barton Creek Resort and Country Club
www.bartoncreek.com, 4/3
Dallas National Golf Club, 4/2
Shadow Hawk Golf Club, 4/5
★The Quarry Golf Club
www.quarrygolf.com, 4/4

UTAH
★Entrada at Snow Canyon Golf Course
www.golfentrada.com, 1/20
★Green Spring Golf Course
www.greenspringgolfcourse.com, 1/21

VERMONT
Ekwanok Golf Club, 9/26
★Equinox Resort
www.equinox.rockresorts.com, 9/25

VIRGINIA
★Homestead Resort, The
www.thehomestead.com, 4/25
Kinloch Golf Club, 4/26
Robert Trent Jones Golf Club, 4/28

★Royal New Kent
www.traditionalclubs.com/royal, 4/27

WASHINGTON
★Desert Canyon Golf Club
www.desertcanyon.com, 5/28
★Port Ludlow Golf Club
www.portludlowresort.com, 5/26
TPC at Snoqualmie Ridge, 5/27

WEST VIRGINIA
★Greenbrier, The
www.greenbrier.com, 4/29
Pete Dye Golf Club, 4/30

WISCONSIN
★Blackwolf Run
www.destinationkohler.com, 6/22
★Lawsonia Links
www.lawsonia.com, 6/21
★Whistling Straits
www.destinationkohler.com, 6/23

WYOMING
★Powder Horn Golf Club
www.thepowderhorn.com, 5/19
★Teton Pines Resort and Country Club
www.tetonpines.com, 5/20

International

ARGENTINA
★Arelauqen Golf and Country Club
www.arelauqen.com, 2/6
Jockey Club, The, 2/4
★Llao Llao Resort & Hotel Golf Course
www.llaollao.com, 2/5
Martindale Country Club, 2/7

AUSTRALIA
★Brookwater Golf Club
www.brookwatergolf.com, 12/26
★Dunes Golf Links, The, 12/23
Ellerston Golf Course, 12/27
★★National Golf Club (Moonah Course)
www.nationalgolf.com.au, 12/24
★★New South Wales Golf Club
www.nswgolfclub.com.au, 12/21
★★Royal Adelaide Golf Club
www.royaladelaidegolf.com.au, 12/25
★★Royal Melbourne Golf Club
www.royalmelbourne.com.au, 12/22

AUSTRIA
★Gut Altentann, Golf and Country Club
www.gutaltentann.com, 8/19
★Dachsten-Tauern Golf and Country Club
www.schladming-golf.at, 8/20

AZORES
★Furnas Golf Club
www.verdegolf.net, 3/19

BAHAMAS
★Four Seasons Resort Great Exuma at
Emerald Bay

www.fourseasons.com/greatexuma,
2/21

BARBADOS
★Green Monkey Golf Course at Sandy Lane
www.sandylane.com, 2/14
★Royal Westmoreland
www.royal-westmoreland.net, 2/13

BELGIUM
★★Royal Golf Club de Belgique
www.golf.be/ravenstein, 9/1
★Royal Zoute Golf Club
www.zoute.be, 8/31

BERMUDA
Mid Ocean Club, 10/20

BHUTAN
★Royal Thimphu Golf Club, 11/25

BRAZIL
★Commandatuba Ocean Course
www.transamerica.com, 2/11
★Costa do Sauípe Golf Links, 2/10
Gavea Golf and Country Club, 2/8
★Terravista Golf Course, 2/9

CANADA
★Banff Springs Golf Course
www.fairmont.com, 6/1
★Bell Bay Golf Club
www.bellbaygolfclub.com, 9/22
★Big Sky Golf and Country Club
www.bigskygolf.com, 5/30
Capilano Golf and Country Club, 5/31
★Chateau Whistler Golf Club
www.chateauwhistler.com, 5/29

*Nirwana Bali Golf Club
www.nirwanabaligolf.com, 12/19
*Ria Bintan Golf Club
www.riabintan.com, 12/18

IRELAND
*Ballybunion Golf Club (Old Course)
www.ballybuniongolfclub.ie, 7/29
*Carne Golf Links
www.carnegolflinks.com, 7/30
*County Sligo Golf Club
www.countysligogolfclub.com, 7/31
*Doonbeg Golf Club
www.doonbeggolfclub.com, 7/28
*European Club, The
www.theeuropeanclub.com, 7/24
*Island Golf Club, The
www.theislandgolfclub.com, 7/23
*Lahinch Golf Club
www.lahinchgolf.com, 7/27
*Old Head Golf Links
www.oldheadgolflinks.com, 7/25
*Portmarnock Golf Club
www.portmarnockgolfclub.ie, 7/22
*Rosapenna Golf Links (Sandy Hills)
www.rosapenna.ie, 8/1
*Waterville Golf Links
www.watervillegolflinks.ie, 7/26

ITALY
*Biella, Golf Club
www.lebettule.com, 11/16
*Milano Golf Club, 11/17
*Olgiata Golf Club
www.olgiatagolfclub.it, 11/18
*Pevero Golf Club, 3/30

JAMAICA
*White Witch, The
www.ritz-carlton.com/resorts/
rose_hall_jamaica, 2/20

JAPAN
*Bonari Kogen Golf Club, 12/8
Hirono Golf Club, 12/6
Kawana Golf Club, 12/7
Segovia Golf Club, 12/9
Tokyo Golf Club, 12/5

KENYA
*Karen Golf Club, 3/9

LATVIA
*Ozo Golf Club
www.ozogolf.lv, 8/16

MALAYSIA
*Hornbill Golf and Jungle Club, 12/16
*Mines Resort, The
www.mines.com.my, 12/15

MAURITIUS
*Belle Mare Plage Resort
www.bellemareplagehotel.com, 3/5

MEXICO
*Cabo del Sol Golf Club (Ocean Course)
www.cabodelsol.com, 1/31
*Cabo Real Golf Club
www.caboreal.com, 2/1
*Four Seasons Resort Punta Mita
www.fourseasons.com/puntamita, 2/2

MOROCCO
*Royal Dar Es Salaam Golf Club (Red
Course), 3/11

MYANMAR
*Bagan Golf Resort, 11/26
*Pun Hlaing Golf Club, 11/27

NEPAL
*Gokarna Forest Golf Resort
www.gokarna.com, 11/23
*Himalayan Golf Course, 11/24

NETHERLANDS
**Noordwijkse Golf Club
www.noordwijksegolfclub.nl, 8/29
**Royal Hague Golf Club
www.khgcc.nl, 8/30

NEVIS
*Four Seasons Resort Golf Course
www.fourseasons.com/nevis, 2/15

NEW ZEALAND
*Cape Kidnappers Golf Course
www.capekidnappers.com, 12/30
*Kauri Cliffs Golf Course
www.kauricliffs.com, 12/28
**Paraparaumu Beach Golf Club
www.paraparaumubeach
golfclub.co.nz, 12/29

NORTHERN IRELAND
*Portstewart Golf Club
www.portstewartgc.co.uk, 8/3
*Royal County Down Golf Club
www.royalcountydown.org, 8/4

*Royal Portrush Golf Club
www.royalportrushgolfclub.com, 8/2

NORWAY
*Oslo Golf Club
www.oslogk.no, 8/13

POLAND
*Krakow Valley Golf Club
www.krakow-valley.com.pl, 8/17

PORTUGAL
*Penha Longa Golf Club
www.penhalonga.com, 3/18
*San Lorenzo Golf Club, 3/15
*Tróia Golf Club, 3/20
*Vale de Pinta, 3/17
*Vilamoura Golf Club (Old Course), 3/16

PUERTO RICO
*Palmas del Mar Resort and Country Club
www.palmasdelmar.com, 2/16

SCOTLAND
*Carnoustie Golf Links
www.carnoustiegolflinks.co.uk, 7/13
*Cruden Bay Golf Club
www.crudenbaygolfclub.com, 7/15
*Gleneagles Resort
www.gleneagles.com, 7/18
*Gullane Golf Club (No. 1 Course)
www.gullanegolfclub.com, 7/19
*Kingsbarns Golf Links
www.kingsbarns.com, 7/12
*Machrie Golf Club
www.machrie.com, 8/9
*Machrihanish Golf Club
www.machgolf.com, 8/8

**Muirfield, 7/21
*Nairn Golf Club
  www.invernessonline.com/
  nairngolfclub, 7/17
*North Berwick Golf Club
  www.topweb.free-
  online.co.uk/nb/xnbhist.htm, 7/20
*Old Course at St. Andrews
  www.standrews.org.uk, 7/11
*Prestwick Golf Club
  www.prestwickgc.co.uk, 8/6
**Royal Aberdeen Golf Club
  www.royalaberdeengolf.com, 7/14
*Royal Dornoch Golf Club
  www.royaldornoch.com, 7/16
**Royal Troon Golf Club
  www.royaltroon.co.uk, 8/7
*Turnberry Resort (Ailsa Course)
  www.turnberry.co.uk, 8/5

SINGAPORE
Singapore Island Country Club
  (Bukit Course), 12/17

SOUTH AFRICA
Durban Country Club, 3/4
*Fancourt Resort and Hotel
  (Links Course)
  www.fancourt.co.za, 3/2
*Fancourt Resort and Hotel
  (Montagu Course), 3/1
  www.fancourt.co.za, p. 126
*Hans Merensky Country Club
  www.hansmerensky.com, 3/6
*Lost City Golf Course
  www.suninternational.co.za, 3/7

*Wild Coast Country Club
  www.suninternational.co.za/
  resorts/wildcoast, 3/3

SOUTH KOREA
Club at Nine Bridges, The, 12/4

SPAIN
*El Saler, Campo de Golf, 3/22
*Masia Bach, Club de Golf, 3/23
*Montecastillo Hotel Golf Resort
  www.montecastillo.com, 3/14
*PGA Golf de Catalunya
  www.pgacatalunya.com, 3/24
*Real Golf Club de Pedreña, 3/25
**Real Sociedad Hipica Española Club
  de Campo, 3/21
*Torrequebrada, 3/13
**Valderrama, Club de Golf
  www.valderrama.com, 3/12

SRI LANKA
*Victoria Golf Club, 11/22

SWEDEN
*Barseback Golf and Country Club
  (Old Course)
  www.golf.se/barsebackgcc, 8/12
*Falsterbo Golf Club
  www.falsterbogk.com, 8/11
*Ullna Golf Club
  www.ulnagolf.se, p. 8/14

SWITZERLAND
*Crans-Sur-Sierre, Golf Club
  www.swissgolfnetwork.ch, 8/21

THAILAND
*Blue Canyon Country Club
  www.phuket-golf.com/blue-canyon-
  country-club.htm, 12/14
*Dragon Hills Golf and Country
  Club, 12/11
*Springfield Royal Country Club
  www.golfhuahin.com/
  sfield.htm, 12/12
*Royal Hua Hin
  www.golfhuahin.com/
  royalhuahin.htm, 12/13

TUNISIA
*Tabarka Golf Club
  www.tabarkagolf.com, 3/10

TURKEY
*National Golf Club, The
  www.nationalturkey.com, 11/19

UNITED ARAB EMIRATES
*Dubai Creek Golf Club
  www.dubaigolf.com, 11/20
*Emirates Golf Club
  www.dubaigolf.com, 11/20

VENEZUELA
Lagunita Country Club, 2/12

VIETNAM
*Dalat Palace Golf Club
  www.vietnamgolfresorts.com/htmls/
  dalat.html, 12/10

WALES
*Aberdovey Golf Club
  www.aberdoveygolf.co.uk, 11/2

*Nefyn & District Golf Club
  www.nefyn-golf-club.com, 11/1
*Royal St. David's Golf Club
  www.royalstdavids.co.uk, 11/3

ZIMBABWE
*Elephant Hills Golf Course
  www.elephanthills.com, 3/8

*Open to the public
**Limited access to the public

PHOTOGRAPHY CREDITS

PRINCIPAL PHOTOGRAPHERS: John and Jeannine Henebry: January 1 (right), 2, 4, 6, 11, 13, 17, 22, 23, 25, February 1, 2, 15, 25 (right), April 3, 7, 10 (right), 13 (left), 20 (right), 22, 25 (right), May 3, 9, 13 (right), 16, 18 (right), 19, 20 (right), 21 (left), 23, 24, June 1 (right), 5, 6, 7, 22, 23 (right), 25, July 4, August 25, September 18, 19 (right), 20, 23, October 7 (right), 17 (left), November 23, December 2, 19, 20 (right), 22; Eric Hepworth: March 12 (left), July 11 (left), 13 (left), 15, 16, 17 (right), 19, 20, 27 (right), August 4 (right), 5 (left), 6 (right), 7–9, September 5 (right), October 21, 22 (left), 24 (left), 26–31, November 1–4, 5 (right), 8; Russell Kirk/GolfLinks: January 10, 19, 31, February 26 (left), March 12 (right), 13 (left), April 20 (left), 21, 27–29, May 6, June 15, 17, 23 (left), July 5, 9, 17 (left), 18, August 10–12, 26, 27, September 2, 5 (left), 9, 11 (left), 14, 19 (left), October 7 (left), 11 (left), 22 (right), 23, 24 (right), 25, November 7, December 22 (left), 25 (left), 28 (left); Mike Klemme/Golfoto: January 12 (left), 14, 15, February 14, 26 (left), 27, March 9, 11, April 2, 4, 8, 11 (left), 12 (right), 24, 25 (left), May 4, 5, 7, May 13 (left), 14, 15, 26 (right), June 18–20, 29, July 1 (left), 2 (left), 3, 10, August 14, September 15, 21, November 16–18, December 4 (right), 7, 20 (left); L.C. Lambrecht: 1, 2, January 12 (right), 18, 29, 30, February 4–11, 16, 19, 22–24, 25 (left), March 1, 3, 4 (right), April 5, 9, 10 (left), 11 (right), 12 (left), 13 (right), 14, 15, 17, 18, May 2, 27, June 10, 16, 24, 26, 27, July 6–8, 13 (right), 14, 21–26, 27 (left), 28–31, August 1–3, 4 (left), September 7, 8, 10, 11 (right), 12, 13, 25, 27–30, October 1–4, 6, 8–10, 11 (right), 12–16, 17 (right).

CONTRIBUTING PHOTOGRAPHERS: Phil Arnold/Golfscape: January 27, 28, June 11, July 2, September 16; Beckenham Golf Library-www.pocket.golf.com: March 16 (left), 19, 21, 23, 24, August 28, November 5 (left), November 15 (right); courtesy Bell Bay Golf Club: September 22; Aidan Bradley: February 20, June 1 (left), 2, 3, 12; courtesy Constance Hotels: March 5; Jordan Coonrad/Airborne: Introduction, January 3 (right), 20 (right), 24, May 20 (left), 21 (right), 22, 26 (left), 29, 30, June 9, 13, July 11 (right), August 5 (right); courtesy Czech Tourism: August 18; courtesy Dachstein-Tauern Golf and Country Club: August 20; courtesy Desert Canyon Golf Club: May 28; courtesy Tom Doak/Renaissance Golf Design: February 17, March 4 (left), May 1, 31, August 30, October 20, November 6, December 21; Joann Dost: January 7–9, July 12, October 18, 19, December 30; Dick Durrance II: January 1 (left), 3 (left), 20 (left), 21, 26, February 28, May 10–12, 18 (left), June 28, December 29; courtesy James Engh Golf Design: June 8, December 11; Markus Erdmann: August 23; courtesy Four Seasons Resort Great Exuma at Emerald Bay: February 21; courtesy Ronald Fream/GolfPlan: March 10, April 1 (left), August 15, 17, November 24–26, December 4 (left), 8; Jorge Gamboa: February 3; courtesy Lester George Golf Design: April 26; courtesy Grove Park Inn: April 23; courtesy Golf and Country Club Güt Altentann: August 19; courtesy Hans Merensky Country Club: March 6; Matthew Harris/TGPL: March 8, August 13; courtesy James Haver: May 17; courtesy Hidden Lakes Golf Resort and Jonathan Cummings: June 4; courtesy Hornbill Golf and Jungle Club: December 16; Paul Hundley: June 21; courtesy Bradley Klein: January 16, April 6,

16, 19, 30 (left), May 25, October 5; Bob Labbance: September 26; courtesy Lake Sunapee Country Club/Ron Forse: September 24; G. Lavasha/TGPL: March 2; Jean-François Lefèvre: March 7, 26–28, 31, April 1 (right), August 6 (left), November 10–13, 15 (left), 20 (left), 21; Patrick Lim: November 27, 28, December 1, 10; Ken E. May/Rolling Greens Photography: February 18, April 30 (right), June 30, July 1 (right); Taku Miyamoto/photolinks: March 15, November 14, December 5, 6, 9, 12; courtesy Oahu Country Club and James Tam: January 5; courtesy Ozo Golf Club and Armands Puce: August 16; Robert Reck: May 8; courtesy Royal Golf Club de Belgique: September 1; courtesy Royal Westmoreland/Phil Inglis: February 13; David Scaletti: December 23, 24, 25 (right), 26, 27; Phil Sheldon Golf Picture Library/Richard Castka: front cover, November 29, 30 (right), December 3, December 13, 14 (right), 15, 18, December 28, 31; Phil Sheldon Golf Picture Library/Patrick Eagar: March 16 (right), 17, September 4, November 9, 22, back cover; Phil Sheldon Golf Picture Library/Phil Inglis: March 30, August 21; Phil Sheldon Golf Picture Library/Larry Petrillo: February 12; Phil Sheldon Golf Picture Library/Hugh Routledge: September 3; Phil Sheldon Golf Picture Library/Phil Sheldon: March 13 (right), 14, 18, 20, 22, 25, 29, August 31, September 17, November 20 (right), November 30 (left), December 14 (left), 17; Phil Sheldon Golf Picture Library/Jan Traylen: August 29; Stefan V. Stengel/TGPL: August 24; David J. Whyte/Linksland: September 6, November 19; courtesy Wittelsbacher Golf Club: August 22

Project Manager: Margaret L. Kaplan
Editor: David Barrett
Editorial Assistant: Jon Cipriaso
Designer: Robert McKee
Production Manager: Justine Keefe

Library of Congress Cataloging-in-Publication Data
Sidorsky, Robert.
 Golf courses around the world : 365 days / by Robert Sidorsky.
   p. cm.
 Includes bibliographical references and index.
 ISBN 0–8109–5893–7 (hardcover : alk. paper)
1. Golf courses. I. Title.
GV975.S535 2005
796.352'068–dc22

2004028158

Text copyright © Robert Sidorsky

Published in 2005 by Abrams,
an imprint of Harry N. Abrams, Inc.

Front cover: Blue Canyon Country Club, Thailand. Phil Sheldon Golf Picture Library/Richard Castka
Back cover: St. George's Hill Golf Club, England. Phil Sheldon Golf Picture Library/Patrick Eagar

Printed and bound in China
10 9 8 7 6 5 4

HNA ▮▮▮▮▮
harry n. abrams, inc.
a subsidiary of La Martinière Groupe
115 West 18th Street
New York, NY 10011
www.hnabooks.com